A Pastoral Leade

Also available from Continuum

How to be a Successful Head of Year, Brian Carline
How to be a Successful Form Tutor, Richard Rogers and Michael Marland
Running Your Tutor Group, Ian Startup

A PASTORAL LEADER'S HANDBOOK

Strategies for Success in the
Secondary School

Marilyn Nathan

continuum

Continuum International Publishing Group

The Tower Building	80 Maiden Lane
11 York Road	Suite 704
London	New York
SE1 7NX	NY 10038

www.continuumbooks.com

British Library Cataloguing-in-Publication Data
A catalogue record for this book is available from the British Library.

ISBN: 978-1-4411-0256-0

Library of Congress Cataloging-in-Publication Data
A catalog record for this book is available from the Library of Congress.

Typeset by Pindar NZ, Auckland, New Zealand
Printed and bound in India by Replika Press Pvt Ltd

Contents

Introduction

The purpose of this book is to explore the role and responsibilities of the pastoral leader in the current educational climate. There are still very few books that focus on the role of a pastoral leader. There is a need for a new book because the whole structure of the pastoral system is changing in response to the government's restructuring agenda and to new approaches to behaviour management. Chapter 1 will particularly focus on the changes and how they might affect you if you are or aspire to be a pastoral leader.

A Pastoral Leader's Handbook is also an introduction to middle management for pastoral leaders in schools, and is relevant both for teachers who hold pastoral posts and for non-teaching year heads. If you have or are about to take on a middle management role as a year head, achievement/progress manager, or head of house in a secondary school, this book aims to provide a compendium of information and advice which you can adapt to fit your needs and which help you to answer the question: What are my responsibilities as a year leader and how do I carry them out most effectively? It is also relevant for experienced pastoral leaders because it enables you to reflect on your practice.

The book can also be used as a development programme. Very few pastoral leaders receive any substantive training before taking up their posts. Once you are in post the range of courses available for pastoral leaders is limited and most courses are one-day events. Although the NPSLBA programme is now being developed to deal with issues around 'attendance, and social and emotional aspects of learning (SEAL)', this may not be what you want. This book aims to fill that gap and to support you in your role as a pastoral team leader; it could help you if you are looking for a pastoral post and want to prepare yourself.

Similarly, if you have been in a post for some years and want to check that the way that you work fits new perceptions of the pastoral system, this book will help you to focus on current problems and issues. The case studies that feature in every chapter can be used for personal reflection or to focus group discussion. SLT members with responsibility for the school's pastoral system can also use this book to help them support and develop year leaders in their role.

A Pastoral Leader's Handbook is a practical compendium of information and guidance which surveys the main aspects of a pastoral manager's role and provides information, exemplars, checklists and suggestions to help you deal with the situations that you are likely to face. Where relevant, the findings of recent reports or research are summarized for you and their impact on your role is discussed.

Integrated throughout the book are case studies, which are all based on the experience of pastoral leaders in real schools. They describe how year leaders in different schools have approached dealing with aspects of their pastoral responsibilities. Most of the case studies are fully worked through. This is to give you a chance to see how someone else handled a situation that you might have to face and to benchmark your own practice. Other case studies give you the opportunity, either on your own or in a group, to work through the case study and offer your own solutions. Leadership is contextual; what works in one school and one situation may not work for another, but the ideas presented could spark off your thinking about what might work in your own situation. Not all the examples show best practice. Both good and bad examples are included because you can learn from both, though the emphasis will always be on the positive.

References and links to useful websites are provided at the end of chapters. We try to keep these as up to date as possible, but contact names, phone numbers and internet addresses frequently change, so if the link doesn't take you to the reference, you may need to browse using your own search engine to follow-up some points.

The Department is rationalising the number of websites it owns, and migrating content onto www.education.gov.uk. All required content from Teachernet, the Standards Site and GovernorNet has been migrated onto this site. For more information about this please see p. 23.

Acknowledgements

I'd like to thank all the pastoral leaders, most of whom I met through their attendance on my middle or senior leadership courses, who helped me by providing materials and case studies, which I have drawn on to write this book. I'd particularly like to thank Sotira Michael, who was so very helpful in answering my questions.

Marilyn Nathan

Marilyn delivers in-school seminars and consultancy, offers distance learning modules and publishes her own short e-books. Training and consultancy, which includes leadership training for pastoral leaders, can be tailor-made to fit your needs. For further information contact her at: marilyn.nathan@realemail.co.uk or marilynrnathan@gmail.com

Marilyn's website: www.marilynnathan.co.uk

CHAPTER 1

New times, new titles – pastoral leadership in the current climate

Roles and titles

This chapter explores how the pastoral system is changing and the new roles and structures that are being put in place. In the current climate, if you are a pastoral leader the first question you are likely to be asked is 'Are you are teacher?' Some of you will be pastoral leaders because you have followed the traditional pastoral route for teachers and become a year head or head of house, responsible for the behaviour, welfare and progress of the pupils in a year group or vertical section of the school. You will probably still be the larger group of staff. Others will not have QTS (qualified teacher status), but you bring other qualities to the equation. You could have followed a variety of routes into the post. You may have been a learning mentor; often you have a background of youth work; you may have a long association with the school as one its welfare assistants or teaching assistant; or you may come in directly from business or industry. Currently, some pastoral leaders have backgrounds in professions such as recruitment, banking or the police.

Titles have changed. Until recently if you were a pastoral manager in a secondary school, you would probably be a head of year or head of house, dependent on which system your school uses. Now, although 'Head of Year' is still the title most frequently used, there are a whole range of other possible titles, such as 'Progress Manager', 'Achievement Manager', or Director of/for Learning', and these reflect the trend towards an increasing focus in the role on managing pupil achievement. In this book, for consistency, the term 'year head' or 'year leader' will normally be used to cover all variants of the pastoral middle leadership position and titles.

One new title is 'Behaviour Manager'. In the past responsibility for the behaviour of the pupils in the year group would have been just one part of the year head's overarching pastoral responsibilities, but increasingly the role may be split. The behaviour manager is usually a non-teacher. Again titles vary. There is no consistency of practice. Often if you are a non-teaching pastoral leader with a role covering behaviour management you are simply called 'Assistant Head of Year', but titles vary from 'Investigative Officer', 'Behaviour and Welfare Manager' through to titles more concentrated on pupil progress, such as 'Pupil Achievement Manager'.

Background to changes to the pastoral system

The changes to the pastoral system have come about because of restructuring. The restructuring programme, also known as remodelling, was staged over three years. Head teachers had to produce a 'remodelled' staffing structure, which reflected the changes to school management posts. The title 'Behaviour Manager' appeared in Year 3 of the new arrangements in a list of jobs which would no longer be done by teachers, and pastoral leaders began to ask, 'Will there be jobs for us in the new system?' The answer is currently 'Yes', because more schools have kept to the traditional approach than have changed it, but you need to be aware that an increasing number of schools are taking a more innovative approach to school organization. The move from management allowances (MAs) to teaching and learning responsibilities (TLRs) has focused them on asking, 'What is the teaching and learning component in the role?' and in this respect the pastoral system, especially managing behaviour, is a grey area.

Restructuring has led to a move to focus the teacher's pastoral role on pupil progress and achievement, as this clearly meets the TRL requirement, and this has generated a range of new titles such as 'Progress Manager', 'Learning Manager' or 'Achievement Manager', or some combination of any or all of these (see the sample job descriptions later in this chapter). You could be called 'Learning Manager', 'Head of Learning', 'Learning Director' or 'Director of Learning' and yet do much the same job. These posts may be attached to a year group or, as a more senior post, attached to a Key Stage, e.g. 'Head of Learning for KS3'. This change is still evolving. Most pastoral managers find their role in overseeing the academic progress of the pupils in their year group or section is growing. They are doing more data analysis than in the past in order to set targets for groups or individuals (see Chapter 9), but often, although they have a new job description, their role hasn't really changed much yet and many pastoral leaders still find that the majority of their time is spent on dealing with disruptive incidents. Case study 1.1 describes the model adopted by one school.

CASE STUDY 1.1: MANAGERIAL CHANGES

This school changed from the traditional pastoral system to having Key Stage managers. The aim of the change to the pastoral structure was to free up teachers to teach and give non-teachers all the jobs that teachers did not need to do. Four Key Stage managers were appointed: Year 7, Key Stage 3, Key Stage 4 and the Sixth Form. Their job is to raise attainment using a positive model. The Key Stage managers oversee the mentoring system, contact and deal with parents, monitor what goes on in the classrooms through classroom observation and interviews with students, and take assemblies. Key Stage managers are teachers.

The school also appointed six full-time year managers, who do not have QTS, to deal with poorly behaved children and welfare/pastoral issues. Each became the manager of a year, one for each year from Year 7 to Year 11, plus one for the Sixth Form. Two of them were existing members of staff, the other four were new appointments. Their job is to deal with issues that prevent teachers from teaching, e.g. student attendance and lateness, school dress, student misbehaviour, and manage contact with parents, attendance at case conferences where the issues are primarily social, exam invigilation and duties, and whole school detentions, etc.

The SLT line manages and provides support for the new structure. One assistant head teacher supports the year managers and two others oversee the Key Stages, one for Key Stage 3 and another for Key Stage 4.

Reactions to the changes

Some pastoral leaders, year leaders or house heads welcome the change because they experienced a conflict between their caring role in dealing with pupil welfare and progress, and their discipline role in managing pupil behaviour and dealing with disruptive pupils. Most of you manage this dual responsibility well, but some year heads resented this part of their responsibilities because they felt that too much was unloaded onto them and that they were regarded as the sin bin or dumping ground for disruptive pupils. This happens particularly in schools in which the form tutor has very little pastoral responsibility. Usually the tutor is the first point of reference in dealing with the pupil's behaviour, as generally, when they are concerned about a pupil, teachers go to talk to the tutor first. In some schools, however, the tutor's role is underdeveloped, and the year head has to do rather more than would otherwise be the case and consequently every minor problem is brought to the year leader.

Most existing pastoral leaders were concerned, however, because it is often difficult to separate the behaviour from welfare issues and from the effect on the pupils' overall performance. Another issue is unfairness, because in some schools a teacher is still undertaking the whole of the traditional head of year responsibilities on top of a teaching timetable; whereas in other schools the role is split between two staff, one of whom is non-teaching.

Advantages and disadvantages of the separation of roles

Advantages

- A major advantage of non-teaching pastoral managers is their availability. If you are a non-teaching year leader, you can follow-up a problem immediately after it happens rather than having to leave it until you have a free period and there is no interruption to your teaching.
- It also frees up teachers, who are year leaders, to concentrate on their teaching. It addresses one of the main issues that face teachers who are year heads, i.e. the interruption to their lessons and difficulty in focusing on their teaching. However much they contributed to the subject department, guilt about this issue is a frequent problem for teachers with pastoral posts.
- An objective of remodelling was to ease the administrative burden on teachers and free them up to spend more time on planning and preparation of their lessons. Having a non-teacher deal with administrative matters, especially following up behaviour and attendance, removes a particularly time consuming part of role.
- It enables school to explore innovative ways of working with families in school and through home support that teachers with a teaching timetable cannot undertake.
- It can sometimes be easier for a non-teacher, e.g. a family support officer, to engage with hard to reach parents.

Disadvantages

- The separation of roles has created tensions because there could easily be boundary disputes over 'who does what'. There are grey areas between behaviour and welfare and, as the sample job descriptions given below will illustrate, there is no consistency in the tasks and responsibilities included in the role. Case study 1.2 describes one year head's personal experience and what she has to do to make the new relationship work.

- It also means that teachers planning their career are less likely to be able to learn a management role as assistant heads of year.
- The issues about non-teaching staff having leadership roles have not yet been addressed and resolved. Most frequently the non-teaching behaviour manager is the equivalent of an assistant head of year and the teacher is the progress manager, holding a year head equivalent post. In a significant proportion of secondary schools, however, non-teaching 'year heads', who are not teachers, do manage a year group and give leadership to the team of tutors. It is usually easier for the teachers to accept the non-teacher as assistant head of year than if the non-teacher is in charge of a team of teachers.

Addressing these problems is partly a question of time, as people adjust to new arrangements. What is important in the interim period is to behave professionally and to treat people with respect.

Case study 1.2 illustrates what it could mean for you in practice if your role as year leader is restructured.

CASE STUDY 1.2: CHANGED ROLE

I'd been a year leader for four years when restructuring came in and the pastoral system in this large 11–18 comprehensive school was completely remodelled. My existing job was divided in two and my job title was changed. I was now the learning manager for a year group; it happened to be Year 9, but we go up the school with our year. A behaviour and attendance manager, who is not a teacher, was appointed as my assistant. The behaviour manager had actually been in the school for some years and had started out as the lab technician, so she did know the children.

I found the change very different at first. My teaching commitment was now higher than in the past, because now that I have a behaviour manager I am not meant to be disturbed in lessons. I had been trained as a BeCo (like a SENCO but for behaviour) but could no longer use this training. My line managers, the Key Stage manager and the deputy head kept telling me to let the behaviour and attendance manager get on with the responsibilities, which were now in her job description. 'Keep your finger out of attendance', the Key Stage manager would tell me.

The behaviour and attendance manager is a non-teaching post so she is on call to deal with incidents as they arise. They put most of the administration connected with the pastoral system into her job description, and she is expected to do these tasks when she is not busy with pupil behaviour. For example, she is responsible for inputting the attendance data and pupil incidents into our behaviour and attendance software program and to give the tutors weekly and monthly lists for their tutor groups, and she provides me with an overview of what is going on. She liaises with the EWO and the social workers and reports back. There are grey areas, however. For example, currently she conducts some of the meetings with parents but usually we do them together, so that she can watch how I handle the meeting and if I think the parents are likely to be intimidating, I take the meeting, but this part of our partnership is still evolving.

I've had to accept that she does things differently from me, but this doesn't mean that she does them badly. My delegation skills have had to improve. We get on OK, so we work quite well together. It is a bit more difficult for her with my tutors. It is a large team of ten tutors and she had to tell them to do things, and there are tensions, as they don't really like a non-teacher telling them what to do.

For reflection/discussion
- How does this case study compare to what is happening in your own school?
- What are the issues raised by this case study and the implications for pastoral leaders?

What the job might look like: sample job descriptions for pastoral roles

A good starting point is always to look at job descriptions. You can easily find exemplars on the internet, using your preferred search engine. Some sample job descriptions are provided below for comparison with your own current job description or for you to look at if you are considering applying for a pastoral post.

Comparing the exemplar role descriptions will show the variation in what is currently required. Exemplar 1.1 uses the title 'Learning and Progress Leader' and focuses on your role in supporting the learners' academic and social development and in using data to support pupil progress. Exemplar 1.2 comes from the same school as Exemplar 1.1 and shows how in this school the non-teaching pastoral support assistant, who used to be called 'Assistant Head of Year', deals with most of the administrative tasks as well as monitoring attendance and punctuality. Exemplar 1.3, which calls the post 'Pastoral Manager', does not separate monitoring behaviour from academic progress and focuses the role on identifying and providing support for the pupils, whose behaviour, attendance or lack of social/emotional skills affect their likelihood of achievement. This support includes classroom observation and individual mentoring.

Exemplar 1.4 is basically the traditional year head role description in which the latest initiative is tacked on the end of a long list of tasks irrespective of how time consuming and demanding it will be. Exemplar 1.5 is the job description for a non-teaching head of year. It could be useful for you to compare its requirements with those in Exemplar 1.1. If you are seeking a pastoral post, you need to look carefully at how the school views its pastoral posts, what are the main responsibilities and how they are grouped, and whether the school wants a teacher or someone who may not have QTS but brings other qualities and experience to the post.

EXEMPLAR 1.1: JOB DESCRIPTION – LEARNING AND PROGRESS LEADER, TLR

Purpose of the post
- To lead, manage and support the learning and progress of students in a designated Year Group
- To ensure that the students in the Year Group attain successful academic outcomes
- To enhance the personal and social development of students and promote their well-being
- To identify barriers to learning and plan appropriate intervention strategies
- To lead, manage and develop a team of tutors in taking prime responsibility for the learning and social progress of a group of students
- To be a key link with home and other support services involved in student welfare

Responsible to
- Designated SLT link
- Deputy Head i/c learning and progress
- Head Teacher
- Governing body

Responsibility for
- Team of tutors
- Assistant learning and progress leader

Main operational tasks
- To support the Form Tutor in day-to-day management of their students
- To monitor attendance and punctuality of students and act to improve these as necessary
- To monitor student compliance with all school expectations
- To use meaningful data and information to track, monitor, and support student progress
- To intervene and work with Teaching and Learning Leaders to overcome any identified underachievement
- To implement the agreed school rewards and sanctions systems
- To ensure Enrichment Days provide effective personal development opportunities
- To ensure the activities are carried out in each Form Period according to the specified programme including: academic monitoring and aspects of personal development
- To organize the transition process from Key Stage 2 to Key Stage 3 and from Key Stage 3 to Key Stage 4
- To use assemblies to promote the personal development of the students and establish the school ethos
- To report progress to parents and students as and when required
- To liaise with internal support services and outside agencies involved in student welfare and progress
- To ensure that full and accurate records are available to the Head Teacher or any external partners as when required
- To contribute to the development of Pastoral Support Plans and facilitate their implementation
- To induct students into the school who arrive after the normal admission date
- To induct and train the tutor team, especially NQTs and staff new to the school
- To contribute to the Performance Management process with regard to tutor role
- To undertake such tasks as may reasonably be asked by the Head Teacher

EXEMPLAR 1.2: JOB DESCRIPTION – NON-TEACHING PASTORAL SUPPORT ASSISTANT (SCALE 4)

Purpose of the post
- To assist the Learning and Progress Leader (LPL) for a designated Year Group (see Exemplar 1.1)
- To support the personal social and academic development of students and promote their well-being
- To contribute to the overall ethos, work and aims of the school
- To assist in maintaining links with home, internal and external support services involved in student welfare

Responsible to
- The LPL
- Designated SLT link
- Head Teacher
- Governing body

Main operational tasks
Attendance, punctuality and uniform
- To liaise with the Attendance Officer, assist with the follow-up on students not swiped
- To monitor student punctuality and assist with detentions for lateness
- To update the LPL and make contact with parents where appropriate, e.g. regarding uniform, punctuality

Behaviour management
- To issue reports and assist in the monitoring of them
- To assist with Year Detentions
- To assist with the investigation of incidents under the direction of the LPL
- To liaise with the inclusion room and contact parents under the direction of the LPL
- To undertake duties at break time according to the duty rota
- To collate information on student successes, e.g. merits, rewards
- To be another point of contact for the Student Supervisors in relation to the Year Group

Communication
- To ensure the issue of the Communication File to tutors on a daily basis
- To liaise with the Cover Manager and step in where needed for tutors

- To attend a weekly meeting with the LPL and all meetings relevant to the Year Group
- To liaise with all staff on behalf of the LPL
- To manage information on students and maintain accurate and up-to-date records

Family and student support
- To deal with day-to-day concerns of families and respond and refer appropriately
- To communicate with parents as required at the request of the LPL
- To organize meetings and make appointments on behalf of the LPL
- To assist in the organization of information for internal and external support services
- To attend student support meetings as required
- To support Year Council meetings
- To order and organize Year Group resources
- To supervise as required classes in the Year Group, during the short term planned absence of teachers, with the agreement of the LPL
- To invigilate examinations for the appropriate Year Group
- To supervise students on educational trips and in school clubs
- To report all concerns about child protection, health, safety and security to the appropriate person

---

EXEMPLAR 1.3: JOB DESCRIPTION – KEY STAGE 3 (KS3) PASTORAL MANAGER, TLR 2

The KS3 Pastoral Manager is line managed by a member of the SLT.

The SLT line manager has oversight of the academic progress and pastoral welfare of pupils in KS3. The SLT line manager coordinates the work of the KS3 Form Tutors and the KS3 Pastoral Manager.

The primary role of the KS3 Pastoral Manager is to help to create a positive and productive atmosphere in which teachers can teach and pupils can learn by providing prompt support when a pupil's poor behaviour, attendance, self-organization or social skills are having a detrimental effect on their own education and/or that of their peers. The KS3 Pastoral Manager may be alerted to these issues by a member of staff, a parent, a pupil, or by their own observation of events.

The KS3 Pastoral Manager is not a counsellor. Counselling pupils requires a different skill set from that of the role of the KS3 Pastoral Manager and to attempt to combine the two roles will result in confusion in the minds of pupils. If the KS3 Pastoral Manager believes that a pupil would benefit from professional counselling, the pupil's parents should be so advised.

The KS3 Pastoral Manager also plays an important role in helping the school to identify and celebrate pupils' personal, non-curriculum achievements.

Main responsibilities

1. To implement the school's behaviour and attendance procedures with respect to KS3 pupils, liaising as appropriate with staff, SENCO, parents, the Education Welfare Service, social services and other outside agencies.
2. Personally to mentor, individually or in groups as appropriate, pupils who have been identified by the SLT line manager as having challenging behaviour, anger management problems, poor self-organization skills or poor social skills. To arrange, in liaison with the SLT line manager, for mentoring by others when appropriate.
3. To set up and monitor a peer-mentoring system.
4. With the prior approval of the SLT line manager, to make classroom observations of KS3 pupils who may require an Individual Education Plan (IEP) for Emotional or Behavioural Difficulty (EBD), or who may require a Pastoral Support Programme (PSP) because of the possibility of permanent exclusion.
5. To attend KS3 parents' evenings to meet specific parents by appointment, in order to follow-up behaviour and attendance matters.
6. To monitor and record the personal non-curriculum achievements of KS3 pupils both in and out of school (e.g. charitable endeavours, the acquisition of awards/certificates, success as members of school teams, participation in school productions, etc.) and to bring them to the attention of the SLT line manager so that they can be celebrated by the school community.

EXEMPLAR 1.4: ROLE DESCRIPTION – HEAD OF YEAR (TLR 1)

The Head of Year is responsible to the senior leadership team for all pastoral matters. The following duties and responsibilities cover the main areas of this post:

- To lead a team of tutors within the year group
- To ensure that the form tutors meet regularly and understand the policies of the school on all relevant matters

- To promote a year team approach, which will enable all students to develop their academic and social capabilities to the fullest extent
- To supervise attendance and punctuality, checking attendance registers at least once a week, checking reasons for absence, possible truancy and punctuality
- To encourage and cooperate with form tutors in discussions with other members of staff, e.g. heads of department and other senior staff
- To arrange meetings with individual parents in order to discuss welfare and general problems arising with any particular student
- To play a major role in organizing and assisting with relevant parents' evenings for the year and to attend such evenings where necessary, by arrangement with the Head Teacher
- To record and coordinate all information received from staff, parents and outside agencies regarding individual students and to ensure that this information is distributed correctly and to check that action is taken where necessary
- To liaise closely with other schools as necessary
- To prepare and hold morning assemblies with the year group as required
- To direct the preparation of reports, records of achievement and references
- To supervise and direct the report card system in use in the school and to hold year detentions when necessary
- To monitor the academic progress of individual students across all curriculum areas and to inform heads of department of any discrepancies
- To contribute to school self-evaluation (SEF)

This role description may be re-negotiated in the light of changes in staffing and with reference to the school development plan.

EXEMPLAR 1.5: JOB DESCRIPTION – NON-TEACHING HEAD OF YEAR

Job title: Head of Year – KS4
Duration: Permanent
Responsible to: Principal and Head of KS4
Grade: Grade 12

Job Purpose
To be responsible for the pastoral support of a KS4 year group.

Objectives

- To provide tutorial and pastoral support in a proactive way
- To ensure high levels of student attendance, behaviour and punctuality
- To work closely with students, teachers, parents and support staff to ensure students flourish within the college environment and achieve their learning goals.
- To raise standards of attainment at KS4

Key tasks

- To work with the Head of KS4 on the transition of students into the year group
- To lead and support a team of tutors in their pastoral support of the year group and their delivery of the PSHE curriculum
- To work with Heads of Department regarding pastoral issues
- To ensure the day-to-day arrangements for the year group are managed to secure an ethos and culture of learning
- To create a year identity by setting high expectations, having a high profile around the year group, presentation of assemblies, organization of extra-curricular events, e.g. social events, study clubs, lunchtime clubs, etc.
- To implement and support developments in the college rewards policy
- To implement and support developments in the college behaviour policy
- To monitor the attendance and punctuality of the year group and to take action when appropriate
- Use the college monitoring systems to identify problems and take appropriate action
- To ensure that the behaviour of students at lunchtimes in and out of College is in line with the College Code of Behaviour
- To attend and organize parents' evenings
- Be responsible for producing Pastoral Support Plans and monitoring their effectiveness
- To integrate students back into college following exclusion
- Work in a proactive way in order to reduce conflict
- Work with the Post-16 Coordinator to ensure students successfully progress onto appropriate courses

Your job description will be reviewed and may be amended from time to time, within the terms of your conditions of employment, after consultation with you and your head of department.

Main areas covered by your responsibilities

Schools have reached different decisions about how to organize the pastoral system. The sample job descriptions included here illustrate that pastoral responsibilities may be delegated either to a teacher or to a non-teacher pastoral leader or a both; they may be divided into two posts, most usually focused on progress and behaviour, or they may be combined. A lot of pastoral staff say that, regardless of what their job description says, they still spend a majority of their time on day-to-day disciplinary issues. This occurs for a number of reasons: it is partly because the new requirements are not always fully understood, the school has not adapted or the postholder has not yet acquired the new skills required to be a progress manager. Usually it is a combination of the reasons; nevertheless, the role clearly is changing its focus and over time will change further. Whatever the format of the job or the job title, your current responsibilities now cover three main areas of the pupil's schooling.

1. Providing a positive environment for learning

This means providing a secure environment in which the pupil is able to concentrate on his/her studies. The student's welfare and providing support for social and emotional aspects of his/her development fall into this category. The extent to which you will be personally responsible for developing and embedding the SEAL programme will vary from school to school, but it will need to be in place for your year group. It also links into the other areas of responsibility because in a positive environment the student is motivated to want to learn.

2. Managing the learning programme for the pupils

You coordinate the pupil's studies and act as the director of studies for the pupils in your year group, Key Stage or house. You are responsible for providing personalized learning through a flexible learning programme targeted to the learner's needs. The curriculum, especially at Key Stage 4, now includes a much wider range of courses than in the past and is still evolving. This means for example that you will need to liaise with the inclusion department, the gifted and talented coordinator, and the key members of staff developing the vocational diplomas in order to provide the necessary interventions or appropriate curriculum for an individual student.

3. Monitoring pupil progress through use of the available data and setting targets with the pupils

Target setting based on good data analysis is now a very high priority in secondary schools. It is regarded as the key to ensuring student achievement and to school improvement. For this reason your role as progress manager supporting pupil achievement has become one of your most important responsibilities. This is explored in Chapter 9.

Ways to develop yourself
Learning on the job
Most pastoral leaders learn their trade on the job. They come to the role with qualifications and experience in other areas. The teachers have subject degrees and may have had the opportunity to shadow a pastoral leader or act as deputy head of year/house, though this kind of very useful job experience is becoming rarer. Non-teacher pastoral leaders may have degrees in a wide range of subjects and you will have useful career or life experiences, on which you can draw. Some of you will have had management experience in a previous career; this is rarely valued by schools, but it may actually help you on the job. Nevertheless, basically you are learning by doing and by building up experience of what strategies and approaches tend to work in your particular school with the pupils for whom you have pastoral responsibility. The more often you do something that works, the more confident you became.

In-school support
People are your biggest source of support, so don't try to do everything on your own. Your first port of call to help you on the job is your colleagues, the other year leaders; they will have a lot of experience on which you can draw and will be able to advise you. Middle leaders are rarely provided with a mentor when they take up a new post; this is a pity as mentoring would help you at the time when you have least confidence in handling the job. Where no formal mentoring or induction is provided, watching how your colleagues approach dealing with the job will give you plenty to think about even if you disagree with their particular approach. You will quickly learn which year leaders have a reputation for being effective, and in what ways. The experienced pastoral leaders will have systems in place that are tried and tested. Asking them about these could save you from having to reinvent the wheel. Similarly, if you have a good relationship with an effective year leader, use him/her as a sounding board to consult when dealing with situations that are complex or difficult. Discussing an issue with a colleague helps you view a problem more objectively and to come up with more possible solution than trying to do everything on your own. Be sensitive to how busy your colleague is, and whether your need can be met by a short informal conversation over coffee in the staff room – you may need to ask for half an hour's help at a time they can manage.

Your line manager is likely to be an deputy/assistant head with a relevant responsibility, such as ECM (the Every Child Matters agenda), the pastoral system or pupil welfare. They should be there to support you when needed. Some schools have a clearly developed system in which senior managers take direct line management responsibility for supporting particular subjects or sections of the school. Others have rather less formal structures. Traditionally, senior managers tend to spend less time on their role as developers than middle managers. This is partly because their teams are often less permanent than year or subject teams. If you are lucky enough, however, to have a line manager with whom you have regular high quality dialogue, having this support available will help you become more effective and develop in your role. The relevant deputy/assistant head can also be a source of information for the developments/initiatives for which they hold responsibility.

You may have a different member of the SLT as your reviewer for performance management, so you could utilize your performance management review as a way to get the school to focus on your professional development. In this case make sure that you have given your own development needs a lot of thought before the annual review and take the initiative.

Training courses

There are plenty of behaviour management training courses on offer and consultants who will come into school. They tend to advertise by sending their fliers into school or through their personal websites. LAs regularly provide counselling courses, which can help you handle pupils or parents with problems and give you the techniques to get a dialogue going. Check their websites for the year's programme. Data training is also usually provided via the LA and each time things change you will need to update. Most pastoral management courses are one-day general courses because courses of two or more days don't attract enough participants to be economically viable, unless they are management courses provided by the LA, which are rarely specifically pastoral.

Cluster groups

If your area runs a pastoral network or cluster meeting this could act as an INSET forum as it can book speakers from within or outside the LA or hold discussion sessions on relevant subjects. Networking with pastoral leaders from other schools in the area gives you the opportunity to look outside your own school at how things are done elsewhere, and attending cluster meetings will help you keep up to date with current developments which affect the pastoral system.

Development programmes
NCSL's Leading from the Middle (LftM)
Pastoral leaders can participate in the NCSL's LftM development programme, a generic nine-month development programme for middle leaders which provides excellent online materials and the opportunity to experience in-school coaching in the role and attend some whole-day and twilight sessions with middle leader colleagues from other schools. The LftM does not aim to address the full range of pastoral issues, however. Spending nine months on this programme enables you to undertake a diagnostic to help you identify your own strengths and development needs and understand how your colleagues perceive you, and to develop your abilities through undertaking an initiative which makes you use specific skills. It is a good developmental experience which also gives you access to time with senior managers. To participate you should already be in post; it is not intended for aspiring pastoral leaders. Currently it is not accredited.

National Programme for Specialist Leaders of Behaviour and Attendance (NPSLBA)
The NPSLBA is a professional development programme which aims to strengthen practical and theoretical knowledge, develop leadership skills and build a professional community of specialists in behaviour and attendance.
It supports the national outcomes for children in ECM by focusing on:

- developing the SEAL programme
- reducing persistent absence
- promoting anti-bullying strategies
- improving behaviour
- raising attainment
- encouraging parental responsibility.

NPSLBA is delivered locally through small self-tutored cluster groups which are guided and supported by the LA. Regional advisers work intensively with LAs and provide support and guidance to develop and sustain the programme. It is open to all LA and school staff working with behaviour, attendance, and social and emotional attendance. There are no formal entry requirements, apart from a desire to develop leadership skills and to work collaboratively with others. Your workplace, however, will need to commit to support you during the programme, so talk to your line manager or head teacher before applying.

The programme is designed to support and enhance current work through self-reflection and active learning in the workplace. Each cluster selects its own 'learning path' dependent on prior experience and interests using learning materials available on the web or from other sources.

During this year-long programme, participants will attend three study days and will take turns in facilitating up to ten self-directed twilight study sessions. Participants will also be expected to undertake some study at home. Financial support may be available for those wishing to incorporate behavioural, emotional and social difficulty (BESD) topics into their learning.

Participants on the programme work towards the DCSF NPSLBA Certificate, which is recognized in LAs and Children's Services, and if you undertake the training you are expected to submit evidence of attendance, work-based learning activities, and reflective logs. The programme is moderated by the LA and/or the regional adviser.

NPSLBA may provide opportunities to gain further accreditation, including City and Guilds qualifications, foundation degrees and postgraduate certificates. Participation may also assist towards meeting the National Occupational Standards for Learning, Development and Support Services (LDSS). See www.teachernet.gov.uk/npslba for more information.

Keeping yourself up to date

Although the relevant deputy/assistant head should provide you with updates about the national initiatives for which he/she holds responsibility, this doesn't always happen, and it is always safer to check for yourself. The easiest starting point is to use TeacherNet, which puts summaries of new initiatives onto its own website and gives plenty of links to other useful sites, such as the DfE's website. As well as information, TeacherNet has useful case studies on a range of issues. Check the date of these as they are sometimes a few years old. It also has a publications section. You can sort this in different ways. Checking 'New publications' every so often, say once per half term, will show you if there is anything relevant for you. Often there is a summary of the report's main findings which might be all you need. If, for example, you need more information about curriculum developments, which may affect the students in your charge, e.g. what is happening about development of diplomas or introduction of IGCSEs, simply typing keywords into your search engine should enable you to find the information you need.

References and web links

Department for Education (DfE) – formerly the Department for Children, Schools and Families (DCSF): www.education.gov.uk

Department for Education and Skills (DfES) – existed between 2001 and 2007; see www.direct.gov.uk

The National College for Leadership of Schools and Children's Services (formerly the National College for School Leadership (NCSL): www.ncsl.org.uk

- This website is useful for both publications and details of the National College's development programmes.

National Programme for Specialist Leaders of Behaviour and Attendance (NPSLBA): www. teachernet.gov.uk/npslba

- Contact the NPSLBA support team on 0118 918 2555 or email support.npslba@ nationalstrategies.co.uk

National Strategies: www.standards.dcsf.gov.uk/nationalstrategies

Ofsted: www.ofsted.gov.uk

- For inspection and SEF guidance.

Standards Site: www.standards.dcsf.gov.uk

TeacherNet: www.teachernet.gov.uk

- This website is particularly useful for surveys of recent developments.

TeacherNet publications: www.teachernet.gov.uk/publications

Teachers TV: www.teacherstv.co.uk

- This website has a wide range of useful topics, especially for benchmarking your practice and for training. Check the menu as new programmes are added regularly.

NB: The Department is rationalising the number of websites it owns, and migrating content onto www.education.gov.uk. All required content from Teachernet, the Standards Site and GovernorNet has been migrated onto this site. Redirects will be put in place to help you find the appropriate sections of content. These sites are currently being archived onto the Government Web Archive, based at the National Archives. The DFE will announce when these sites will be closed at a later date. Other Department for Education websites will be migrated in the coming months.

Pages without the following disclaimer have been created or updated since the formation of the new Government on 11 May 2010, and reflect current policy.

'All statutory guidance and legislation published on this site continues to reflect the current legal position unless indicated otherwise.' Pages with this disclaimer were created before 11 May but have been retained for a number of reasons. For example they may:

- continue to reflect the current legal position; or
- provide useful historic or reference information; or
- provide a time series of research or analysis over a number of years; or
- be reference materials or case studies that schools' or children's workforces have told us they find useful.

This disclaimer will be kept in place until content is amended or removed by the Department. You can get further information by contacting the Department.

CHAPTER 2

Becoming effective in the role

What does it mean to be a middle manager?

There is no simple definition of middle management in schools. The closest one can come to a definition is to say that middle managers are the people whose role places them between the senior management team and those colleagues whose job description does not extend beyond the normal teaching and pastoral functions. It is a key role because schools are heavily dependent on the hard work and commitment of their middle managers for their success. This is often described as distributive leadership. At best there is a real partnership between the levels of leadership in the school and a shared aim to create a positive learning environment in which all children can achieve.

The jump from teacher to manager can be a difficult one to negotiate successfully. It is a truism that a good teacher is not necessarily immediately effective in a management role. There are some born leaders and managers, but most of us have to learn the skills, usually on the job. It is rare that a school provides induction for new managers, but finding yourself a buddy among the more experienced pastoral leaders could give you someone to use as a sounding board and an informal mentor.

Similarly, the move into schools from business or industry, if you become non-teaching pastoral leader, can be fraught. You may have had management experience but will know less about the intricacies of education and how schools work. Even if you have had management experience, transfer of skills is not easy as leadership is situational. You have to work hard to gain acceptance and too often any previous management experience that you may have acquired is not valued.

What is the difference between management and leadership?

The terms management and leadership are often used interchangeably, but they are different.

Management is about getting things done, achieving your goals and objectives, with the best possible use of the available resources. It is usually defined as focusing on systems structures and resources. Your biggest resource, however, is people, and that is why there is a grey area between management and leadership. Management is currently less high profile than leadership but should not be undervalued. Poor management can adversely affect the success of your leadership. Advice on putting in place effective management systems can be found further on in this chapter.

Leadership is harder to define than management. It usually regarded as setting vision and direction and focusing on people. It is about winning commitment, inspiring, motivating, developing and supporting people. Currently, leadership is high profile because your leadership can make a huge difference to what your team members and the students can achieve.

Whatever your job title, to be effective in your role you have to be both a manager and a leader. For example, you both lead and manage change.

The core purpose of the middle leader's role

This definition of the core purpose and list of roles that a middle leader might currently have to undertake was complied by a group of middle leaders at a training seminar:

- The emphasis is on leading other adults in the school. An increasing number of these adults will not be teachers.
- Impact on whole school development – your role in raising and maintaining standards.
- Enable and facilitate learning and development.
- Make a critical difference to children and adults in the whole school.
- Ensure an effective learning environment, for adults and pupils, which will enable pupils to reach their potential.

Leadership roles

In the course of your duties you undertake a variety of leadership roles in order to motivate your team and to get them to perform well. You may well be undertaking several of these roles at the same time and need to use different roles with different people. It could be useful to compare the list of roles, which follows, with your own job/role description as a middle leader and to think about which are the most significant roles for you. You may wish to add other roles to this list.

Key roles: Here are some ideas suggested during discussion by a group of pastoral leaders.

- **Expert/role model** – demonstrating your knowledge, confidence and expertise and modelling for others.
- **Facilitator** – enabler; spots opportunities and makes things happen.
- **Performance manager/developer**; providing constructive feedback, training or coaching.
- **Networker** – networks with middle leaders and other adults within the school and in other schools.
- **Representative** – representing the year/phase to parents and external agencies.
- **Parent figure** – your caring and supportive role.
- **Quality assurance manager** – monitoring, data analysis, performance management.
- **Scapegoat** – someone to blame when things go wrong.
- **Strategist and policy maker** – development planning, managing change.
- **Visionary** – demonstrating creativity when setting long-term goals.
- **Servant leader** – doing more for the team than would otherwise be the case because members of the team lack time or commitment.
- **Moral educator** – committed to high educational values. This role is high on the current educational agenda.
- **Social architect** – sensitive to the needs of pupils and staff. This role is frequently assumed by pastoral leaders; uses emotional intelligence (EI) effectively to promote good professional relationships.
- **Manager of the learning environment** – overarching role; secure and stimulating.

Approaches to leadership

To be effective in your role you need to be able to use the leadership styles most suited to the situation, the purpose, and the needs of the group or individual. Sometimes the task itself will influence the style that you adopt. This means you have to flexible. You will have a natural leadership style – your default style that you use most frequently – but you also need to be able to employ other styles when they are more appropriate. A lot of research has been done in this area by Daniel Goleman and others (see the end of this chapter). The six most commonly used styles are:

Dictatorship

Occasionally you will have to use a tough style. It is often described as coercive or dictatorial. It is appropriate when dealing with emergencies, or if you need to kick-start an unpopular project and you have to push people into doing something. It is hard work because you have to use it in situations where people are not self-starters and have to be constantly supervised. It works in the short term, but you have to know when to stop using it. The trouble with autocratic leaders is that once the emergency is over, too often they don't want to give up their full powers and they become tyrants, running the kind of regime which represses freedom and creative thought. This is when it is least successful.

Authoritarianism

A directive approach to leadership tells people clearly what they should be doing and how to do it. People know exactly where they stand and they tend to like this, because it provides security and they know that the directive leader will take the responsibility. Sometimes it is described as a visionary style because this kind of leader provides a clear vision and direction for the team. It is a straightforward, uncomplicated style. It usually works, but works best with an inexperienced team or with team members who lack confidence and want clear guidance and like you to take all the responsibility, or in turbulent situations where people are looking for certainty. It is time effective, productive and usually delivers good results, but over a period of time it could limit the development of capable team members.

People-centred leadership

This approach focuses on people in the team. Not surprisingly, they like this style, because it puts their interests high on the agenda. You need to use this style and it is most successful when previously there has been conflict within the team or the team has not been valued. Probably it should be a short term style because you have to watch becoming too cosy with your team members. If this happens, you lose sight of the objectives. What is important here is to judge when it is time to change to a different more challenging style.

Democracy

A democratic approach gives team members the opportunity to be involved in project development and participate in decision making. Their views matter and being able to contribute is developmental for them. This approach works best with the confident, capable, experienced team who understand what they are doing and will get irritated by being told what to do and how to do it. It may not be appropriate to use this approach when you first take over the team, because the previous leader may have used a very directive approach and they are used to being told, which makes them over-dependent. Genuine consultation takes time, but as long as decisions are reached and prove to be good decisions, it pays dividends because there will be real team spirit and the team will have ownership of the initiatives. For this reason using a democratic approach is a long-term strategy. Used appropriately, it can be very effective.

Pace setting

Sometimes you need to model for the team, but use this style with care because if you are the only exemplar of good practice it can be a real turn off. The element of coercion implied in 'You have to do it my way' can make this approach very unpopular with team members. Diversity isn't valued, which limits their contribution to the team. There is also the problem that team members are not clones of the leader and will not be able to operate in exactly the same way as you. Often team members forced to work in a way that does not come naturally to them go backwards and the style is unsuccessful and unpopular.

Coaching

Coaching is both a skill and a style. Really it is a process. It is a complementary style because you can use it with other styles. You may use a directive coaching style with a very inexperienced colleague and something much more like co-coaching with a very experienced or capable colleague, who may be the best tutor on your team. It has increased in importance over recent years, especially in helping the members of your team tackle a difficult issue or develop a skill. You will need to use it as part of your role as a developer. You may not provide the coaching personally, but it is your responsibility to see that someone appropriate provides the coaching. It takes time to develop the coaching relationship and to begin to reach real solutions, so don't expect it to provide a quick fix, but it could deliver good long-term solutions, as the coaching owned by the 'coachee'.

What is different about being a pastoral leader?

What are the main differences between pastoral and subject leadership and why do pastoral leaders need highly developed management and leadership skills?

Lack of pastoral expertise

- Very few pastoral managers have done any strategic units of study on pastoral issues before taking up the post, whereas a subject leader usually has a degree in the subject. You will probably have to build up your pastoral skills on the job and while managing a section.

A lot of crisis management
- Dealing with other people's crises occupies a lot of your in-school time. If the subject area is managed effectively, crises should not be a daily occurrence.
- Because people regularly unload their problems and emotions onto you, pastoral leadership is particularly physically demanding, tiring and stressful. It can be difficult to cope with this on a daily basis.

It is more difficult to win commitment from team members
- The team is usually not the most important aspect of the job for most members. They tend to be subject teachers first, and tutors a bad second. This can make them very reluctant tutors.
- You can sometimes get an impossible team member moved out of your team for the next year, whereas the subject head of department cannot transfer a difficult subject specialist to another subject team.

You may have less 'clout' than the subject leaders
- Your status and/or pay, especially if you are a non-teaching pastoral leader, may be less than that of the middle managers, who lead subject departments.

Leadership skills and how to acquire them
There are two main sets of skills that you will need to succeed in your role; the interpersonal skills and the thinking and planning skills.

Interpersonal skills
These are all the skills involving dealing with people. They include:

- Team building
- Motivating
- Delegating
- Counselling
- Coaching
- Chairing meetings
- Communicating

You need highly developed interpersonal and communication skills to interact successfully with the students, your team, parents and outsiders. Sometimes this is described as having 'emotional intelligence' (EI), that is being able to manage your own emotions so that you don't overreact or lose control, and having the social skills which enable you to develop effective relationships with others. It is so important because you probably meet more outsiders than subject leaders and you have to be able to interact successfully with a wide range of different audiences. Having a low level of interpersonal skills or low EI can lead to frequent confrontations and affect your ability to get people to cooperate.

Within the interpersonal skills, communication is a key skill. It covers such large area and needs subdividing.

It is about listening to what people say and making it clear:

- what the expectations are
- what is going on
- what the vision means – sharing the vision.

Thinking and planning skills
These include:

- Assimilating information
- Analytical skills
- Problem solving skills
- The ability to set goals and objectives for the team
- The ability to work out how to achieve the goals

The thinking skills are less high profile than EI, but if you don't use your thinking skills early on, you are likely to be ineffective or to make unnecessary mistakes. You have to deal on a daily basis with a lot of information, which you have to assimilate and analyse. You have to be able to both cope with a lot of detail and be able to tell the wood from its trees. You need your problem solving skills for dealing with both situations and people. You have to develop good planning skills to set the goals and objective for and with the team, and the ability to work out the best method of achieving the objectives in a specific situation and with a particular set of people.

Developing your leadership skills
The saying that practice makes perfect isn't true if you just keep making the same mistake over and over again. Getting feedback on how you use the skills will help you improve and develop. Use your colleagues to help you do this. Members of the team could provide some upwards appraisal or another year leader could act as learning partner and coach you. Get the feedback and discuss how you could adapt or improve and then have another go at using the skill or technique.

Guidelines for becoming effective
Communicate clearly
Good communications are vital to your success because you liaise with a wider range of audiences than other middle leaders. Information and decisions must be passed quickly and efficiently to the people who need to know, both within your team and outside it. If you haven't communicated effectively, the members of your team cannot achieve the department's goals or vision or work to your deadlines, because they don't know what they are. If communications are poor, the team feels left out and it affects their motivation. Communication is always a problematic area, especially in large organizations. We usually prepare very carefully when we have to communicate major change and try to provide full information to support innovation, but often we fall down on communicating the day-to-day information. Occasionally, as a result of the pressures of the job, we think that we have told people more than we have, so sometimes we need to check what we have actually said and to whom.

You need good skills for both written and oral communication. How you choose to communicate is up to you. Within your team you can use memos, emails, a regular department bulletin, tell people personally, or most likely, a mixture of approaches. The test is: Do the people who need to know actually know everything necessary to do the job properly? Sensitive issues, however, are always better dealt with face to face because your expression and body language are likely to be warmer than the words you have to use.

Listen actively
We also have to listen to what people tell us even if what they say is uncomfortable to hear. Effective communication involves actively listening to what your team members have to say. A frequent criticism made of leaders is that they don't listen; they just talk. But don't expect that your team members will always have listened carefully to you, especially if you are saying things that they don't want to hear. If your ideas are received in silence, this usually means that the team are unenthused, particularly if the silence is accompanied by negative body language. Sometimes their silence speaks volumes, especially when you are communicating yet another new initiative. It is as important to listen to what they don't say as to the words that they use.

Be pro-active about managing time
A pastoral leader has to be a good manager of time because of both the sheer volume of tasks with which you have to deal and the crisis management that occurs on a daily basis and which is a major component of the job. Time management is essentially concerned with managing all the demands and

tasks efficiently and effectively. **Efficiency** means getting right how and when to do the job; **effectively** means doing a job or task to the right standard.

You must be realistic about the time needed to do a job well. Experience in the post will help you develop this essential skill. You will do jobs less well if you rush them, or keep breaking off to do other things. Set a time limit for jobs that should not take long or that are low priority, and free up enough time for those which require thorough analysis. Sometimes attempting less and concentrating on priorities can increase your productivity and effectiveness.

Establish good systems and make them work for you
Giving the appearance of being on top of the job can make a real difference to how your team members perceive you and to the impact that you make.

Why administration matters
Administration focuses on the paperwork – collecting and correlating information. It is often seen as reactive – carrying out someone else's instructions. Although there are now restrictions on the kind of administrative tasks teachers are allowed to undertake, administration remains time consuming and unpopular.

Getting the administration right is important, however, because it secures the basic conditions of work – it can make a real difference to how your team is able to work. If, for example, your responsibilities include PSHE and you fail to keep the resources in good order so that the team can't find the books and equipment they need to teach the lesson, it will lead to dissatisfaction and resentment among the team and it will be very difficult to motivate them. They won't trust you and this will affect their willingness to work with you and for you.

The following short exemplar contrasts two ways of dealing with the same organizational task. A Year 8 team received hand-written PSHE materials on the day of the lesson and often after the start of the session soon became very negative about the subject. They resented being put in this position in front of the pupils and became vocally critical of their team leader. In stark contrast, the Year 9 team, whose lesson materials were easily accessible from the year tutor's learning platform, and the approaches discussed and agreed at the team meeting the previous term, were much more positive about teaching PSHE. (See also Chapter 3 – particularly the section on needing to be a manager as well as a leader.)

Poor administration can make a real difference to people's lives. If you get it wrong, for example essential records are not kept or cannot be located when they are needed so that information about a pupil is not to hand when it is needed for a case conference about a child, it will make you and the school appear inefficient but, more important, it could affect or delay the decision being made about the child's future. Inaccurate information also has a negative impact. If the administrative assistant in charge of making entries for examinations makes mistakes over the entry list and pupils in your year group are not entered for subjects that they should be entered for, and some are entered for subjects that they don't study, it will make a real difference to them, and if not put right, it could affect their future.

You don't need to reinvent the wheel. Most schools have good systems in place and plenty of templates and so forth available on their ICT system for you to use. Check what is available during the first half term you are in post and ask your colleagues about the systems that they use. You will know from their reputations which year leaders are considered to be good organizers and will be likely have good systems.

The internet can provide examples against which you can benchmark your practice. If you are looking for sample formats or useful software systems, use your web browser to find examples. A lot of schools put their structures and procedures onto the internet, but treat these with care as they are not always exemplars of good practice. Chapter 9 provides information about some of the most popular software systems to use in monitoring behaviour and achievement.

Once you have audited what is already in place talk to the team about what might need tweaking a bit to make it work better. Acting on their suggestions will gain you good will at the same time as improving how the department works. The systems and structures need to be in good working order as you don't have time to think about them – they are the tools not the end in itself, so check them occasionally. A good time to do this could be towards the end of an academic year since it is important that the new academic year gets off to a flying start.

Distinguish between what is urgent and what is important

The demands made on a teacher, particularly the demands placed on middle managers in schools, may seem endless, but some of the jobs are much more important than others. Urgent things must be done immediately but they are not necessarily important in themselves. If a teacher is absent that day, someone will have to cover the lesson. The matter is urgent and needs sorting out, but it is only important that day. Your development plan for the next three years is important, but you may not have time to do anything about it that day. The important things are strategic; they are concerned with helping you achieve your vision. Ask yourself:

- What are the most important things?
- What are the most urgent things?

Using this approach will help you clarify and keep sight of your real priorities.

Being able to prioritize effectively will make all the difference to your success as a manager.

- Clarify what goals are the most important.
- Don't have too many priorities – this could affect your chances of success (see Chapter 3).

Analysing how you spend your time

Analysing how you are managing now could help you to take control of time. It will certainly show you how little time you are actually spending on the really important things. It has been claimed that around 90 per cent of a manager's time is spent not in managing but in doing – does this apply to you? Pick a day sometime soon and log all your activities for the working day (sometimes people survey a week so that they can see the spread of activities).

- How much of the day is teaching/administration/interaction with pupils or interaction with adults? Work out the proportions and list them on the chart.
- Log what happened in the free periods/non-contact time.
- If you hold some management responsibility, how much time is devoted to this and is it maintenance, development administration or personal contacts/team building? What percentage of your time in that period did you actually spend thinking strategically or in making plans for the future?
- What percentage did you spend dealing with people, responding to either pupils or colleagues or sorting out their concerns?
- How much time do you have to spend on supervising or supporting colleagues?
- What is the proportion of time spent on other people's crises?
- How much of your time was spent fire fighting? Are you having to run fast to stand still?
- Include the work done at home in the evening.

Try not to lose sight of the big picture

What matters is to keep your eye firmly on the main objectives that you want to achieve. Schools are pressurized so this can be difficult. It can be particularly difficult for a pastoral manager because so much of your time is spent dealing with other people's crises. Keep track of the big picture by:

- clarifying your key objectives for a term or half a term at a time
- setting yourself realistic deadlines and trying hard to keep to them
- refocusing every ten days or so.

Refocusing helps you see whether you can still see the bigger picture and distinguish the wood from its trees. It helps you remember the important things which you have forgotten or neglected because so much else is going on. It reminds you that some things are now nearing their deadlines and have become urgent as well as important, and that you need to allocate some protected time during the next few days to completing the task.

Make the jobs manageable

- Make sure that you have with you all the information that you need to do the job so that you can get started straight away and don't waste the free time that you have.
- Break a substantial task down into its component parts so that a major task becomes a series of smaller jobs, with which you can deal step by step.
- Get someone else to check you haven't left out something important – someone else is always better than you at seeing your mistakes.
- The more clearly your file system is labelled or subdivided into sections, the easier it is to find the information you need. This applies to computer files as well as paper. Avoid having a file labelled 'miscellaneous'!
- Review the classification annually so that it always relates to the needs of your job.

Do not put things off

A poor manager of time always puts off doing the job until he or she is always engaged in brinkmanship. This may be because:

- the task is dull or difficult, so you put off doing it
- it will take you a long time, you are tired and you don't fancy starting it now
- it is not urgent; you could do it tomorrow
- you are not sure how to deal with it, so you convince yourself not to start it yet, in case you get it wrong.

If you delay on tasks, the problem tends to get worse. If you put off dealing with dissatisfied pupils, staff or parents, their attitude worsens and eventually a small thing can trigger a major confrontation. Try to take initial action on a job on the day it arrives. Only very simple straightforward jobs can be dealt with in one touch or action, but your initial response to acknowledge receipt or get things started should be immediate. You will then need to make time for thinking and to investigate further, but the initial swift response brings good will and indicates that you will be following up and getting things done.

Delegate effectively

Good delegation helps you to manage the role effectively. It is about not trying to do everything yourself and not dumping jobs that you don't want to do on someone else; this only creates resentment. Good delegation is meant to be developmental for the people who take on the delegated tasks, so it is worth thinking about how to achieve it.

What makes delegation work?

- Good planning – thinking it through first and involving the delegatee in the planning.
- Choosing the task carefully – matching the task to the level of expertise and ability of the delegatee with the right degree of challenge to enable the delegatee to succeed.
- Being clear what it means – delegation is not the same as dumping tasks that you don't want to do because they are time consuming or difficult; it should be useful experience for the person involved and contribute to their professional development.
- Clear parameters being agreed at the start – time span, degree of autonomy/supervision, etc.
- Being unselfish – sometimes it involves giving up a task you enjoy.
- Giving the person the freedom to do the job – control freaks find delegation difficult so try to avoid unnecessary interference.
- Not expecting the person to clone your approach – they will do it differently from you.
- Not expecting it to be faster – delegation takes time.
- Being pleased if the delegatee does the task better than you would have.
- Recognizing achievement and ensuring that the person gets the credit for what he/she has done and giving the recognition publically. As a rule of thumb: If it succeeds they get the recognition; if it fails you take the responsibility.

You must not delegate high risk tasks that are very likely to fail. You do not set someone else up for failure.

Don't keep difficult problems to yourself

Make it a principle to talk problems through with someone else. When you hit a problem, trying to solve it on your own can be unproductive. The longer you worry about the problem the less likely you are to solve it and the more depressed you become. Talking it through with someone else is about getting another perspective on the problem. The other person will see it differently from you and care less. Your mountain is their pimple! This means they can be much more objective than you about your problem and can help you to view it from a different angle and move forward.

Think about the effect your time management has on others

CASE STUDY 2.1: THE EFFECT OF INAPPROPRIATE TIME MANAGEMENT

Sophie was a night owl. Head of Sixth Form in a comprehensive school, she did all her planning and preparation late at night or in the very early hours of the morning. She was also an avid bridge player and midnight was often the earliest she got home. As a result, she found getting up difficult and arrived at school just in time for registration. She was distinctly not at her best at this time, and leaving aside the fact that she was not there to see them before school, sixth formers who caught her on her way into school received short shrift and her colleagues tended to avoid interacting with her at this time. At the end of the day, she was prepared to stay late and see sixth formers, but they did not want appointments at this time. They had jobs and had to get to work. They felt that Sophie did not care about them, and this adversely affected her relationship with her year group, but a lot of the problem was about the way that she worked and used her time.

Try to work within your deadlines

Some of us are much better than others at working within deadlines. Failure to deliver on time has the same effect on colleagues as poor administration and can make you very unpopular. Rushing around at the last minute trying to deliver on time really irritates others, particularly the steadier, more methodical members of the team. They won't appreciate that you are really very creative; they will remember how bad tempered and impatient you were at that time. If you are late completing an important initiative, they will feel it reflects on them.

If meeting deadlines is a problem for you, it can help to work with some-one else who will keep you up to the mark. There are no miracles but try to work back from the end – this means that you have to work out when the job has to be finished and the steps you need to take to get there and match this to a timetable. This matches the planning strategy of identifying the outcome and then working out how to get there. Planning out your time could help you manage it better.

Similarly, if one or more of your team members has this problem, you need to be aware of the problem and work with them to try help your colleagues manage better and prevent unpleasantness developing between team members with different working styles.

References

The Curriculum Publishing Company: info@edu-fax; www.edu-fax.com

Goleman, D. (1998), *Working with Emotional Intelligence*, London, Bloomsbury.

Goleman, D., Boyatziz, R. and McKee, A. (2002), *The New Leaders*, London, Time Warner Books.

Murdock, A. and Scutt, C. (1993), *Personal Effectiveness*, Oxford, Butterworth-Heinemann, Institute of Management.

Nathan, M. (2005), *The Leadership Team Edu-fax*, Ipswich, Edu-fax (chs 1 and 4).

Nelson, I. (1995), *Time Management for Teachers*, London, Kogan Page.

CHAPTER 3

Leading the tutor team

In education a team may be groups of teachers and other staff who have these characteristics:

- They share objectives and the commitment to achieving them.
- They have the necessary authority, autonomy and resources to achieve the objectives.
- They have well-defined and unique rules.
- They may be permanent or short term.
- They include no more than 15–20 people.

Some special challenges in leading a pastoral team

Your role as team leader constitutes one of the main challenges for you as a year leader.

Particular problems and issues

Lack of choice in membership of the team

It is rare that pastoral leaders get much choice in assembling their tutor team. You may or may not be consulted, dependent on your own standing and influence and the ethos of the school. Often the team is put together late in the summer term when the last staff appointment has finally been made. This means that you are likely to have ill-assorted team members who did not choose to be on your team. If you are regarded as good at dealing with difficult people, you may find that you are given a disproportionate number of these 'characters'.

Team members lack motivation

You have to be realistic about the level of motivation of the majority of your team members. Few tutors are really enthused about being tutors. It is not their main role in the school and many want to concentrate on their role as subject teachers. They regard it as an additional burden on an already pressurized workload. In practice most grumble a bit but do a reasonable job. A minority, however, are really reluctant tutors and getting these horses to water is an ongoing problem for year leaders and house heads; they take up a disproportionate amount of your time, and challenge your authority as a leader.

Lack of good quality tutors

Naturally good tutors do exist, but in small numbers; this means that while you may have one or two really good tutors on your team, several may leave much to be desired, either because they lack motivation and commitment or they do not have the ability to do the job well.

Inconsistent practice

Some of your tutors won't share the objectives. This makes it difficult to win commitment. These tutors won't bother with uniform checks or enforcing rules with which they don't personally agree.

Lack of continuity

Your team is meant to go up with the students through to the end of Year 11. By the time the team reaches Year 11, the composition of the team is likely to have changed totally, either because members have left or been promoted or because the team has been reconfigured because of problems elsewhere in the school.

Lack of training for the team members

Tutoring is a skill, which needs developing, but there is little training available for tutors and even if there were, the tutors who most need it would be least likely to apply for it. Tight INSET budgets don't help; colleagues are much more likely to choose a training session which will help them consolidate their subject skills than a session to help them enhance their tutoring skills. This means that developing the tutoring skills of your team is down to you and this is no easy task as schools rarely give time on school INSET days for tutor training, or if some training is provided, normally in the after-lunch session, there is no follow-up and the training is quickly forgotten.

Role tensions

If you are a non-teaching year leader the traditional problems may be compounded because the teachers find it difficult to accept you as leader and question both your authority and your expertise.

These issues challenge you as a leader, but they are not insurmountable. It means that you need highly developed leadership skills. For this reason, this chapter aims to present you with ideas and suggestions for getting the most out of your team and some materials that you could use or adapt when working with your tutors, and with some detailed case studies based on real schools so that you can compare these scenarios and possible solutions with your own team's problems.

Strategies for team building

Sharing the problem

Working together with other pastoral leaders on common problems makes sense because the problems identified at the beginning of this chapter are common to leading tutor teams. A sharing session focused on 'This has worked for me . . .' can be very useful. Drawing on the experience of other pastoral team leaders who have been in post for a while can give you ideas and strategies that you could apply or adapt. You need a range of strategies because the different members of your team are likely to respond in very different ways.

Team leaders can catalyse effective team working through

- alignment to the school or 'subject' vision
- critical review of the impact of the team – team audit
- expecting the best – while remaining realistic
- motivation
- effective communication
- shared leadership and appropriate delegation
- encouraging creativity
- setting aspirational goals for the team and individuals
- professional learning
- mutual accountability.

For reflection/discussion

This list was created by a group of pastoral leaders in a discussion focused on how to get the best out of the team. You may want to do this in your own school as a group of year heads and create your own list from first principles. The other way that you can use this list is to take it as it stands as a piece of stimulus material and, working in pairs or as a whole group, reflect on and discuss how you could deliver any of these approaches.

Auditing the team

You need to know where you stand. A team audit which your team members complete will indicate how they view the team. Analysing it will indicate:

- whether the team's perceptions are similar to or very different from yours
- whether they all feel the same way about things
- the areas that are perceived as strong
- the areas that are perceived as problematic
- whether the issues and concerns raised are areas that you can address or relate to whole school issues beyond your control ('Can I do anything about this?').

The team audit below is not specific to pastoral teams, but focuses on the factors needed for a team to function effectively, so it is a good starting point for you. You may want to use it as a whole so that you can get an overview or you can focus on particular sections and tailor-make it to fit your particular requirements. You might also find it useful to add an empty line at the end in which they can write one comment on something they think works particularly well or would like to see improved.

To complete the audit, team members have to grade each bullet point on a 1–5 scale, with 1 being the top grade and 5 the bottom. It is also useful to get them to assess each section. Advise them not to average the grades for the section, but to take an overview of how the team is functioning in this particular category. Tell your team members not to give all '3's as this is fence sitting and not helpful.

Usually audits are anonymous; those with particular axes to grind are likely to put their names on the form as they will want you to know what they feel. If you have the school's resentful person on your team, this person's completed questionnaire will stand out from the others even if they don't sign it, so expect to receive all '5's. Try not to take this personally.

Normally, people are prepared to say what they think, but if their previous leader was very directive, and did all the thinking for the team, there will be a culture of dependency, which you will need to break. Similarly in an early stage of team building, the members are rarely honest with each other and more likely to bite their tongues or tell you what they think you want to hear. This is because the trust between team members and the team leader hasn't yet built up. Developing a more open culture takes time; you will have to run some sessions which encourage the sharing of views in an unthreatening way. If it doesn't appear to work at first, persevere. In this situation, it might be appropriate to wait until the end of the first year before you conduct a team audit.

What really matters is that you act on the results of the completed questionnaires, otherwise the team members will feel that this was merely a paper consultation and that their time has been wasted. Analyse and chart the results and present them to the team using a team meeting to focus on how to move forward on the areas which are most underdeveloped. Consulting the team about next steps is an important aspect of team building because it is easier to win commitment from team members who feel valued.

What do you do if the problem lies with the leadership section, i.e. you are the problem? Give yourself time to absorb what they have said and try not to take it too personally. Think about why they have given the low grades and against which criteria. Are they expecting you to be the clone of the previous leader and your style is different? Is it really a reflection of whole school issues? Is it particular actions that you have taken, or the way that you have carried them out that caused the team's resentment? Focusing on issues helps to make it less personal. Then think about how you can resolve the issue. Showing that you have taken on board some of the points made about your leadership is likely to earn you respect.

A team audit

1. **Shares clear objectives and agreed goals, and**
   - agrees on what the team is trying to do and its priorities for action
   - agrees on what differences are tolerable within the team
   - clarifies the role of team members
   - discusses values and reaches a general consensus on its underlying philosophy.

2. **Has clear procedures**
   - for communicating information and expectations
   - for holding meetings
   - for making decisions and delegating responsibility.

3. **Reviews its progress regularly and**
   - reassesses its objectives
   - evaluates the processes that the team is using
   - does not spend too much time discussing the past.

4. *Has leadership appropriate to its membership*
- The leader is visible and accessible.
- The leader utilizes the strengths of all the team members.
- The leader models the philosophy of the team.

5. *Has open lines of communication*
- Team members talk to each other about issues, not just to the team leader.
- Each person's contribution is recognized.
- Positive and negative feedback are given.
- Members are open-minded to other people's arguments.
- Ideas and advice from outside the team are welcomed.
- Members are skilled in sending and receiving messages in face-to-face communication.

6. *Has a climate of support and trust*
- Members give and ask for support.
- Members spend enough time together to function effectively.
- Members' strengths are recognized, valued and built upon.
- There is respect for other people's views.
- The audit relates positively to other teams and groups.

7. *Recognizes that conflict is inevitable and can be constructive*
- Issues are dealt with immediately and openly.
- Members are assertive but not aggressive.
- Feelings are recognized and dealt with.
- Members are encouraged to contribute ideas.
- Conflicting viewpoints are seen as normal and dealt with constructively.

8. *Is concerned with its members' personal- and career development*
- Each team member receives a regular review.
- The leader looks for chances to develop the members and they to develop the leader.

Matching your vision to the school or subject vision

One of the key elements of leadership is setting the vision and direction for the team. Teams are often ineffective when there is no vision or a lack of clarity about the vision. Focusing your team on how as a pastoral/year team it contributes to the overall school vision and what its particular objectives should be for the year/long term is actually a team building activity. The most productive team building activities involve the team members working together on a real piece of development. In most schools the school improvement plan (SIP) focuses on achievement. In the current climate, with the emphasis on the learners' achievement, there should be no difficulty in aligning your goals to the whole school goals.

Involve the team in determining the goals

Harnessing commitment is usually easier if the team members have been involved in formulating the goals. A top-down directive approach often produces resentment. In a time limited world, however, you may not have the time to work totally from first principles. What could work very well is for you to develop the overall aim focused on the students in your year/section achieving or surpassing expectations and involve the team in setting and working out how to achieve the objectives, which are usually short term and more concrete – your one-year action plans. This shows that you have exercised your leadership role in setting the direction and that you do have some vision, but also that you value their input. If nothing else, this exercise will develop their understanding and awareness of the goals.

Don't have too many priorities

Chapter 2 highlighted the importance of distinguishing the urgent from the important and identifying your priorities, but it is also important that there aren't too many priorities as this will affect the likelihood of success. Research has indicated that effective managers can deliver three major initiatives successfully in a year. Often the government's agenda forces us to deliver far more than three major initiatives. This means that you have to identify what really matters and be realistic when you decide your long-term priorities with the team. It could mean putting on the back burner a scheme you would like to implement so that other priorities can be delivered, or you may have to phase an initiative over two years rather than one. Make the rationale for the choices clear to your team.

Maintaining direction

Sadly, because schools are so pressurized, it is often difficult to focus on the long-term goals because too much of the time is actually spent on fire fighting and you become reactive and your leadership suffers. You need to demonstrate to your team that you haven't lost sight of the big picture, even in the worst weeks of term, and that you are able to maintain your direction.

Set clear and realistic expectations

You have to take into account that your tutors were appointed as subject teachers; being a tutor is not their main job, so expectations should realistic. This doesn't mean, however, that they should be low. One way to deal with this is to set the expectations by providing a tutor's job description or a code of practice. Examples of each approach are provided below; they could complement each other.

Below is the description of their duties and procedures that School B issues to its tutors to clarify their responsibilities. It is really a job description. This exemplar illustrates a top-down directive approach and is designed to ensure consistency, which is an important feature of an effective pastoral system. In School B, all the tutors know what the expectations are, but as they may not have been involved in deciding what the responsibilities should be, you may have your work cut out with some tutors to make them toe the party line.

EXEMPLAR 3.1: TUTOR JOB DESCRIPTION

Form tutor responsibilities, duties and procedures
The Form Tutor is the personal link with the child, parent and the school. The Form Tutor's responsibilities, duties and procedures include:

Attendance: Register/oversee swipe (ensure there is silence when paper register is taken), monitor attendance, collect absence notes and pass to the PSA, identify problems, establish reasons, contact home (via student diary, letter, telephone), refer persistent problems to the Learning and Progress Leader (LPL)/Pastoral Support Assistant (PSA) for parental meeting, EWO referral.

Punctuality: Monitor punctuality – students late to school will get a detention on the day from the LPL/PSA; those late to registration to get detention from tutor; inform parents via student diary of any concerns, or by letter (standard letter available/email).

Uniform: Monitor uniform/jewellery; with persistent problems contact home (as above) and refer to the LPL/PSA, give warning, confiscate item (standard letter available/email), ensure no banned items.

Student diary: Monitor and signed by tutor ONCE A WEEK.

Academic progress: Monitor academic progress.

Social progress: Monitor social progress, health matters, any personal problems, give advice/counselling, refer any problems you are unable to deal with to the LPL/PSA.

Discipline: Monitor, liaise with subject teachers and teaching and learning leaders (TLLs). Refer persistent and ongoing concerns to the LPL/PSA, contact home, Form Tutor daily or weekly report. Submit general behaviour reports to the LPL and behaviour in lesson reports to the specific subject leader.

Commendations and rewards: Recommendations from tutors/list of names to the LPL/PSA.

PSHE/Citizenship programme: Contribute to the effective delivery of this programme when required.

Assembly: Tutor to lead form into the hall, in register order and in silence, oversee class assembly (please refer to specific notes on rules for assemblies).

Social activities: trips, parties, sports events.

During form time: PSHE/Citizenship, form tutor report (daily or weekly), silent reading 'free time' as a reward, finishing off work revision notice, letters home, etc.

For reflection/discussion

Benchmark/compare this exemplar with any guidance put out by your own school:

- How similar are the expectations?
- Which responsibilities cause you the most problems?
- How much form/tutor time does your school allocate?
- How does your school use form time? What is the balance of PSHE/SEAL to individual working?

Developing a tutors' code of practice

If you want to get a higher level of involvement from your tutors you could do some work with them to develop a code of practice.

Involve the team in the process but don't make them do all the work. Have some stimulus points that will help focus thinking, but ensure full consultation on the draft so that they get a lot of input, and have to think about the role, but don't have to take way homework. This ensures that it isn't too top-down and also isn't burdensome. Taking this approach is good use of meeting or INSET time because it is developmental and it helps clarify what it means to be a tutor in your school or team.

Here are a few stimulus statements that you could start from. You can adapt this list to fit your needs. It is set up as a 'diamond nine' – eight statements and a blank line so individual tutors can add a statement that they think should be included. You might want to organize the session in stages: team members look at the list individually then share their thoughts with one other team member, and then the whole team discuss it.

WHAT IT MEANS TO BE A TUTOR

- Tutors are a vital part of the pastoral care process.
- Tutors are the first line of reference for the members of the tutor group.
- Tutors are responsible for the conduct of the form on a daily basis.
- Tutors take a consistent approach and ensure that routine procedures are carried out.
- Tutors have oversight of the welfare of the tutor group.
- Tutors have oversight of the personal learning programmes of members of the tutor group and monitor the progress of the individuals in the tutor group.
- Tutors need access to relevant information which will help them support individuals within the tutor group.
- Tutors should liaise closely with the year head and vice versa.

The discussion should help you focus your tutors on what really matters in the role – the key responsibilities. The stimulus list is deliberately short – the idea is that there is plenty of opportunity for input. Completing the blank line should produce several points you can add to the list. This could for example give you the opportunity to highlight where the tutor fits into the school's agenda of raising achievement and the blank line could be used to draft what this means for the tutor. If you have real philosophical disagreements, the group might also need to resolve the thorny issue of what are tolerable differences. This would mean that expectations are clear to all and that you are in a strong position able to say 'This is what we agreed'. It also means that you shouldn't have to waste your time trying to make a recalcitrant tutor enforce something that the team has agreed is of minor importance. If differences are irreconcilable, involve and endeavour to get support from your line manager, the SLT member with pastoral responsibility.

Take a similar approach to developing the vision by using a set of stimulus statements as your starting point for discussion.

Motivating the team and its members

A vitally important factor in leadership is winning the commitment of the team members – a lot of this is about motivating the team. This means that you need to understand what makes people willing to cooperate and what makes them reluctant to work with some managers.

Being a manager as well as a leader

To succeed as a team leader, you also have to be a good manager (see Chapter 2). Management is all about providing the conditions through which the team can function effectively and do its job. As a pastoral manager, your ability to organize so that everything runs smoothly is crucial to your success because whatever you do, so much of your time will be crisis management, dealing with other people's crises, which always occur at the most inconvenient times. How well you deal with things impacts on your team's motivation.

Start by removing the negative factors or demotivators. You may or may not be the person who has responsibility for the administrative side of the role (see Chapter 1), but you are responsible for the management. What does this mean in practice? Your team members are entitled to clarity about what to do and how to do it. This means that you have to put in place detailed steps and timetables to ensure results and to organize the allocation of the necessary resources. You also need systems to monitor the implementation of your action plans.

Poor administration makes it difficult for people to their job properly; it affects how they feel about it and influences their attitude towards 'the management'. For example, if your tutors regularly receive inaccurate or late information, try to use it and have to deal with the consequences, or they don't have resources or equipment available when they should have, it affects their attitude towards doing the job. Ongoing inefficiency makes people feel annoyed and frustrated and that their time has been wasted. This can have a really negative effect on motivation, and the result will be that if your tutors are asked to collect information or complete a task, they won't want to make the effort because the arrangements won't work, or nothing ever comes of it and their expectations are very low. Meetings that are talking shops and never reach decisions can have the same effect. Case study 3.1, illustrates good procedures and getting the most out of the meeting time available.

Good school management information systems and ICT should make it easier than it was for pastoral leaders in the past to handle the administrative side of the role, so that all the information about a particular pupil is to hand when you need it for a case conference or session with parents. In many schools non-teaching administrative assistants deal with a lot of this.

You still need to use your supervisory role, however, to ensure that the procedures are working properly and are clear to everyone involved. Once you have clear procedures in place, you need to monitor them by checking them occasionally to see that they still work. You may find that they don't work as well as in the past because circumstances have changed. In that case tweak or modify the procedure or structure to get it working again.

Although in motivation terms, poor administration and management can turn people off, you need to be aware that good systems and structures rarely turn people on; they are an entitlement, not a motivator, so it is important to understand what does motivate people.

Inspirational leadership
The quality of the leadership you provide is one of the key factors in winning commitment from your team. Leadership is contextual; different models fit different schools and particular teams. The state of development that the team is in when you take it over will also make a difference to the style you should use. If the team are used only to being told what to do, it will take a while before they are use a democratic approach successfully. Because they are used to a directive approach, they will think that you are not doing your job as a leader. In these circumstances you will have to develop them out of dependence at an appropriate pace. What really matters to your success is to be able to be flexible and able to adapt your approach to the needs of the team and the situation.

The best leaders are often described as inspirational. Although it regularly features on people's list of what makes a successful leader, it is always difficult to define 'inspirational'. Leadership focuses on people, your 'followers', and what you do to attract and keep them. Research indicates there is no blueprint for effective leadership or one particular characteristic that all leaders will have. Current thinking about leadership in both Britain and America suggests, however, that successful leaders exhibit many of the features from a range of characteristics. The findings from successful schools suggest that the more of these characteristics that you have, the more successful you are likely to be in your leadership role.

For reflection/discussion
The list below comes from a pastoral training seminar in which the participants focused on what characteristics the leader would need to demonstrate in order to motivate and inspire his/her team.

- Clarity of vision and direction
- Accessibility – involves others and shares

- Leads by example/role model
- Demonstrates energy and enthusiasm
- Uses the right blend of challenge and realism
- Takes a constructive approach
- Creates a climate of openness and trust
- Treats people with respect and earns respect
- Knows when to take risks
- Innovative without being over-burdensome
- Good organizer
- Communicates well and regularly
- Unselfish – 'takes care of team members'; protects their security.

Being a role model

All school leaders model leadership for the team and for the pupils on a daily basis. Often this is unconscious. Hopefully you will go home and say to a member of your family, for example, that the deputy head acted in a particular way in his leadership role and that you learnt a lot from this and would like to model your own practice on his approach. More frequently, we react negatively and what we actually say is: 'The deputy did such and such today. It was a disaster and I'd never do it that way!' Your team will react to your leadership actions and style. You can't expect to please all the people all the time, but you do need to think about the impression that you make. You can't expect your tutors to develop a positive relationship with their tutor groups if you fail to bother to do this with your team. If you clearly demonstrate this to your team – that you care about them in a professional way – they are more likely to do what you ask and with fewer complaints.

Similarly, making the time to ask after their health or families if you know that there have been issues, or from time to time simply remembering to ask how their children or partners are, can make a real difference to a team member's attitude. Being able to remember a few family names usually helps. Keep a note of these in your file. It doesn't mean that you want or need to be 'best friends' with your team members; it means that you treat them as people, not just as tutors. It is part of accessibility and makes it easier for them to raise issues with you. A lot of this advice shouldn't take extra time; it is a matter of how you use your time.

Recognition and encouragement

The best motivator is the way that you use praise and encouragement. For your tutors it really makes the difference because it isn't their main job in the school and so it is important to give recognition for the work that they do. Not surprisingly in these circumstances, nagging is a turnoff and just demotivates people, so you have to focus on the positive. A cheerful word of encouragement to a tutor, which indicates that you are aware of the efforts that he/she is making with individual pupils or simply that they have done everything asked of them uncomplainingly often makes a real difference to how people feel about the job. This means ensuring that if your tutors come up with good ideas they get recognition and the credit for what they have done or that you comment approvingly on how much time or effort they have put in to dealing with a particular situation or supporting a member of the tutor group. Always be specific, so that the person can see that it is not just grease aimed at getting more out of them, but that you have genuinely noticed and approve of aspects of their work. If you use 'thank you' notes, make sure that they are personalized with the individual's name and make specific mention of what you are thanking them for. This way the team member knows that the recognition is real.

Using social events

At pastoral training seminars there are often discussions of whether it pays dividends to run social events to help weld the team together. Feedback indicates that it works for some teams but not for others, so it is a question of trying it and testing whether it works for you. If only some people enjoy it and other members of your team don't want to participate, either because it creates an additional burden such as paying a babysitter or they don't want to socialize with the team outside work, beware of dividing your team members into two teams rather than team building. Where it does work because meeting other team members off the premises and outside the school context does help the bonding, then go for it. Going on a residential with other members of staff certainly makes a difference. If you do decide to run a social activity, it can be useful to get different members of the team to choose the activity so that it is not your choice and yet another top-down activity. Going out for meal, ten pin bowling and river cruises regularly feature on the list of activities that have worked in welding pastoral teams. Getting the timing right can also help you. Try to avoid the pre-Christmas period as usually there are too many events then. Some firms hold their Christmas event towards the end of January, not just because the Christmas rush is then over, but because this is the darkest, most depressing time of the year and it gives people something to look forward to and enjoy.

Take the 'chocolate cake' approach to leadership

Team meetings tend to be timetabled for after school, when people are tired after a day's teaching. You can't expect people to be really creative in these circumstances and often tiredness can make people irritable and dismissive.

Providing tea and chocolate cake at least helps to create a more positive atmosphere because it shows the team that you care about their well-being. This approach applies to more than just the team meetings. Often bringing in a cake or some chocolates when the team has been particularly pressurized, or after an evening event such as a pupil progress meeting with parents, makes people feel that their efforts have been noticed and appreciated. Making people feel special and that they matter is a key motivator. Don't forget the healthy option – always provide some fruit as well so that people don't feel left out.

Your role as a developer
Shared leadership and appropriate delegation
'Distributed leadership' is an 'in word' in current educational thinking. The idea behind it is that leadership can't just be the role of the head teacher, but needs to be shared with the SLT and distributed to the middle leaders, without whose efforts much of the leadership role could not be managed. For middle leaders there is always a dichotomy, as on the one hand you are expected to delegate and on the other the tasks that you are asking someone else to do are on your job description. It is particularly hard for pastoral leaders to delegate any of their responsibilities or to carry out their role as a developer because tutoring is a secondary role and often members of your team have leadership responsibilities of their own (see Chapter 2 for delegation issues).

Case study 3.2 addresses this issue and explores how one year leader dealt with this dilemma.

Case studies
The case studies which follow are included to illustrate how year heads have approached dealing with this aspect of their role so that you can reflect on how other year leaders have handled problems that you may have to face.

CASE STUDY 3.1: MAKING IT WORK

I've been a year leader for several years now and getting the best out of my team has always been a challenge. Some things have got easier. For example, now that all the administrative data is keyed into the tutors' laptops, I don't have to chase registers for attendance and punctuality as I used to do. Some tutors are less good than others about keying in the information, and accuracy varies, which can cause problems especially when you are seeing parents about the issues arising from the pupil attendance data, but nowadays administrative officers chase this, and this makes my role less confrontational than in the past and it takes some of the hassle out of my team leadership role. I don't have to nag people as much!

I still have to be realistic about what I can ask of them. Meetings may be on the calendar but they are never easy to arrange, so I have to flexible. I make the rationale for the meeting absolutely clear. I use procedures – clear detailed agenda with timings so that the meeting doesn't overrun and I use my role as 'gatekeeper' to bring closure to an item and keep the meeting on track. There is no point putting too many items on the agenda; it only makes me look inefficient if there is a lot of unfinished business. I also use action minutes. This shows the tutors clearly what was decided and what the follow-up will be. This way we don't waste time rehashing the same discussion at the next meeting. I use a standard template for the agenda with a section left blank for the action, and I can key in actions, the time span, if relevant, and the lead person as we agree them, so I'm not spending time after the meeting sorting out the minutes, and team members know that minutes will be available within 24 hours of the meeting.

The meetings are focused on working together to make decisions or progress an initiative. If we are developing an initiative, I like to start by getting them to work in pairs for a short time, say up to ten minutes to generate ideas, basing the pairs on my knowledge of who work most productively together, and then we discuss their suggestions as a bigger group – this way, we get lots of ideas, no one dominates and things move forward quite rapidly. They have got used to this procedure and quite like it.

I always make sure that there are refreshments – coffee, cake and some fruit for the healthy eaters. It's a way of saying thank you to the team and recognizing that they have worked a long day before the meeting starts.

I never hold a meeting just to give out information; I use a year group newsletter for that and for items I can't include in meetings. For example, I have a section which highlights good practice, not just to give recognition for effort and initiative but also to reinforce expectations. I try to make the weekly newsletter an attractive document, brightly coloured and following a regular format so that my tutors know where to look for specific information. Having the newsletter makes it much easier for me to ensure that a lot of the minor stuff, that you would never cover in a meeting and could easily forget to mention to people, does get disseminated. I have clear procedures in place for access to the more confidential information. My tutors know how to access it and can never claim they have been left out of the loop.

Having whole school ICT systems in place has made information so much more accessible, so I've tried to build on this to develop a system to involve and draw in tutors by sending alerts to form tutors when a pupil had received a particular punishment (detention, etc.) or had earned points for the form or received a merit certificate. Similarly, I used a form tutor report as a first level of intervention, again to involve the tutor. I didn't expect them all to react and become involved, but they can't claim that no one told them and some have reacted very positively.

For reflection/discussion
- What issues does this case study raise?
- What are the lessons of this case study for you as a year leader?

CASE STUDY 3.2: DEVELOPER OR SERVANT LEADER?

When I reviewed my team for this year, I realized that I had a head of faculty, two heads of department and an NQT on my team of six. This isn't of course an unusual state of affairs. It seriously affected what I can ask of them, because the head of faculty and HoDs had other manage-ment commitments, which are the first demand on their time and the NQT has a restricted timetable and shouldn't have to be a tutor in the first place. It didn't feel fair to unload everything onto the other two team members and this was a problem for me. I am a teacher head of year and I am on a subject team. I feel guilty about how little time I can give to develop subject materials and always try to do my best with tasks that my HoD asks me to take on. I try to attend some subject training each year as well as departmental INSET, yet the subject leader still grumbles about the pastoral people on her team not being totally focused on their academic role. It doesn't work both ways and I have to be realistic about that.

I use my team meetings as my main opportunities to share and consult the team members so that they are involved in the decision making and I try to keep the time commitment outside meetings and tutor time down to minimum. Unless the item is a directive from the head, everything is always labelled 'draft' to ensure their input. At least their awareness is raised in this way. There is little allocated time for pastoral INSET so I do what I can through discussion of issues or the development work that we do at the year meetings. I came across the concept of 'servant leader', who does the bulk of the job, and I feel that I do this role a lot of the time. I always provide an initial draft, a working document or stimulus materials so that we never have to start from scratch and can get something finished or decided in the time available to us. If someone actually offers additional help, which does sometimes happen, I always accept and try to use this as an opportunity to help the individual develop.

I make it a practice to go through the tutor role description in the first meeting year meeting of the autumn term. This isn't about delegation, but about focusing us on what the tutor role means. I emphasize the need for consistent practice and my clear expectation that these duties will be carried out, and I use my supervisory role to monitor things. They know I will follow-up and that if they raise concerns, I will try to do something about the problem. I don't always succeed, but I always let the tutor know the outcome. The feedback does seem to make a difference; they like to know what has happened. Similarly, I try to see that the tutors are fully informed about any issues concerning form members, and encourage them to become involved and carry out their role of being the first point of reference for the pupils in their form and I feedback any results or progress.

An additional problem is that I am not their performance management reviewer. The school does use a line management approach, but the heads of faculty and some heads of department are the reviewers. There are rarely pastoral objectives for performance management, which makes it difficult for me to address the developer part of my role. I deal with this by holding individual interviews with team members every year, starting as soon after the beginning of the autumn term as I can manage. I have to manoeuvre to fit them in, but I regard them as very important. I use the individual 'interview' to find out about them as individuals and talk to them a bit about their form group.

During these meetings I raise the issue of what they can contribute so that we can reach agreement and I am clear what can expect. If I find a team member who is thinking of a pastoral route for career development, then I try to provide some development opportunities through appropriate delegation. Sometimes, although they don't want to follow a pastoral route, there are insufficient opportunities to learn to lead in a large subject department, so I check what they want to develop and suggest ways that they get skill development on my team, which they could use for their CVs. We negotiate what the brief is, how much time it will take and the extent to which I'll supervise or support. That way it isn't too burdensome for the individual. Feedback from my team is that they value the annual interview because I have taken the time to show an interest in them and usually something comes out of it for them.

For reflection/discussion

- Compare Case study 3.2 with Case study 3.1 – what are the similarities and differences?
- How do these year leaders use negotiation and communication?
- Discuss/reflect on what the year leader in Case study 3.2 means by the role of 'servant leader'.
- What are the lessons of this case study for you as a delegator and as a developer?

Although winning commitment from a pastoral team is particularly challenging for pastoral leaders, there are plenty of examples of success. Case study 8.4 describes how an extra-curricular club was set up for Year 7. In this case study the year team became the planning group for the team. It provides a positive example of team working in a pastoral context.

CASE STUDY 3.3: DEALING WITH THE NEGATIVE TUTOR

What is hard for me to accept is that good teachers don't want to be tutors as well as subject teachers, and that so many regard it as an extra burden. Often in practice, although they whinge about it, they do a lot for members of the tutor group and I do have some fantastic tutors, but a significant number are not really interested. I have learnt not to take it personally. When I was first a year head, I had a really good line manager and she advised me to do the best I could with the team, not to expect miracles and to value the good tutors when I found them.

This is why I set the expectations as clearly as possible, so that everyone knows what the bottom line is, while always highlighting good practice and involving them as much as I can, so that they get drawn in. The line manager also advised me that if I had to manage a difficult interview with a tutor, always to focus on the issue and never to allow things to become personal.

One of my team comes to mind. She was a very capable teacher, and more experienced than me, so it was difficult for me to stand up to her and make sure that she did what was needed. She didn't skip team meetings, but I would be aware that she would move her chair to indicate her lack of involvement. I was never publically critical; this would have been unprofessional and would have given her an audience of potential supporters, but I knew that if I avoided confronting the issue, she would think she had got away with it and would do even less of the job, so I spoke to her individually. When I had to confront her about aspects of her role that she was avoiding, I tried to keep calm, be polite, helpful and professional and not to respond to any statements which distracted from the main issue or were being used to wind me up. I kept things specific, based on evidence; I explained that this was my position and this was what I needed to do and in order for me to be able to do my job what I required her to do. It was time consuming, but usually I got there in the end, though sometimes we compromised. I reckon that over time just dealing with this teacher made me a lead practitioner in assertiveness techniques.

Guidelines for dealing with a difficult tutor

- The longer a poor tutor is allowed to get away with doing very little, the worse the problem will get. It is very important to prevent the problem escalating.
- If you do the tutor's job for her, she will let you. Don't make a rod for your own back.
- It is also very likely that because of the tutor's attitude, the tutor group is developing bad habits – this needs to be addressed.
- If there is a legal requirement, e.g. registers are not done properly, the tutor must fulfil these requirements. This could give you a lever.
- Developing bad habits is not good for her and could lead to professional disaster.
- Do not allow 'winding up' techniques to irritate you so much that it

becomes personal. Emphasize that this is not a personal vendetta but a professional issue.

- Don't allow yourself to become too preoccupied with the difficult member of the team. This adversely affects your ability to get on with the job in hand. It can also make you feel depressed, which affects your self-esteem and your confidence to handle the demands of the job.
- Try to keep a sense of perspective; treat it as a little local difficulty, but one which you are going to sort out. Your ability to approach the matter objectively and with detachment will give you an advantage.
- Focus on the issue and break the problem down into its component parts; this helps you to clarify what the problem is really about so that you can deal with the real problem not its symptoms.
- You are likely to have to deal with two linked issues: failure to do the job adequately and an attitude problem. To get a better job done, you will have to deal with the tutor's negative attitude to the role.
- Be clear what the bottom line is so that you don't get involved in too many unfruitful skirmishes or spend your whole time nagging. Concentrate on the most important responsibilities, e.g. not leaving the tutor group room during tutor time.
- Start what you think you may be able to improve, rather than trying to deal with it all at once. Every little victory will help your morale.
- Keep focused; expect the tutor to use ploys which will attempt to distract you from the main issue. Try to make her feel that the game is not worth the effort that she is putting into it.
- Have your evidence ready and be specific, so that it is hard for the tutor to be evasive. Without the evidence, the tutor can simply deny everything and you can't prove it.
- Talk it through with a colleague who understands but is less involved than you. Another person will bring a different perspective to dealing with the problem and help you be more objective.
- Practising/doing a dry run with a colleague can help you prepare. It is always difficult to think on your feet, but practising the interview gives you a feel of the tactics which could be used against you and advice/feedback on how to handle it.
- It is a sensible move to inform your line manager of the steps that you are taking in case there are problems later. You are entitled to support from your senior managers in dealing with this problem. At the very least, you want the opportunity to use the senior manager as a sounding board.
- If you have referred the problem, but are not receiving the help that

you need, you have to keep trying. The advice here is that however difficult, you must persevere. You may prefer to choose your senior manager rather than use your direct line manager. You may need to put in writing what you have done.

- Keep a record of the issues raised and outcomes; if no agreement is reached, that needs recording. Later on it could prove important that you have kept a record of the failures to conform to good practice and the measures you took to rectify the situation.

In the case study which follows, a year leader describes the most effective tutor in her team.

CASE STUDY 3.4: WHAT DOES GOOD TUTORING LOOK LIKE?

The form tutor who comes to mind was new to the school and quite inexperienced. She was an overseas teacher – a trained teacher from abroad. I think that this was one of the positive factors as she didn't bring any prejudices about to the job. She simply accepted that being a tutor was one of her responsibilities as a teacher in our school and she gave it her best go.

She was an English teacher, which gave her the advantage of teaching her form, so she met them in class as well as in tutor time. She used her English skills to build up a very good relationship with the pupils in her form. She took time to find out about the students, their interests, their family life, and at the end of each day she asked the pupils how their day had gone and if there had been a lesson where there had been problems, such as behavioural issues, she discussed it with the individuals and sometimes with the form. She congratulated pupils who had received merits or points each day. She wished them luck if they had a test and asked them afterwards how it went. Some pupils in the form did cheerleading after school – she took the time to go and watch them occasionally. The same thing happened with games tournaments and charity events for the year group. She took an interest, encouraged, advised and came to watch. She arranged assemblies with the form to be performed to the year group.

She always made herself available for the pupils to talk to her if they had a problem or wanted help, or needed to discuss something. The pupils were willing to talk to her because they saw her as unbiased and always prepared to listen to them. They accepted that this didn't mean that she would always side with them, but she always explained the reasons for the view that she took and this often helped them understand the other person's perception. She worked hard to resolve disagreements between form members when they occurred and also between pupils and their teachers. She often helped the pupils see the teacher's point of view if there was any conflict and made them write apology notes or apologize personally to the teacher.

Similarly, she would reprimand them if they had caused problems for a cover teacher or had done something wrong, but the main part of her discussion with the pupils focused on talking the issue through with them, looking at what would be the best way forward to put things right or resolve the issue. They certainly didn't regard her as a pushover, and I watched her build up the respect of the group. They realized that she cared about them, so they listened to what she said. She was prepared to use her initiative and was in regular contact with some parents, who spoke very highly of her. Within a few weeks of her taking over the form, the subject teachers of her form started to approach her instead of going directly to the year head if they had any problems with anyone in the form. She knew them better than any other teacher, including me, and certainly gave me good advice when I approached her with any problems I had in dealing with pupils in her form. It was all about her taking time to build a relationship with the pupils and taking time to talk to them. I think almost every teacher is capable of that, but many don't want to spend the time doing it. What it made me realize though was that most of her involvement with the form didn't take any extra time; it was how she used her tutor group time and a bit of follow-up.

This case study highlights some key factors about the form tutor role:

- It is the tutor's attitude which makes a crucial difference – a positive attitude enables the relationship to develop.
- There is a time commitment – but not an overly burdensome one – much of the interaction came in tutor time.
- Having sufficient tutor time can make a difference to what a tutor can achieve – but how the time is used matters more.
- Pupils don't expect or want the tutor to be soft, but they do want him/her to be unbiased and to focus on achieving a positive outcome.
- Being interested in form activities and willing to listen is the first step to developing a positive relationship with the group.

• Teaching at least some of the form group helps tutors to get to know form members in a different context.

Using the case study with your tutors

If you use this case study as stimulus material for a discussion on what makes good tutoring, you may want to use it without the list of key factors, or you could get the tutors to amend or add to the list.

References

Belbin, R. M. (1996), *Team Roles at Work*, Oxford, Butterworth-Heinemann.
  • Dr R. Meredith Belbin is one of the leading thinkers on team building. Belbin promotes and develops team role theory. His website has information about software, games and books produced by Dr Belbin and a summary of the Belbin team roles is given. There is a page of frequently asked questions about Belbin's team role theory. Contact Belbin Associates at 01 223 264 975; Belbin's website is www.belbin.com
Nathan, M. (2005), *The Leadership Team Edu-fax*, Ipswich, Edu-fax, Curriculum Publishing Company (ch. 3: 'Leading the team').

CHAPTER 4

Managing pupil behaviour

Who does what? What is your role in managing pupil behaviour?

The purpose of the school's behaviour or discipline policy is to establish a clear framework for pupils so that they know what the expectations are, what constitutes acceptable behaviour and what is considered unacceptable. Having strong policies for behaviour in place, and seeing that they are implemented, affects the school's standing in the local community.

Case study 4.1 illustrates how one head teacher met the need to create a secure learning environment through a clear framework of rewards and sanctions.

CASE STUDY 4.1: ESTABLISHING CLEAR SYSTEMS TO IMPROVE BEHAVIOUR

The candidates for the head teacher post were sitting in the head teacher's study for the briefing about the interview day when John saw the paper darts come down outside the window and began to get a gut feeling about the standards of behaviour accepted in the school. As he toured the school, his initial impressions were confirmed. He was disturbed by the classroom and corridor behaviour. At interview he was asked about his views on pupil discipline and said that establishing a clear framework for the pupils would be a priority and that this could initially mean taking a tough attitude. He was told later that this was one of the reasons why he was given the post.

Downtown High School was an inner-city school, with new buildings on an older site, and a large influx of pupils for whom English was an additional language and who kept moving home, which meant many of them came and went as pupils, as they moved across borough boundaries. For John, the lack of personal stability in the lives of many of his pupils meant it was even more important to establish a framework of acceptable behaviour to provide a secure learning environment within the school. He also felt strongly that there were too many fixed-term exclusions – the school needed to address the problem.

The school had a discipline policy, but no one was using it, so John redrafted it as the 'Positive Discipline Policy' that rewarded good behaviour. A key statement in the policy was that the end purpose of behaviour management was to establish a secure and effective learning environment. This gave the framework and made clear to everyone what the expectations were. The central feature was to be a uniform approach to classroom management to replace the variety of approaches that existed. John made it very high profile so that staff and pupils alike understood the SLT was clearly expecting the policy to be followed.

Without strong backup the new system would quickly fail, so he appointed three non-teaching behaviour officers to manage pupil behaviour. Their responsibilities included removing children from class when they had reached a fifth warning and to patrol corridors. Another major part of their role was to work with children with behaviour problems. This gave a clear message to the pupils that poor behaviour would not be tolerated and to the staff that they would be supported.

To reduce the number of exclusions, John set up an in-school exclusion unit, which he called the 'Education Withdrawal Unit'. Pupils who would otherwise be excluded are sent to work there in silence for one or two days. The pupils are referred to the Key Stage learning managers, who take an overview of the pupils' behaviour. Within the Education Withdrawal Unit, John set up a small unit for pupils whose behaviour was so extreme that they needed to be taught outside the normal curriculum. This reduced the need for permanent exclusions.

The unit is staffed by teaching assistants who have received training in managing pupils whose behaviour is likely to be challenging. Learning mentors also work with the pupils in the centre and carry out exit interviews. Overall responsibility went to the head of the unit and the post carried a TLR 1 allowance.

John and his learning managers liaised closely with parents over this, both when the pupil entered the withdrawal unit and in the period after they returned to normal lessons. He emphasized to the parents and carers how much better it was for their children to be withdrawn within school and continue learning than to be excluded and wander the streets.

To support the positive behaviour system, John had reviewed the role of the year leaders, who became learning managers with a responsibility for a year group or a Key Stage. They were teachers and became the line managers for the non-teaching behaviour officers. Their responsibility focused on pupil achievement.

John provided new software for the behaviour managers to monitor attendance and record incidents so that the learning managers could gather an overall picture of the behaviour and performance of a pupil or a set of children. This could then be used to set targets. The behaviour officers also monitored attendance and liaised with the school's EWOs, as a target for the school was to improve attendance. He also created a school support officer post (see Chapter 7), initially to deal with truancy but as time went on increasingly the school officer helped students whose lives had a high element of instability deal with and resolve issues that came between them and their schooling and impeded their progress.

As part of the initiative he introduced 'restorative conferencing', an initiative in which pupils, who have been involved in misbehaviour, and their parents or carers were required to attend a meeting with the member of staff they offended. Usually the learning manager acts as convenor. Both sides have a chance to say their piece and an apology is made. The aim of this process is to make pupils face up to the consequences of their actions. It has also had the effect of making teachers to become more aware of the needs of pupils.

As a result of these changes, behaviour in lessons and about the school significantly improved. When John evaluated progress after a year, the feedback from the teachers was that they are now able to focus more of their attention on the classroom, curriculum and learning.

The school's results at GCSE are also significantly up, though, as often happens, it is more difficult to unpick which of his initiatives have contributed most to the change. He is developing a wide programme of diplomas to ensure that the curriculum meets the diverse needs of his students and delivers personalized learning. John is currently focusing his learning managers to use their software programs to track the achievement of pupils from entry to enable early intervention. They also use the information provided by the behaviour managers to contribute to the school's SEF on behaviour of the learners. He is pleased with progress so far, but aware that the hardest part of any initiative is to sustain improvement.

For reflection/discussion
- What are issues raised by this case study?
- What are the lessons of this case study for you as a pastoral leader?

Role restructuring
Case study 4.1 illustrates how restructuring has brought changes to the way that responsibilities for behaviour are delegated. In the past, as a year or house head you had overall responsibility for the behaviour of the pupils in your charge. In most schools, though not all, the subject leader was responsible for what happens in the classroom, and the year leader was responsible for everything else. If the pupil's behaviour affected his/her work in a number of lessons, however, then as the year leader the problem was yours to investigate and to try to resolve. Now it is much less clear (see Chapter 1).

In some schools the traditional role where the year leader has overall responsibility for the behaviour as well as the progress of the learner still applies; in other schools a non-teaching behaviour manager, with one of a range of titles such as 'Investigative Officer', is now the first line of contact for pupil behaviour. Additionally, in a lot of schools and academies there is now a police presence on the premises and a lot of issues are referred directly to the school's police person; this brings a third person into the equation. This division of responsibilities highlights the need for good liaison between those who share responsibilities, especially as in many cases boundaries are still being determined. Who, for example, deals with pupil welfare and does it come under behaviour or progress? Different schools will have different answers to that question.

Issues affecting how you manage the role
Role conflict
One of the traditional issues for year leaders was that some year leaders or house heads found a conflict between their caring role in dealing with pupil welfare and their discipline role in managing pupil behaviour and dealing with disruptive pupils. Most of you manage this dual responsibility well, but occasionally this part of your responsibilities may have been resented by year heads, who feel that too much is unloaded onto them and that they are regarded as the sin bin or dumping ground for disruptive pupils. This happens particularly in schools in which the form tutor has very little pastoral responsibility (see Chapter 3). In the large number of schools where the tutor's role is underdeveloped, the year head has to do rather more than would otherwise be the case and consequently every minor problem will be brought to the year leader.

Time issues
The other problem for teaching year heads was time. Problems arose during lessons. All too frequently in many schools, teaching was interrupted because procedures were not in place (or more often not followed) for dealing with pupil issues that occurred when the year head was teaching. Another issue was that sometimes problem pupils were dumped into the back of the year head's class, which could affect how you teach your own lessons.

Even if your lessons were not interrupted, making the time to deal with the problem during the school day was always an issue. The proportion of free time allocated to year leaders is often insufficient to deal with serious issues. The result was that often it took longer than was ideal for an issue to be dealt with or resolved and that sometimes this made a real difference, because you needed to act immediately. One of the aims of introducing non-teacher behaviour managers was to free up the teachers to concentrate on their teaching. If you are not a teacher not only do you bring a different perspective to the job, but you can get on with it immediately and have the time to focus on it.

Setting the expectations
Whatever your background, when you manage pupil behaviour your aim is to enable pupils to control and manage their own behaviour better. Discipline implies 'doing something to someone'. Unacceptable behaviour will arise from time to time even in the best-regulated systems. When this occurs it needs be dealt with quickly and effectively so that pupils are able to reflect on it and strategies can be employed to try to prevent the situation from arising again, and so that, in the longer term, the pupil is better able to cope. Often a

pupil's behaviour is adversely affected by other issues, such as difficult family circumstances or mental health issues. These are covered in other chapters, especially Chapter 6. This chapter focuses on managing behaviour – your main responsibilities and how to deal with them. It will also summarize current approaches to dealing with behaviour issues.

The head teacher is responsible for formulating the policies, but if you are the behaviour manager for the pupils in your year group or section of the school, you are the person who is actually responsible for implementing the school's behaviour policy and the first point of contact for pupils, parents and other staff. The end purpose of behaviour management is securing effective learning behaviour. This means that you have to ensure a high standard of behaviour on a daily basis, deal with incidents that occur, liaise with staff and parents and outside agencies, and monitor whether the systems are working effectively. You are likely to have to contribute to completing the section of the school's SEF which evaluates pupil behaviour. The descriptors, which set out the expectations for pupil behaviour, are given in Table 4.1.

Communicating and reinforcing the behaviour policy

One of your first tasks is to emphasize to the pupils and their parents the importance of observing the school's behaviour code. It is important to keep it high profile. To do this you will use a range of communications. For example:

- The Year 7 induction pack and parents' pack will contain the behaviour code and you are likely to send the behaviour expectations home again at the start of the school year.
- It is often featured on the school's website.
- Year assemblies deliver and reinforce your expectations for behaviour within the classroom and about the school.
- PSHE periods enable the school to discuss behaviour issues, e.g. the year code of conduct is revisited and revised at the beginning of each school year to give group ownership of the code and reinforce core values.
- The year code of conduct is likely to displayed in classrooms.

Schools are also at very different positions in terms of use of technology and software programs for communicating and monitoring behaviour and attendance (see Chapter 9). The exemplars given in this chapter can be paper based or computer generated, depending on your school's current practice. Often schools use a mixture of the two.

Exemplar 4.1 is an extract from the letter to parents and pupils put out by one year leader to explain and reinforce the behaviour policy.

Table 4.1 *Evaluating the standard of learners' behaviour – Ofsted's descriptors*

Outstanding	Learners' mature, thoughtful behaviour is an outstanding factor in their successful learning and creates an extremely positive school ethos. Learners are very supportive of each other in lessons and show great consideration of each other's interests around the school.
Good	Learners' behaviour makes a strong contribution to good learning in lessons. Their behaviour is welcoming and positive. They show responsibility in responding to routine expectations, set consistent standards for themselves and need only rare guidance from staff about how to conduct themselves. They behave well towards each other, showing respect and encouraging others to conduct themselves equally well.
Satisfactory	Learners' behaviour is acceptable in the classroom so that it does not interfere with learning and time is not wasted. They can work on their own or in small groups. Around the school, learners' behaviour is secure and well-ordered so that public spaces are normally safe and calm. Learners themselves feel secure and understand how to deal with bullying or other problems. Learners generally respond appropriately to sanctions.
Inadequate	Learners' behaviour inhibits progress or well-being in lessons more frequently than very isolated occasions. Time may be wasted through persistent low-level disruption or occasional deliberate disobedience, for example by interfering with others' concentration during independent work. It may also be reflected in lateness and a lack of attention such as extensive off-task chatter. Some learners show a lack of respect for – or direct challenge to – adults or other young people, including instances of racism, sexism and other forms of bullying.

EXEMPLAR 4.1: BEHAVIOUR POLICY LETTER

Good behaviour and discipline in schools are essential to good teaching and learning. At Middletown Academy the discipline code provides a consistent approach to our expectations of pupil behaviour. The code is modified to be appropriate for each year group and a copy of the code for Year 10 is attached. The whole school discipline policy can be found in the policies section of our website and can be downloaded.

Pupils and parents need to be fully aware that bad behaviour is unacceptable and will be punished.

> Parents can have a powerful effect on children's behaviour. They should ensure that pupils arrive in school on time in uniform, have necessary books and equipment and that homework is completed on time and that they behave themselves while at school.

Aggression, defiance and creating a disturbance in lessons or about the school are the keynotes of unacceptable behaviour.

Table 4.2 *Common behaviours that disturb lessons*

Arguing	Arrogance	Swearing
Fighting	Bullying	Uncontrolled anger
Loss of self-control	Fear of losing face	Exhibiting boredom
Need for superiority	Humiliating another pupil	Rudeness
Avoiding work	Persistent off-task talk	Butting in
Talking out of turn	Defacing work	Missiles
Lack of concentration	Attention seeking	Persistent interrupting
Not having equipment	Delaying tactics	Seeks help for work well within capacity
Avoiding failure	Not working	Singing or chanting
Impressing peers	Non-cooperation	Laziness

For reflection/discussion

The tone and language of a communication can make a real difference to how the recipient reacts to it.

- What impact would you expect this communication to have on the parents who receive it?
- How would you frame a communication to parents to get them to support the school's behaviour policy?

The purpose of a communication to parents about pupil behaviour is to get parents on side. While it is important not to sound aggressive or patronizing, what really matters is that they appreciate and agree with the rationale for your actions. Different schools need different approaches, so you will need to reflect on what would be suitable for your students and parents.

Should you use a behaviour contract?

Some schools use a behaviour contract which pupils and parents have to sign. These used to be much more popular than they are now. A lot of schools have found that getting agreement to the contract is very time consuming, and it is then difficult to enforce. All too frequently in practice, schools found that the contract proved not to be worth the paper it was written on and the promises made in it were broken. For this reason, many schools prefer to promote positive discipline because the findings of recent research indicate that in the long term a positive approach is more effective.

Implementing the policy: systems for monitoring pupil behaviour

Whether you are a teacher or non-teaching pastoral leader with responsibility for pupil behaviour, you are often in the position of having to monitor a pupil's behaviour over a period of time to see if there is improvement. In any week you may have several pupils on report. This means that you want to have in place systems which indicate very clearly what the progress over the week has been. In the past pupils were often issued with blank time-table forms for a week and teachers were asked to comment on behaviour. These forms were rarely specific and the comments tended to be bland or vague: 'OK' was frequently used. Now monitoring is much more precisely targeted and often computer generated. Case study 4.2 illustrates how one school used its integrated data system to monitor pupil behaviour systematically in order to apply appropriate interventions. In this school the year leaders are teachers.

CASE STUDY 4.2: A THREE-LEVEL INTERVENTION PLAN

My pastoral intervention plan it was very simple. It involved three levels of alerts, which triggered different intervention at different levels.

Level 1 Intervention was for the form tutor. This was when a pupil had been sent out of a lesson to the referral room or had received an after-school detention that day. The action taken was for the form tutor to discuss the incident with the pupil and set targets to improve this behaviour and place the pupil on form report for at least two days. I used a pro forma with space to set targets at the top (based on the reason for the initial detention/being removed from lesson) and then the pupil was to take this report to all lessons during the subsequent days and for subject teachers to write whether the pupil had met the targets (if the problem was just within one subject, this could be adapted for just one subject). If the tutor felt it appropriate, they could discuss this with the child's parents, or get the parents to sign the report. If this intervention did not improve matters then the pupil was referred to Level 2 Intervention.

Level 2 Intervention was if the child had been sent out of a lesson to the referral room (we called it C5) or had received an after-school detention twice during a half term, or he/she had a single fixed term or internal exclusion. The action taken was that the head of year was alerted, who discussed problems with the child who was placed on year head report for at least two weeks. Parents were also called or a meeting arranged. At this point the year head could also refer the pupil to other intervention strategies if deemed necessary such as a learning mentor/school counsellor. If behaviour did not improve pupil would be referred to Level 3 Intervention.

Level 3 Intervention was for five C5s in a term or five after-school detentions in a term (or combination) or two fixed term/internal exclusions in a year. This alerted the assistant principals in charge of behaviour and inclusion. At this point the child's behaviour and progress would be discussed at an inclusion meeting. The inclusion team consisted of relevant year head, the assistant principal in charge of inclusion, the AP in charge of behaviour, the school nurse, the school counsellor, the senior learning mentor, SENCO, the LA pre-exclusions officer, the school policeman, etc. At this meeting appropriate interventions are discussed such the pupil spending some time in the learning support unit attached to the school and various programmes and projects such as the Life project or Teens and Toddlers, in conjunction with the interventions put into place at Level 2.

The school's database was set up to send these alerts automatically to the relevant people. The database also allowed an evaluation of whether the interventions were having an impact. I also designed this. All interventions and the date they started for each pupil are recorded in the database and the evaluation system simply allowed the time period to be typed in before and after the intervention start date and allowed a comparison of number of behavioural incidents, attendance issues, academic point score, etc. This enabled us to keep an overview and monitor whether the behaviour intervention strategies were effective. It made presenting information about a pupil to the inclusion group or to the student's parents much easier than in the past.

Its value was not that it involved new ideas for working with the student, but that it used them in a systematic way. Using a stepped approach meant that we did not rush into using heavy measures for first offences; pupils could not be sent straight to the deputy principal as had too often happened before we introduced the intervention plan. We now had a very clear structure that the pupils and their parents understood which brought together all information that we needed and helped us focus on the problem and apply a range of interventions.

Obviously, all pupils are different and some may require earlier intervention and the system needed to be flexible, but this was stated clearly in the policy. For me it met the need to have directed intervention that was available to all pupils if they met the criteria in order to ensure no pupil slips through the net. It was also essential to be able to evaluate the impact of the intervention strategies, and for this to not just be qualitative but also quantitative. Because we now had an integrated information system, the school's database system allowed this to happen without the need for excessive paperwork and time.

Sample monitoring forms

A range of monitoring forms is used by schools to check pupil behaviour in class, or to record incidents that occur. Some exemplars of the most common student monitoring forms are included below. Schools can adapt these forms to fit their requirements.

Often you need feedback from staff to tell you how they perceive a pupil or monitor how a pupil is behaving over the week or in particular lessons. It will also illustrate differences in staff perceptions of a particular pupil.

EXEMPLAR 4.2: A PASTORAL FEEDBACK FORM

Staff Questionnaire

Name: Tutor Group:

Subject: Set:

Subject Teacher

	Very poor					Very good
Please rate his/her behaviour this term	0	1	2	3	4	5
Please rate the behaviour of the class	0	1	2	3	4	5

Please tick on the continuum on general attitude

Negative to teacher	0	1	2	3	4	5	Positive to teacher
Off task	0	1	2	3	4	5	On task
Attention seeking	0	1	2	3	4	5	Self-contained
Inappropriate behaviour	0	1	2	3	4	5	Appropriate behaviour
Negative to peers	0	1	2	3	4	5	Positive to peers
Out of place	0	1	2	3	4	5	In place
Inappropriately equipped	0	1	2	3	4	5	Appropriately equipped
Work behind deadlines	0	1	2	3	4	5	Work up to date
Ignores instructions	0	1	2	3	4	5	Ability to follow instructions

Please list the things this pupil does well:

Please list the *specific* behaviours shown by this pupil regularly cause concern?

Any recent test results/NC levels, etc.:

Other comments you may wish to make:

EXEMPLAR 4.3: CAUSE FOR CONCERN

Name of pupil: . . . .

Form: . . . .

Type of cause of concern (Please tick – you can tick more than one item):

Academic progress
Effort
Attendance
Behaviour
Homework
Other (Please specify)

Signed:

Date:

Please return this form to the year head and copy it to the form tutor.

EXEMPLAR 4.4: AN INCIDENT FORM

Name/s of pupil/s involved

....

....

....

Form/Set ....

Form/Set ....

Form/Set ....

Form/Set ....

Location (please circle): during lesson, on corridor, break, lunchtime, after school

Date:

Action taken:

Signed:

Please return this form to the year head and copy it to the form tutor of each pupil involved.

EXEMPLAR 4.5: A PUPIL BEHAVIOUR REPORT CARD WITH TARGETS

MIDDLEHAM ACADEMY BEHAVIOUR TARGET CARD

Please give this card to the teacher at the START of every lesson

Name: Form: Date:

Reporting to:

Agreed targets:

1. . . . .

2. . . . .

Signed: (Pupil)
Signed: (Staff)

You must report DAILY to . . . . to check and sign the card.

You must show this card to your parents/guardian to check and sign DAILY.

All STAFF – Please check and sign the card at the end of each lesson.

Thank you for your cooperation.

Scores key:
1 = Excellent   2 = Good   3 = Satisfactory   no score = Unsatisfactory

Week beginning:	1	2	3	4	5	6	Total	Staff signs	Parent signs
Monday									
Tuesday									
Wednesday									
Thursday									
Friday									

End of week review: Total for week:

Communicating concerns to parents

EXEMPLAR 4.6: SAMPLE STANDARD LETTERS

Punctuality

Date. . . . .

Dear (Parent/Guardian)

Re . . . .

I am sorry to have to write to you to inform you that I am concerned about your child's punctuality to school. Our school records indicate that your child has been late on (number/dates)

Although I have spoken to your son/daughter on a number of occasions about his/her timekeeping, your child continues to be late to school.

We are concerned about this situation. As a matter of urgency please assist the school in ensuring that your child's punctuality improves from now on. Thank you for your support in this matter.

If you wish to discuss the matter further please do not hesitate to contact me on the school number.

Yours sincerely,

Signed: . . . . Year 8 Pastoral Support Assistant

The line between pastoral and curriculum is often a grey area, but in many schools the year leader will be the person who writes home to the parents when a pupil has misbehaved in particular lessons. The letters give details of the misbehaviour and inform the parent what action the school is taking. Usually it also offers the opportunity for the parent to contact the year leader. Here are two examples:

Dear Mr and Mrs Ghosh (Parent/Guardian)

Re: Ali Ghosh 10B

I am sorry to write to you to inform you that on Wednesday 2 March your son disrupted his GCSE Technology lesson taught by Mr Smith. Your son disrupted the learning of other students by throwing items around the classroom. Behaviour like this will not be tolerated and if repeated Tariq will be excluded from the lesson.

As you are aware Ali is currently on report for his behaviour, given the above he will serve a **Technology Faculty detention on Monday 7 March in Room 6 at 3.30 p.m. for one hour.** Failure to attend this detention will result in further sanctions being imposed.

Thank you in advance for your support in this matter.

Yours sincerely,

Signed: . . . . .Y10 Progress Leader

More often you have to write home because a number of subject teachers have raised concerns about a pupil's behaviour which is impacting on the smooth flow of the lesson and affecting the progress of the pupil and of others in the class.

Re: Benjamin Grant 9C

Dear

I am writing to express our concern about Ben's attitude and behaviour in a number of his lessons. His constant talking, interruptions and failure to follow instructions makes it difficult for him to achieve to the best of his ability and his disruptive behaviour makes it difficult for others to concentrate. He has also failed to complete and hand in homework which affects his overall assessment in several of his subjects.

I am unhappy with this situation and am writing to ask you to work with us to ensure that Ben's attitude and behaviour in class improve. In the short term, we are putting Ben onto lesson report, which you will need to check and sign daily to show that you have seen it. It will start today 3 November, and continue in the first instance for a two week period. Hopefully this will provide a structure and a sufficient period of time in which we can monitor and Ben can demonstrate an improved attitude

If you would like to discuss this matter further, please do not hesitate to contact me on the pastoral leader's direct line (given above).

Yours sincerely,

Signed . . . . Year 9 Progress Leader

EXEMPLAR 4.7: RE-INTEGRATION ARRANGEMENTS AFTER EXCLUSION

Support and re-integration after exclusion

The year staff and the year head should monitor all incidents, using a variety of support mechanisms within and outside the school. Discussions with pupils should include:

- a restating of the school policy and expectations of the school
- the pupil's difficulties
- coping strategies
- liaison with the SENCO if necessary
- liaison with the head of faculty or member of staff, if required.

In addition, for those who have been excluded, there should be a meeting with the parents to discuss re-integration. Those at risk of permanent exclusion should have a Pastoral Support Plan (PSP) drawn up for them. At this meeting with parents and pupils, SMART targets should be agreed. A date for another meeting to discuss progress should be made for eight weeks' time

At the eight-week review, there is another date for a meeting in a further eight weeks. If there is no improvement after 16 weeks when the PSP finishes, the pupil may be permanently excluded, although this rarely happens.

For statemented pupils it is important to involve the SENCO at every stage. It may be necessary to update the individual education plan (IEP).

Strategies for supporting staff

Most pupils behave well most of the time, but incidents occur in the best-regulated places. What is important to the staff is that they feel supported. Some short case studies illustrate possible approaches.

CASE STUDY 4.3: PATROLLING THE SCHOOL

In the past we struggled with behaviour management. One problem was that children truanted from lessons or were removed from lessons by teachers. Under the new head a system of corridor patrol during lessons was instituted. The year leaders were asked to participate in this initiative and agreed because we had to lead by example and it clearly supported other staff. We also felt it was better than having children sent to sit in the back of our lessons. To support all members of staff we have a member of the leadership or middle leader team on duty every lesson of the week. This person is on duty and patrols – he/she walks the school 'on duty' to ask any pupil out of a lesson who has given them permission to be out and why. The person on patrol carries a duty mobile phone so that he can be contacted immediately if any member of staff needs support. Since we put this system in place, we've found that the number of referrals has decreased due to the immediate action that can be taken. Records of pupils out of class are made and a member of the support staff undertakes an analysis to look for patterns or individual pupils who are out of class. Both the teaching and the support staff say they like the system as they feel more visibly supported.

Should you have a sin bin?

Schools vary in their views on whether to use a sin bin. There are two main approaches. Sometimes it is used as a kind of sin bin for short term exclusion and pupils do their lessons in the unit for a couple of days supervised either by a designated member of staff, often a member of the non-teaching staff. For example, Case study 4.1 featured a school with an Education Withdrawal Unit. Other schools use it to help pupils on a short trigger to cope with anger management issues. Here is an example of this approach:

CASE STUDY 4.4: SETTING UP A TIME-OUT ROOM

We do have a room for pupils who need to be withdrawn from class for a short time, but it's not called a 'sin bin'. We spent a lot of time in our year leaders meeting discussing the issue and deciding whether to have this facility. The teachers were in favour because they felt strongly that confrontation situations could be dealt with immediately and they could get on with their teaching. In the end we felt that we had to provide some sort of time-out space managed by one of our most experienced non-teaching staff, who would come to collect the child if necessary. In most cases the pupil is given a time-out card which he presents to the Time-out Room manager on arrival. We log all children sent there – which children, which lessons, which teacher, which times of day. This gives us valuable management information, which we follow-up with class teachers, subject heads of department, pastoral staff and parents. The Time-out Room manager is trained in anger management because the pupil often arrives in a very angry state. She tries to create a dialogue with the pupil and to help them unpick what has happened and to develop strategies to help them manage better next time.

CASE STUDY 4.5: SUPPORTING SUPPLY TEACHERS

When we analysed our data on incidents occurring during lessons, we realized that supply teachers accounted for the majority of the incidents and that they clearly needed more support. We drew up and provided them with a clear set of guidelines of how support staff can be involved in managing pupil behaviour in classrooms. This clarified what each side could expect of each other. Knowing that support is available and how to access it appears to have given them more confidence to handle issues which they might have backed off from, or which might have caused confrontations in the past. It is more difficult to monitor this now though increasingly our own support staff, who know our pupils and are familiar with our behaviour management strategies, are acting as cover staff, so supply teachers are only used in real emergencies.

CASE STUDY 4.6: SUPPORTING NEW STAFF

Newly qualified teachers (NQTs) traditionally have the most difficulty with classroom management, so we thought that if we put some support into this area, it could cut down the number of times we had to deal with pupils who misbehave in their lessons and help new members of staff. We decided that this should apply to all new staff, not just NQTs, because even experienced teachers can encounter difficulties in new situations and some of us recalled from our own experience that part-time staff or returners are rarely given induction or support when they join the school and often struggle. We liaised with the NQT mentor and the CPD coordinator; produced some guidelines that could be given to all new and supply staff and offered to lead some sessions focused on teaching and classroom management strategies. These sessions are now offered annually in the autumn term as part of our staff training programme.

Unpicking behaviour problems

Teachers often label pupils as disruptive but what does this mean? In order to deal with the behaviour, you have to be clear what the problem is. There are two stages to unpicking behaviour problems before you move to applying solutions:

1.   Observing and recognizing the symptoms
2.   Analysing what the problem is really about.

The first thing that you need to know is what is going wrong. Are you dealing with rudeness, lateness, internal truancy, failure to complete work or, as often happens, a combination of factors? This will tell you what the symptoms of the problem are, and indicate what kind of behaviour modification should be applied.

Pinning down what is happening in the lesson

If you have a student or group of students who are persistently referred to you as misbehaving in a particular lesson, you need to know what kind of misbehaviour is occurring. Often the complaint isn't specific, as the teacher is expressing his/her negative feelings about the impact that the pupil/s had on a carefully prepared lesson. Often the problem is low level but persistent disruptive behaviour. This really erodes teacher patience and undermines confidence. Unpicking the kind of behaviour exhibited enables you to clarify what is really happening, and to address the actual behaviour problem not just a generalized issue. It also helps you to support the teacher because the design of the teaching activity may be a cause of the problem. The strong link between engaging the pupils in their learning and their classroom behaviour is now clearly recognized (see the findings of the 2009 Steer Report), but in order to address the teaching issue you have to start by unpicking the symptoms of the problem

---

EXEMPLAR 4.8: PART OF SCHOOL B'S MONITORING FORM FOR DISRUPTIVE BEHAVIOUR

(*This can be paper or computer generated.*)

Problem: Please tick 1 or more of the list below or write in the problem in the line left blank.

- Resistance to teacher direction
- Argumentative
- Defiant – disregards teacher's role
- Sullen – passively negative – slow starter – needs reiterated instructions
- Attention seeking – needs a personal explanation each time
- Does not listen to instructions
- Insolent/persistently rude
- Calls out/interrupts
- Talks – talks during teacher exposition
- Too chatty – talks during pupil activity
- Prevents others from working by one or more of the above
- . . . .

Agreed targets for the week:

1.
2.

Signed: (pupil)   Signed: (teacher)

Guidance on your powers in respect of discipline

'I know my rights; you can't confiscate my mobile!' This response is typical of pupil reaction when teachers and support staff attempt to exercise their right to discipline a pupil. The primary responsibility of teachers is to teach and not to act as law enforcement officers, but sometimes the members of your tutor team will have to deal with issues that can affect the pupils' rights. Often the teachers and support staff don't have confidence in this area because they are unsure what they are allowed to do. This makes them reluctant to act because they fear that the pupils know their rights only too well and that their parents will support them. In recent years, however, there have been changes which actually give schools clearer and broader powers than in the past. In particular, the Education and Inspections Act 2006 gave schools the statutory power to discipline not only within school but also off the premises.

You have an important role in supporting your team. Providing your tutors with clear information about what their rights are will give them more confidence to manage pupil behaviour in difficult situations. This means that you need to be clear yourself about what the position is. Little training is provided in this area so you will need to keep yourself up to date. Check the TeacherNet/DfE websites before the beginning of the school year for any new legislation which could affect the position or for new information leaflets that you should distribute to your team members and use as basis for awareness raising sessions. For example, the DfE's leaflet *School Discipline: Your Powers and Rights as a Teacher* provides basic information and is a useful starting point. Making copies of this available to your tutor team and spending a few minutes going over and expanding its main points at a tutor meeting so that your staff can counter the pupils' claims could pay dividends. Key areas include searching pupils, use of restraint, detentions, confiscations and the power to discipline outside the school gate.

Searching pupils

Searching pupils and confiscating their property even short term is a minefield. Fear of a charge of violating a pupil's human rights dominates this area and is likely to get worse. You would like the right to search for any item that is banned under the school rules, but you have to be very careful about what you search for and how you carry out the search, and must make this very clear to your tutor team. Having a police presence on the premises can be an advantage as the police have wider powers of search than head teachers, but it also tends to mean that the police are involved at an earlier stage than if the rules were less stiff.

Currently the Crime Reduction Act 2006 gives heads and authorized staff statutory power to search pupils if they have a reasonable suspicion that they are carrying a knife or other offensive weapon.

- Searches must be in a private place – not in the classroom in front of other pupils.
- If you carry out a search you must be of the same sex as the pupil

and accompanied by another adult of the same sex as the pupil.
- You cannot require the pupil to remove any clothing except outer wear and a search of the pupil's possessions must be carried out in the presence of another adult. The search can be undertaken using 'such force as reasonable in the circumstances'.
- If the search reveals offensive weapons or knives, or evidence in relation to an offence, the school must call in the police.
- The head cannot demand that you or other staff conduct the search, only authorize you to do so. Authorized staff must be properly trained, so you may need to find a source of training for this.
- Since October 2006 schools can screen pupils at random for weapons using 'arch' and 'wand' metal detectors to protect pupils and staff from violent crime.

New legislation in the Apprenticeship, Skills and Children and Learning Act 2009 (section 2.23) extends and clarifies the power of search. It gives school staff the right to search in three areas which threaten pupil safety: illegal drugs, alcohol and stolen property. The final Steer Report (2009) recommends that this change should be reviewed after three years.

Use of restraint
Use of force to control of restrain or control pupils is governed by section 93 of the Education and Inspections Act 2006. It enables schools to use such force as is reasonable in the circumstances to prevent a pupil from doing or continuing to do any of the following:

- Committing any offence (or for a pupil under the age of criminal responsibility, what would be an offence for an older pupil)
- Causing personal injury to or damage to the property of any person (including the pupil himself)
- Prejudicing the maintenance of good order and discipline at the school or among any pupils receiving education at the school whether during a teaching session or otherwise.

This applies both to any teachers who work at the school and to any other person whom the head has authorized to have control or charge of pupils, such as the TAs, learning mentors and lunchtime supervisors and to people who are given temporary authorization, such as volunteers, which includes parents accompanying trips. You need to be quite clear that it doesn't include prefects and sixth formers. The Apprenticeships, Skills and Children and Learning Act 2009 introduced the obligation to record the use of force on pupils.

The problem, of course, is in defining reasonable force. There is no legal definition – it will always depend on the precise circumstances of individual cases and needs to be in proportion to the consequences it is intended to prevent. In an emergency it can be difficult to keep your head and think clearly, so it makes sense for year leaders to prepare themselves, for example, by organizing some training on how to handle situations in which they might have to use force, such as 'A pupil's rough play is risking causing injury; what should you do?' The best guidance that you should pass on to your tutors is to use the minimum force needed to get the desired outcome.

Detentions

Any detention taking place after school hours and lasting more than a few minutes needs to be communicated at least 24 hours in advance to parents. They can question the date if there are problems about the child attending but they cannot question your right to impose the sanction. There is no longer an automatic right for parents to receive notification in writing for lunchtime detentions and detentions are now permissible at a wider range of times.

Confiscations

It is OK to confiscate mobile phones on a temporary basis. There is now a legal defence for staff confiscating (keeping hold of or disposing of) inappropriate items. If you suspect that images of bullying or violent behaviour may be on the phone, you can't 'search' the phone, however, as this comes under the rules governing the right to search. You would need to use your SSP officer.

The power to discipline outside the school gate

Schools are now expected to deal with incidents of disorder that occur beyond the school gate when children are going or coming to school. You have to follow-up on complaints about your year group's behaviour in the local shops and on the school bus using the same methods as you would for incidents about the school, taking statements from witnesses to give you an overview and talking individually to those concerned. Sometimes this will mean liaising between parents and angry householders, shopkeepers or bus companies. Involving the parents sooner rather than later makes sense – for example if the bus company threatens to refuse to take a child or group of children on its bus because of persistent bad behaviour which could affect the safety of others, the parents would be entitled to complain if they hadn't been informed and involved at an early stage.

The more difficult problem to resolve is off-site bullying. A lot of bullying takes place off the premises but has its origins in school. The advice is to draw on the support of the police and other agencies where possible, especially if you have a SSP officer on the premises or a local police community officer.

The power to exercise discipline beyond the school gate should be included in the school's whole school behaviour policy and schools are also advised to include it in the home–school agreements. This aspect of discipline is always unpopular with pupils who rarely see why the school should have any power over their behaviour outside school. Sometimes they are supported in this attitude by parents, particularly those whose own experience of school was negative. For this reason, it is a good idea to remind pupils and parents at the beginning of each school year that this power exists.

Research and reports that influence current practice

Research over a long period (from the Elton Report, *Discipline in Schools* [1989] onwards) indicates that a positive approach to managing pupil behaviour tends to work better than a sanction-heavy system. Since the 1990s much of the government's research has drawn on the findings from inspection evidence.

The Practitioners' Group on school behaviour and discipline, known as the Steer Committee

Here are some of the main findings of the 2005 Steer Committee.

School ethos is directly supportive of pupil behaviour

- School ethos is highly correlated with school behaviour. Research indicates that, in all Early Years settings and at least two-thirds of primary and secondary schools, a positive and consistent ethos is promoted by the head teacher and senior management team, reinforced by staff and understood by pupils. This is reinforced when there is close liaison with parents.
- Within schools this creates a secure environment where children thrive, develop confidence and begin to take responsibility for their own actions. This generally has a positive impact on their attitude to learning. High expectations for behaviour are shared with parents so that there is consistency between home and school.
- SLT is responsible for the development of a school's ethos but its growth and maintenance depend on the involvement and cooperation of the whole staff.
- Consistency in the way staff themselves behave and act in and around the school is very important; in particular it helps boys behave better and achieve more.

Staff training
- CPD focused on developing staff knowledge in child development and classroom management is a key factor in addressing challenging behaviour.
- Regular training linking classroom practice to an understanding of how children develop socially and emotionally is central to understanding and managing behaviour. In the schools which have difficulty managing behaviour, more systematic training for head teachers and senior staff is needed.

Systematic behaviour tracking
This facilitates effective behaviour recovery strategies.

- The more effective schools carry out detailed tracking of behaviour and learning, identify pupils' needs and quickly take action, e.g. they use this information to timetable lessons, to organize teaching groups, and to focus attention on subjects where teaching and learning is less effective.
- Research indicates that pupils' needs are often identified too late and there is insufficient analysis of patterns of behaviour and it is usually a crisis that leads to belated action.

Effective teaching and classroom management
These impact on addressing challenging behaviour.

- The most effective teaching for learners with the most difficult behaviour is little different from that which is most successful for all groups of learners.
- Learning is best when the staff know pupils well and plan lessons which take account of the different abilities, interests and learning styles.
- A positive classroom ethos with good relationships and strong teamwork between adults encourages good behaviour.
- Late starts to lessons, disorganized classrooms, low expectations and unsuitable tasks allow inappropriate behaviour to flourish.
- Pupils often react badly when the staff show a lack of respect for or interest in them.
- Consistent experience of good teaching promotes good behaviour.

Pastoral support needs to be consistent and focused
- Research indicates that the most effective pastoral support systems are consistent and focused.

- A key feature is careful and regular tracking of pupils' learning and behaviour.
- The role of the tutor in secondary schools and colleges is of great importance in supporting those with the most difficult behaviour.
- Research indicates that the effectiveness of tutor support varies considerably within pastoral programming.

These findings have led to the development of behaviour strands in the national primary and KS3 strategies and to the development of the SEAL initiative.

The Steer Committee's first report: *Learning Behaviour* (October 2005)
This influential report made it clear that there is no single solution to the problem of poor behaviour and it provides the basis for current approaches to managing pupil behaviour. It spelt out good practice, including:

- a consistent approach to behaviour management
- a strong supportive leadership team, which sets high standards
- support and CPD opportunities for school staff
- involving parents and other agencies
- engaging pupils through good teaching and an appropriate curriculum
- regular tracking of pupils' learning and behaviour
- a system of rewards and sanctions
- good pastoral support for pupils
- supporting pupils as they change schools and classes
- good organization and a high quality environment.

Update to the 2009 Steer Report
Sir Alan Steer was asked to undertake a further a review of issues around school discipline and pupil behaviour, particularly to look at what progress had been made on existing issues and what new issues had emerged. His new report is encouraging because broadly he finds that there has been improvement. Nevertheless, there is still a lot that needs doing.

Learning Behaviour: Lessons Learnt (2009) makes 47 recommendations. Many of them, especially the strong link between high quality teaching and good classroom behaviour and the need for a major programme of training for school staff, build on and extend the points identified in the 2005 report. New issues include:

- The link between SEN and mental health issues and pupil behaviour. Much poor behaviour has its origins in the inability of the child to

access learning, rather than as a result of an unchangeable character defect.
- The ways that schools should deal with exclusion, especially the need for effective provision from the sixth day of exclusion.
- Cyberbullying – particularly how schools should support staff who are targeted by cyberbullying.

His main recommendations include
- Intervention early in the primary phase to identify and address potential problems.
- All schools should have a written policy on learning and teaching to ensure that the links between inappropriate teaching and behaviour issues are addressed.
- Significant CPD in behaviour management issues and techniques at all levels; particularly training programmes should provide better preparation for good practice for SEN needs and disabilities.
- Review school pastoral systems for pupils to ensure all pupils have someone who knows them well and who is able to support them and, through effective monitoring, ensure that any needs are quickly identified and addressed.
- Use of learning mentors and other staff with similar roles to support vulnerable pupils should be extended where possible.
- Schools should work closely with and be supported by external specialists, Safer School Partnerships, and Child and Adolescent Mental Health Services (CAMHS), because the behavioural problems experienced by some children are caused by mental ill health. These are particularly important sources of support. The SSP programme should be extended to all schools (see Chapter 7).
- Schools should agree and operate a fair access protocol which ensures that all schools admit a fair share of 'hard to place' pupils and agree a managed move protocol for pupils for whom a move to another school is agreed appropriate.

Positive behaviour management strategies
Supportive behaviour management
This is a strategy aimed at helping pupils whose emotions get in the way of things so that they can't interact appropriately with others or who are likely to have rather more confrontations in class than their peers. All too frequently low-level disruption escalates into a major confrontation between a pupil and a teacher. Applying sanctions on an increasing scale of punishments deals

with the symptoms, but doesn't prevent the behaviour from happening the next time the pupil experiences a similar situation. Supportive behaviour management takes account of the context, there could be ongoing EBD issues or family problems; for example, the pupil may be a carer whose parent's condition is deteriorating.

Creating some space by separating the teacher and the pupil before the situation becomes serious is the first step. This approach also takes account of the fact that it could be that the teacher is also having a bad day and is less able than usual to cope with irritation. A lot of schools have a time-out room which could be used for this purpose. Its first use could be to buy calming time after an incident. The pupil would be sent to the time-out room after an incident and the TAs/pastoral support officers, who would staff the room, would be trained to find out what had happened and to encourage the pupil to talk about the context. This can be particularly good for boys who often find it difficult to articulate their feelings yet need to know that someone is listening to them.

Encouraging techniques would be used to help them to talk through the issue. Comments such as 'I understand how you feel' or 'I understand why you reacted as you did' show sympathy without saying that the behaviour was correct. It can also lead on to saying, 'Now how might you react next time?'

The TAs would also be trained as coaches for the teacher to help them manage the pupil's re-entry so that the both can move on. If the teacher sounds bad tempered or negative, little will have been gained from the work done with the pupil in the time-out room and the whole situation could start up all over again.

Supportive behaviour management could be used to pre-empt difficult behaviour. Some primary schools use a traffic light system to help special needs pupils with a low explosion threshold and this is now increasingly used at Key Stage 3. The pupil holds up an amber alert card to show that he/she is experiencing difficulty and either a TA comes to sit with and support the pupil or the pupil is allowed to go to a time-out room.

Restorative justice

Restorative justice (RJ) is becoming increasingly popular. It developed out of the work being done in schools to help pupils develop their emotional intelligence. It allows those involved to share their emotions and feelings about the situation in a safe environment facilitated by a responsible adult. It encourages the students to think through what has happened and how the behaviours involved have affected people, and it involves them in developing a solution. It enables the offender to redress the harm that has been done to a 'victim', and enables all parties with a stake in the outcome to participate fully in the process.

The four key questions are:

- What happened?
- Who was affected?
- How can things be put right?
- What would be the right or fair thing to do to get this situation sorted?

Schools organize it in different ways – it may be year or Key Stage based. Sometimes a senior manager is in charge, but often implementing the system becomes the responsibility of a year head or Key Stage manager; sometimes it comes under learning support and occasionally an outside psychologist is brought in. Training has to be provided both for the manager responsible and for staff participating. It places heavy demands on the staff involved, especially in terms of time, but it can have significant rewards for both the school and individuals. It is used a lot in dealing with bullying incidents and has been used successfully to resolve situations that could otherwise have resulted in exclusion. All the professionals need to be thoroughly involved in the process and it can only work with the consent of all parties. Case study 4.7 illustrates how this might work.

CASE STUDY 4.7: RJ IN PRACTICE

Lena is the Key Stage 3 pastoral manager. She receives a call that there has been an incident in a Year 9 science lesson and arrives to find Desmond, a boy who is often in trouble, outside the classroom door and the lesson suspended while the teacher interrogates the two back rows of the class. The teacher tells Lena that he had been called out for a few minutes and returned to find that there had been paper throwing and spitting. It was the spitting that had particularly upset him and he points out the globs of spit on the back table. Desmond was throwing paper at another boy as the teacher entered the room so he sent him out immediately, but it was more difficult to find out who else was involved.

Lena offers to remove Desmond and the two back rows to a free class-room and use an RJ approach to sort the matter out and the teacher agrees. She encourages the group to reflect on what has happened, and to tell her honestly if they were involved. This identifies three pupils,

Desmond, Euan and Artie, as the 'culprits', so she sends the other pupils back and continues to work with the three boys. Although they initially say that they were only larking about, the question about who was affected makes them focus on the disruption to the lesson, especially to the practical session and how the teacher might have felt about it. 'It got out of hand and I can see why he might feel angry', Euan says.

When she asks what would be the fair and right thing to do to sort it out, the boys say they should apologize to the teacher. When Lena takes them back to the lesson, they apologize to the teacher, and she asks him how he feels about the incident. 'I'm pleased that they have admitted it and apologized,' he says, 'but I'm still angry because the practical session was spoilt, and I'm upset because I don't have time to repeat it. This will mean that some pupils will not understand the ideas involved, so I'll have to give them extra help.'

At this stage the boys, who can't think of a way to make up the lost time, offer to clean up the classroom during break so that no one else is affected and the teacher accepts this offer. Lena asks if he will now take all three boys back in or whether he would prefer them to remain with her until the end of the lesson. He thinks about this for a moment and then says he will take Euan and Artie back, but Desmond hadn't been working properly before the incident and was rude when caught throwing the paper, so he should stay out until the next lesson. The teacher adds that this would give him time to calm down and get things into perspective.

Case study 4.7 is a straightforward example of using RJ to deal with lesson disruption rather than applying sanctions. It makes the boys involved reflect on the effect of what they did and think about how they might make at least some restitution. See Chapter 5 for a case study on using RJ to help deal with bullying issues

Use of learning mentors
A one-on-one approach has proved a useful strategy to support both pupil behaviour and learning. Individual attention can sometimes help to remotivate pupils. Some schools use community mentors especially as role models, to focus pupils on raising their aspirations. This can work very well and good relationships are formed between the pupil and the mentor, but there can be problems as community mentors do not always turn up for the sessions, so the pupils are disappointed and therefore disenchanted. It tends to work best

when the mentors are on the staff. For example, pupils who are struggling to behave well in class are identified and get special one-to-one coaching from learning mentors, who are members of the support staff and have received specific training on behaviour and anger management strategies. Coaching or mentoring helps give the pupil ownership of the solutions and reinforces the standards of expected behaviour. Academic mentoring is often provided by SLT members, particularly to support Year 11 pupils who have been identified as needing individual support.

Working to improve pupil motivation

CASE STUDY 4.8: WORKING TO IMPROVE PUPIL MOTIVATION

Now that our role as pastoral leaders has been redefined to focus on our responsibility for the pupil's learning programme, we started to think about what stopped pupils from making progress and what we could do to address this issue. It quickly became clear to us that a lot of the problems that occur in the classroom and which are referred to us are low disruptions because children are not engaged in their learning. We were conscious that pupils, who arrive from primary school enthusiastic and responsive, often turn off and lose their initial enthusiasm. At a year leaders' meeting we began to explore how we could get through better to some of the hard-to-reach pupils with low motivation. We decided that improving our own understanding of motivation would help us to handle these pupils more effectively, but we wanted this to be in an educational context, so we asked the LA's psychological service to give us some basic training.

The distinction is usually made between two types of motivation: that which arises from within us (intrinsic) and that which is external or comes from the outside (extrinsic). Extrinsic motivation is usually associated with reward or sanction systems; we didn't think we needed to concentrate on this as we had given a lot of thought to rewards and sanctions, so we concentrated on understanding intrinsic motivation. We learnt that intrinsic motivators can include:

- Giving learner control or choice
- Curiosity
- Challenges, problems or novelty
- Aesthetic experiences

- Positive feedback
- A physically and emotionally safe environment

Under the leadership of the deputy head responsible for teaching and learning, we used this knowledge to analyse the curriculum. We started with the Year 7 learning programme as the approach could go up with the pupils. If we could keep going some of the enthusiasm and curiosity associated with primary education this would be beneficial. One year leader pointed out that the motivators list was actually a list of the main elements of good teaching; but this didn't mean that we did enough of it.

Our aim was to see how we could ensure that the diet included a sufficient amount of the motivators that had been identified for us. We worked with subject leaders to take topics in the Year 7 programme and unpick the approaches to learning activities. This was a much closer association than in the past and both sides found it very useful. The subject leaders drew on the work on learning styles that had been conducted with our pupils and teachers and the wide range of good resources now available through the internet and Teachers TV programmes to give us ideas for more problem solving and challenging activities.

We also did some work on the classroom environment. For this we used the Hay McBer effective teaching questionnaires to help us focus on classroom climate. We used observation, especially for some of the activities that are traditionally difficult to manage such as group work. For this we also involved the pupils – getting feedback on the learning activities and acting on their comments – this was part of giving them control.

We also used our good relationship with our local primary feeder schools to do an exchange of observations. We visited some of our feeder schools and watched a morning of Year 6 lessons. In return we invited the schools to send some Year 6 teachers to come and track and sample the work of some of the pupils who had joined our Year 7 from their primary schools and to comment on their progress and attitude to work in their new school. Their comments really made us think and this link has now become regular feature of our Year 7 monitoring programme.

Monitoring how the pupils feel

Finding how the pupil feels can help you establish a dialogue that could move a situation forward. Sometimes using a questionnaire can be a useful starting point, particularly with a child who is not good at expressing his/her feelings orally. The questionnaire can be used as a means of assessing a pupil's thought's, attitudes expectations and beliefs and can easily be adapted to suit your specific needs. Similarly, you can design a questionnaire that focuses on how the pupil perceives the school. An example appears below.

EXEMPLAR 4.9: MIDDLEHAM HIGH SCHOOL'S PUPIL ATTITUDE QUESTIONNAIRE

For each question put the appropriate number from 0 (very poor) to 5 (excellent) or underline the relevant words, or circle or tick as required. Where it says 'other' you can add your own words.

How would you grade your behaviour in:
Classrooms
Corridors
About the school
Assembly
Playground
Outside school

How do you generally behave?

Which of these words best describes you?
Helpful, unhelpful; rude, polite; loud, quiet; violent; talkative, sullen; cooperative, withdrawn; hard working, lazy.

Do you think you can change your behaviour? (*Tick*)
I can
I can't
I don't want to

What might affect you changing your behaviour? (*Tick*)
Teachers stop me
Teachers help me
Other pupils affect
Other pupils stop me
Other pupils help me

What do you think of yourself? (*Circle*)

Confident	Lacking confidence
Attractive	Unattractive
Sociable	Alone
Clever	Stupid
Involved in things	Not involved
Interested	Not interested

What do you think of teachers' attitudes towards you? (*Circle*)

Interested	Not interested
Helpful	Unhelpful
Friendly	Unfriendly
Polite	Rude
Caring	Uncaring

Other – write the word in:

What do you think of the behaviour of other pupils towards: (*Write what you think*)

You

Other pupils

Teachers

Helping the pupil to move forward: stages in behaviour modification

Trying to get a pupil to improve his/her behaviour is never easy. Often they are resistant to change, they may not see the need to change, and all too frequently the cycle appears to be one step forward, two steps backwards. It is always time consuming and can be frustrating and disappointing. Understanding the stages that a pupil is likely to go through when you are working to modify a pupil's behaviour can help you to manage the process more effectively and not to take the setbacks as personally.

Stage 1: Resistance

At the start of the process, you should expect resistance. At this stage the young person is not contemplating change. The pupil tends to be unaware that there is a problem or any need for change at all or to see it as 'YP' – your problem. There is no recognition that there is a need to change, and the pupil may be very resistant to the idea of any change happening.

Indicators include:

- Denial – 'What problem?' 'I haven't got a problem.'
- Strong non-verbal signs of resistance, e.g. reluctance to make eye contact.
- High level of stress – 'I just can't take on any more' – there is so much stacked up against them in life that change is not on the agenda.
- Complacency – 'I'm alright as I am' – the pupil sees no need to change his/her behaviour as the current pay-offs are heavily weighted towards the existing situation, e.g. peer admiration, behaviour condoned by parents, etc.
- Lack of awareness of the consequences of current actions.
- Lack of self-awareness.
- Lack of awareness of the fact that they can change, or can choose to change.

Strategies include:

- Making contact and building up trust.
- Raising self-awareness – initially of their own strengths and interests.
- Using the language of choice – 'You can choose either to carry on bothering others and get yourself into detention, or you can choose to get on with your work and go home on time – the choice is yours!'
- Making the youngster aware of the consequences of their actions – 'If you do that again, X will happen . . .'
- Making the youngster aware of what they are doing – either by feeding back observational data or video recordings of their behaviour; having specific evidence can help you here, and prevent endless argument.
- Peer feedback about how they really come across – often this approach uses group work and/or an outside facilitator (see the case studies in Chapter 5).

Stage 2: Developing awareness

You will probably notice that what the pupils say and what they do may be quite different. They now understand that there are aspects of their own behaviour that they need to improve and have begun to think about how to do so, but they can't see how, and are not yet ready to do anything about it. They will often see-saw between reasons to change and reasons to stay the same.

Indicators include:

- The youngster begins to talk about themselves and some of the issues.
- Contact has been established and a relationship is beginning to build.
- They become more aware that they have a choice.
- They are beginning to weigh up the pay-offs of change as against the pay-offs of staying the same.
- They are not happy with the current situation, but can't quite bring themselves to act differently.

Strategies include:

- Help them to see the good points and pay-offs for change, while at the same time being realistic about what they will lose if they change.
- Help them to envisage how it would be if they did change – what would their average day look like? How would others respond? How would they feel? Envisaging could include getting them to draw outcomes – it doesn't need to be great art, but could help them articulate the end.
- Develop self-awareness, particularly of feelings, which have often been masked by denial in pre-contemplation.

Stage 3: Taking responsibility

It is only at this stage that the pupil is ready to embark upon change. They begin to focus on the solution, take responsibility for problem solving and decision making in their own lives. They develop an enthusiasm for change and begin talking about how to go about it. It is at this stage that they begin to be able to contemplate targets and strategies for achieving them.

Indicators include:

- An enthusiasm for change and energy to contemplate it
- Readiness to look at targets to work towards
- Sufficient confidence to apprehend change.

Strategies include:

- Supporting the pupil to maintain his/her enthusiasm and positive thinking.
- Consideration of benefits, pay-offs for change and possible rewards (avoid appearing to be bribing the pupil!).
- Target setting and forward planning (using SMART targets – specific, measurable, achievable, realistic and time limited).

- Clearer communication – letting others know of the targets and strategies, e.g. members of staff, parents, etc.
- Setting up support systems, e.g. parents, peer support groups, buddying, etc.

Stage 4: Action

At this stage the pupil engages with the planned strategies to bring about change. Visible change begins and the plan of action is embraced.

Indicators include:

- A more positive sense of self with clearer goals linked to reasons and emotions
- A certain insecurity as to whether they will be able to manage the change
- Obsession with feedback about how they are doing
- The need for positive feedback and clear monitoring of their progress
- A need to tell others about their change.

Strategies include:

- Developing monitoring and feedback systems
- Ensuring regular opportunities for positive feedback and encouragement
- Positive feedback to relevant others, e.g. parents, staff; a good letter home to parents who have only ever received complaints about their child can make a real impact.

Stage 5: Relapse

This is a phase common to all processes of behaviour modification. It is usually triggered by some adverse event such as row with another pupil, a negative or critical comment, bad news, etc. The pupil is thrown into a negative state, all the improved behaviours are forgotten and previous behaviours come once more into play.

Indicators include:

- Negative mood state, loss in confidence, tendency to blame themselves or others for the relapse
- Loss of hope or 'future' orientation
- Tendency to 'catastrophize' – one setback means that all hope of change has gone! This is sometimes described as 'awfulization'!

Strategies include:

- 'Normalization' – seeing relapse as a natural part of the cycle. For successful change one has to go through the cycle several times! Have examples of real catastrophes to use so that the pupil can see the difference and begin to get things into proportion again.
- Review the monitoring and feedback systems to affirm the positive changes that have taken place.
- Ensure that family, staff and friends do not reinforce the negativity – watch for this as in spite of your vigilance it is likely to happen.
- Move swiftly back to the strategies you used in Stage 2 to get the show on the road again.

Stage 6: Maintenance and consolidation

The improved behaviours are beginning to become consolidated. It takes less time to reinstate improved behaviours after a relapse. There is less of an 'intense' feel about the process.

Indicators include:

- Pupil willing to take responsibility for his/her own actions
- Less dependence on you
- Improved self-esteem and confidence
- More willing to try new things/take risks.

Strategies include:

- Occasional reinforcement
- Being available.

Rewards

All schools develop a set of rewards to motivate pupils to work harder and behave better. It pays to discuss with the pupils, for example through your year council or tutor time discussions, what they see as suitable rewards for various actions, or what would motivate them to work. Involving the students in this kind of discussion gives them ownership, so revisit it annually. As Case study 4.9 shows, the rewards don't have to be expensive; what matters is that the students should value them and that they are seen to be fair. Pupils often regard rewarding a badly behaved child for obeying the rules as unfair on the majority who always obey the rules. They also don't like the teachers who hand out merits too easily as 'bribes'. These issues need discussing with the students. An effective reward system will be one that:

- is easily understood, achievable and bureaucracy free
- rewards all aspects of school life
- is fairly and consistently applied by all staff
- is workable, agreed to by the staff and approved by the pupils.

Rewards could be given for:

- school uniform – if your school has one
- attendance
- punctuality
- completing the contact book correctly for a term
- service – helping others
- complying with the class code or year behaviour plan
- complying with work rules for a significant period of time
- an excellent piece of work
- improved effort/attainment over time
- good effort grades on progress cards.

CASE STUDY 4.9: INTRODUCING A REWARDS SYSTEM

In our school, after discussions with year groups and a meeting of the school council, a sliding scale of labels and stars was adopted:

5 stars	=	1 bronze label
10 bronze labels	=	1 silver label
10 silver labels	=	1 gold label
1 gold label	=	school prize

Stars were recorded in mark books and children's workbooks, labels were stuck into the pupil's home–school contact book, and year heads kept records of the silver and gold labels. The head saw all pupils gaining silver and gold labels.

We were surprised to find that even Years 10 and 11 pupils liked and respected the system. The work rules, classroom rules, and form tutor rules were displayed in all rooms, and there was no ambiguity about what merited a label. Everything was geared to the positive, there were no demerits.

In addition, certificates were awarded in assemblies throughout the year. A letter or card home to parents recorded the achievement.

Social and emotional aspects of learning (SEAL)

The SEAL resources were first produced by the DfES in 2005 as part of the Behaviour and Attendance strand of the Primary National Strategy. SEAL aims to develop children's social, emotional and behavioural skills and is currently being rolled out in both the primary and secondary sectors.

The list below sets out the rationale behind the SEAL initiative. Where children have good skills in these areas, and are educated within an environment supportive to emotional health and well-being, they will be motivated and equipped to:

- be effective and successful learners
- make and sustain friendships
- deal with and resolve conflict effectively and fairly
- solve problems with others or by themselves
- manage strong feelings such as frustration, anger and anxiety
- be able to promote calm and optimistic states that further the achievement of goals
- recover from setbacks and persist in the face of difficulties
- work and play cooperatively
- compete fairly and win and lose with dignity and respect for competitors
- recognize and stand up for their rights and the rights of others
- understand and value the differences and commonalities between people, respecting the right of others to have beliefs and values different from their own.

The government has put considerable financial resources behind the initiative to support secondary schools in introducing the new SEAL programme as part of its strategy for improving behaviour. It is encouraging a phased national implementation.

What is the SEAL programme?

The programme aims to help teachers develop pupils' skills in five key areas:

- Self-awareness: knowing and valuing oneself; understanding feelings.
- The management of feelings: improving the management and expression of emotions.
- Motivation: developing persistence, resilience and optimism; improving strategies to reach goals.
- Empathy: understanding the thoughts and feelings of others; valuing and supporting others.

- Forming positive relationships: building, maintaining and improving relationships with others.

How the SEAL programme is implemented
The programme is usually taught across the curriculum rather than in specific lessons. Some examples of how teaching could incorporate SEAL include:

- Exploring the subject of personal motivation through drama and English by exploring the experiences of characters who have overcome difficulties.
- Developing empathy in citizenship by exploring current conflicts and considering why it can be so difficult to keep the peace.
- Teaching children through PE how to work as part of a team and experience winning and losing gracefully.

The SEAL website will give you more about the rationale for the programme guidance for implementation, staff training and explanations of how SEAL links to other initiatives. Curriculum materials can also be downloaded from the TeacherNet website (see the end of this chapter).

Does it work?
Evaluations of the pilots were undertaken and the DfES commissioned an independent study of the impact of SEAL in secondary schools in Autumn 2007 to assess pupils' social and emotional skills before and after starting the programme. The main findings, which are summarized below, were positive and the researchers found that similar benefits gained by using the approach were found in both low achieving schools and high achieving schools.

Impact on teachers
During the five terms that the secondary SEAL programme was tracked, the greatest impact the researchers noted was on teachers' attitudes towards the idea of social, emotional and behaviour skills, and their understanding of how to develop these skills systematically within subject lessons. As a consequence, there was discernible improvement in some teachers' skills in developing these competencies.

Impact on pupils
Among the most heartening outcomes of the SEAL programme were the benefits for pupils. Some benefits were experienced by pupils as a direct result of the SEAL programme and its impact on classroom approaches, teaching and learning. These led to:

- better team working
- better recognition and articulation of feelings
- greater respect for each others' differences and strengths
- greater willingness to take risks in their learning.

Other benefits were indirect, resulting from changes in school systems brought about by the programme. This led to benefits such as:

- more consistent rewards and sanctions in the behaviour system
- improved lesson planning
- more helpful approaches to teaching and organization of learning
- better relationships with school staff.

Some schools encouraged teachers to set a social, emotional and behavioural skills objective for each lesson, such as developing the skills of working in a group, using positive language or being empathetic. Some successful approaches included:

- The regular use of group work to build cooperation and teamwork.
- Weaving references to emotion into a lesson such as in the examination of texts in English.
- Using suspense and intrigue when enquiring into historical events to build resilience and motivation.
- Acknowledging the feelings of fear, anxiety, apprehension, confusion, etc. in maths lessons with lower attaining pupils.
- Using techniques to develop independence and resilience in more passive pupils by suggesting ways in which they could help themselves rather than simply giving them the answers.

It was also found that systematically considering how children are grouped for teaching sessions makes the activities more effective than when the setting or grouping was inflexible.

What has emerged from evaluation so far is that although their experience had been good, schools could not always disentangle the impact of the pilot project from other initiatives to support behaviour and learning, but they were positive about it and considered potential impacts of the programme to include:

- raising standards of achievement
- creating a more positive school environment
- improving pupil behaviour
- improving interactions between pupils and staff
- improving attendance.

A more recent (2009) Cambridge Assessment Research study looked at the possible impact of SEAL on academic achievement. It compared GCSE grades from some 2,000 pupils, who also filled in questionnaires, rating themselves on qualities relating to their well-being, emotional maturity, etc. This research suggests that emotional intelligence has a bigger impact in subjects such as English, English literature and drama than in French or art and design, and that in science it has most impact in applied science and least in physics. Results in maths in this study were inversely related to the level of social skills, which raises the issue that if an individual has a high level of emotion, it might get in the way of logical thinking. This is clearly an area that needs more work, perhaps in targeting SEAL, as it is the introspective person who often needs support in developing and sustaining social and professional relationships. Overall, however, they found that using SEAL has a very important and positive effect on learning.

There are no miracles, but there is sufficient evidence to suggest that SEAL helps to equip students with the tools and skills they need to manage themselves and to develop and sustain relationships with others. SEAL will usually be run in conjunction with other initiatives such as peer mentoring programmes (see Chapter 8) and mental health intervention programmes (see Chapter 7 for the work done by CAMHS), which will make it even more difficult to unpick how much is SEAL and how much is other initiatives. From your point of view it is the outcome that matters.

References

Department for Children, Schools and Families (DCSF) (2009), *School Discipline: Your Powers and Rights as a Teacher*, downloadable in pdf format from http://publications.education.gov.uk/eOrderingDownload/School-Discipline_Leaflet.pdf

Robinson, G. and Maines, B. (1997), *Cry for Help: The No-Blame Approach to Bullying*, Bristol, Lucky Duck Publishing.

SEAL: Social and emotional aspects of learning: www.teachernet.gov.uk; see also the behaviour and attendance sections of the National Strategies website: www.nationalstrategies.standards.dcsf.gov.uk

Steer, Sir Alan (Chair) (2005), *Learning Behaviour: Report of the Practitioners' Group on School Behaviour and Discipline* (The Steer Report), DfES, downloadable in pdf format from http://publications.education.gov.uk/eOrderingDownload/STEER-FINAL.pdf

Steer, Sir Alan (April 2009), *Learning Behaviour: Lessons Learned – a review of behaviour standards and practices in our schools*, London, Institute of Education and Social Research, University of London (www.ioe.ac.uk)

Vidal Rodeiro, C. L., Bell, J. F. and Emery, J. E. (2009), *Can Emotional and Social Abilities Predict Differences in Attainment at Secondary School?* Cambridge, Research Division, Cambridge Assessment.

CHAPTER 5

Dealing with bullying
and cyberbullying

*'I feel safe here. There's almost no bullying, and we know that if
anything happens the teachers will deal with it at once.'*
Pupil comment during an inspection

Preventing bullying

One of the most high profile of your responsibilities is to prevent bullying. It is a major part of your responsibility to create a secure learning environment for the students in your year or section of the school. This means that you have to ensure that a programme is in place to make it clear to the pupils that bullying is unacceptable. It is statutory for schools to have a whole school anti-bullying policy. The school's policy should form the basis of your approach to dealing with bullying. Many schools base their policy on exemplars provided by the LA or the downloadable policy available on the Kidscape website (www.kidscape.org.uk). A sample policy is given below as Exemplar 5.1. It draws on several of the models available. You may find it useful to compare with your own school's policy. If the emphasis is different, you may want to think about why this is so.

How prevalent is bullying? It is an old and widespread problem, but one which has become very high profile last 20 years. Research indicates that as many as one in seven of all children in schools has either been a bully or the target of a bully and that most bullying happens in school or, through the growth of cyberbullying, arises from school. Every year around 16 pupils kill themselves because of bullying, and 19,000 pupils attempt suicide. Generally these are teenagers. In practice, with vigilance you should be able to keep the incidence of bullying low, but it is unlikely that any school can prevent it altogether.

The sample policy below accepts this but its statement of intent clearly shows that it views bullying as unacceptable. Similarly, the pupil's comments, included as Case study 5.1 below, show that students know that whereever there are people, bullying will occur, and that what matters is that action is taken. Notice too that in the exemplar policy, emphasis is put on ensuring that pupils are not frightened to tell teachers when an incident occurs.

EXEMPLAR 5.1: A SAMPLE ANTI-BULLYING POLICY

Statement of intent
We are committed to providing a caring, friendly and safe environment for all of our pupils so they can learn in a relaxed and secure atmosphere. Bullying of any kind is unacceptable at our school. If bullying does occur, all pupils should be able to raise this and know that incidents will be dealt with promptly and effectively.

Aims
1. The principal aim is to reduce to a minimum the occurrence of bullying in the school in all its forms, and to create a non-threatening environment for pupils based on mutual respect and concern for the welfare of each other.
2. To create awareness in the minds of all members of the school, governors, staff, pupils and parents of:
    — what constitutes bullying
    — the strategies in place in school, which help parents to cope with and resolve any problem associated with bullying.
3. To establish a structure of support for all parties involved in the incidents of bullying, i.e. bullies, bullied and parents.
4. To emphasize:
    — the unacceptable nature of bullying
    — the notion that extreme cases of bullying would expect to be dealt with seriously.
5. To establish confidence in pupils that sharing the problem with a member of staff will not create an even more threatening situation, but will instead lead to a resolution of the problem.

Objectives of this policy
*   All governors, teaching and non-teaching staff, pupils and parents should have an understanding of what bullying is.
*   All governors and teaching and non-teaching staff should know what the

school policy is on bullying, and follow it when bullying is reported.
- All pupils and parents should know what the school policy is on bullying, and what they should do if bullying arises.
- To ensure that procedures established in the policy are follow if an incident occurs.
- To make it clear that as a school we take bullying seriously. Pupils and parents should be assured that they will be supported when bullying is reported.
- To ensure that bullying will not be tolerated.

Definition: what is bullying?
Bullying is the use of aggression with the intention of hurting another person. Bullying results in pain and distress to the victim.

Bullying can be:

- Emotional: being unfriendly, excluding and tormenting
- Physical: pushing, kicking, hitting, punching or any use of violence
- Racist: racial taunts, graffiti, gestures
- Sexual: unwanted physical contact or sexually abusive comments
- Homophobic: focusing on the issue of sexuality
- Verbal: name-calling, sarcasm, spreading rumours, teasing
- Cyber: all areas of internet, such as email and internet chat room misuse
- Mobile: threats by text message and calls.

There are three key characteristics that can turn unkindness into bullying: it is ongoing; it is deliberate; and it is unequal, i.e. it gives the person doing the bullying some power over the person experiencing the bullying.

Why is it important to respond to bullying?
Bullying hurts. No one deserves to be a victim of bullying. Everybody has the right to be treated with respect. Pupils who are bullying need to learn different ways of behaving.

Schools have a responsibility to respond promptly and effectively to issues of bullying.

Strategies for dealing with bullying
Our strategies fall into four main categories:
1. Raising the profile/recognition
2. Establishing coping strategies/clear procedures
3. Creating a secure environment
4. Dealing with incidents/sanctions

Recognizing bullying: signs and symptoms

A child may indicate by signs or behaviour that he or she is being bullied. Adults should be aware of these possible signs and that they should investigate if a child:

- Is frightened of walking to or from school
- Doesn't want to go on the school/public bus
- Begs to be driven to school
- Changes their usual routine
- Is unwilling to go to school (school phobic)
- Begins to truant
- Becomes withdrawn, anxious, or lacking in confidence
- Starts stammering
- Attempts or threatens suicide or runs away
- Cries themselves to sleep at night or has nightmares
- Feels ill in the morning
- Begins to do poorly in school work
- Comes home with clothes torn or books damaged
- Has possessions which are damaged or 'go missing'
- Asks for money or starts stealing money (to pay bully)
- Has dinner or other monies continually 'lost'
- Has unexplained cuts or bruises
- Comes home starving (money/lunch has been stolen)
- Becomes aggressive, disruptive or unreasonable
- Is bullying other children or siblings
- Stops eating
- Is frightened to say what's wrong
- Gives improbable excuses for any of the above
- Is afraid to use the internet or mobile phone
- Is nervous and jumpy when a cyber message is received.

Similarly, investigate if you notice:

- Name calling
- Excluding one person from a group
- Stopping talking to someone
- 'Hiding' property
- Physical abuse
- Unwanted conduct of a sexual nature, or other conduct based on sex affecting the dignity of boys and girls at the school
- Unwanted conduct or displayed attitudes based on race, religion or gender.

These signs and behaviours could indicate other problems, but bullying should be considered a possibility and should be investigated.

Raising the profile/recognition

Teaching and welfare staff should be vigilant in their observations of pupil behaviour to recognize and take appropriate action where incidents of bullying occur.

Correct attitudes – i.e. the unacceptability of bullying – should be developed and embedded through our teaching programme:

Anti-bullying material is used as a teaching resource.

- The subject of bullying should be part of our SEAL programme.
- It should used in assemblies and in subject teaching e.g. in PSHE, English, drama and RE and history, to identify to pupils the school's understanding of what is meant by bullying.

Procedures

- All bullying incidents should be reported to staff.
- In cases of serious bullying, the incidents will be recorded by staff.
- Parents will be informed and asked to school to discuss the problem.
- If necessary and appropriate, police will be consulted.
- Bullying behaviour or threats of bullying will be investigated and stopped quickly.
- An attempt will be made to help the bully or bullies change their behaviour.

Create a secure environment

- Pupils should be encouraged to report all instances of bullying immediately.
- There is often an understandable reluctance to tell anyone, so encouraging pupils to find a member of staff with whom they can share their concerns should be reiterated regularly in year assemblies and form time.
- Staff involved in any incidence of bullying should treat all incidents with due concern, which reflects the school's attitude to the problem.
- Appropriate action such as walking away, not retaliating and, in particular, finding an adult with whom to share the problem, should be included in any discussions with pupils on the subject of bullying.
- Anti-bullying material is used as a teaching resource. Pupils should always be sure that concerns will be dealt with swiftly and positively in order to give them security.

- Staff should follow the school's *Strategies for Handling Bullying* handbook when providing individual support for a child. Always seek advice if you are unsure how to proceed.
- External agencies and teacher counselling are used to help children.

Nothing is hidden
- We monitor each reported incident – there is an annual audit and a short report is produced.
- Our policy is reviewed with staff, governors and students annually in the first half of the school year and is available for parents.

Sanctions
- In dealing with incidents of bullying, each party involved should be asked to put into writing his/her own version of any incident. Salient points of any discussions with the pupils should be recorded by the member of staff dealing with the incident. This documentation should be stored in the pupil's file so that any patterns of behaviour which are forming will become evident.
- Each incident should result in a plan of action being formulated, which should be agreed by all parties.
- Any sanctions imposed will depend on the frequency or severity of the incidence of bullying. You will find additional information about sanctions in our *Managing Pupil Behaviour* booklet.
- Parents are expected to work with the school and at the appropriate level of seriousness parents will be invited into the school to contribute to the development of strategies for improvement of behaviour.

Outcomes
- The bully/bullies will be asked to accept responsibility for their actions.
- In serious cases, suspension or even exclusion will be considered.
- If possible, the pupils will be reconciled.
- Each case will be monitored to ensure that repeated bullying does not take place.

Associated school policies
- Behaviour, school rules, code of conduct, equal opportunities, pastoral, etc.

How schools deal with bullying

CASE STUDY 5.1: AN EXTRACT FROM A DISCUSSION WITH SOME YEAR 11 PUPILS

We know that there will be some bullying whatever we do. What I like here is the strenuous effort made by the school to deal with any incident that occurs. What matters to me is that something is done to stop the bully and help the person being bullied. The other thing, that I think is really good, is that in this school you can take the problem to any teacher. I moved here from another school. In that school there were only one or two teachers to whom you could talk. Here all the staff will listen and help. Knowing this really makes a difference . . .

The above comments make it clear that what really matters to pupils is that people will listen and that the school will take action to deal with any bullying situations that arise.

The exemplar which follows is a list of strategies devised by School B to prevent bullying and to deal with it should it arise. It is included as a checklist for you so that you can benchmark your own practice. To ensure that it was comprehensive the school focused on three areas and identified what would be needed institutionally, personally and within the curriculum.

EXEMPLAR 5.2: SCHOOL B'S STRATEGIES TO HELP YOU HANDLE BULLYING

Personal strategies
- Children decide the rights, responsibilities and rules for their class/tutor group
- Showing respect and dignity in all situations
- Intervention
- Interesting and relevant curriculum
- Whole class discussions
- Encouraging responsible behaviours
- Communication with lunchtime supervisors
- No bullying behaviour
- Teaching children about bullying
- Role modelling

- Meeting with colleagues
- Supporting colleagues.

Curriculum strategies
- Case conferences with other staff (consult)
- Novels/films/video/DVD material
- School magazine articles/problem page
- Teaching victims coping strategies
- Countering bullying across the curriculum
- Teaching bullies awareness
- Projects
- Discussion/debates
- SEAL programme and PSHE: social skills, negotiation, arbitration, intervention
- Essays
- Identify opportunities in subjects, particularly, but not exclusively, English, history, drama, RE.

Institutional strategies
- Keep the issue high profile
- Contact with primary schools
- Questionnaires
- Inter-agency contacts
- Changing playground environment
- Developing a telling ethos
- Parents' evenings
- Introducing lunchtime activities
- Safe areas
- Bully box
- Training for all staff
- Ongoing staff meetings
- Management responsibilities
- 'Listeners'
- Buddy system
- Policy development and implementation.

The no-blame approach

The no-blame approach to dealing with bullying was developed by Barbara Maines and George Robinson in the early 1990s. At the time the problem of bullying in schools was becoming high profile and many of the strategies previously adopted in schools were considered ineffective. The no-blame approach is concerned with ending the bullying, rather than punishing the bullies and works as follows:

Step 1: Interview the victim
When a teacher finds out or is informed that bullying is occurring. He/she should talk to the victim about his/her feelings. The emphasis is on finding out who is involved, rather than the specific incidents.

Step 2: Hold a meeting with all the people involved
As well as the leaders, this session could include some of the more peripheral people, or some of those who joined in. Groups of 6–8 pupils tend to work most effectively.

Step 3: Explain the problem
This is essentially a means of sharing the victim's feelings with the other pupils. Generally, drawings, poems or stories are used to convey the victim's distress. The details of particular incidents are never discussed and do not form any part of this procedure.

Step 4: Moving forward
No blame is attributed, but the teacher makes it clear that he/she knows that these pupils are responsible and can change their behaviour towards the victim.

Step 5: Generate strategies with the group
The next step is for the teacher to ask the pupils for their ideas to move the situation forward and help the victim. Although the teacher responds positively to the ideas put forward, he/she does not insist that they are implemented. No promises are extracted.

Step 6: Leave it up to the pupils
This step involves trusting the pupils to take responsibility for rectifying the situation.

Step 7: Monitor progress
The teacher arranges a date on which to meet the group of pupils to see how the situation has developed.

Step 8: See pupils individually
The teacher holds a short meeting with each pupil involved, including

the victim, to see what progress has been made. This helps the teacher check progress and also to share feelings which may not emerge in a group session.

The no-blame approach has met with a mixed response. It takes considerable skill and sensitivity to manage it effectively. Realistically, some pastoral leaders will be much better at using it than others, and some educational psychologists and EBD teachers believe that the impact of this programme is short-lived. There are also some cases which are so extreme that a no-blame approach simply does not apply. Probably the best thing to do is to develop a range of strategies for dealing with incidents of bullying.

Restorative justice (RJ)

RJ (see Chapter 4) builds on the no-blame approach and is often used in dealing with bullying situations. Case study 5.2 focuses on girls' 'friendship' issues, which all too frequently consume a lot of a year leader's time and often include bullying, and shows how using an RJ approach flexibly can help the pupils involved.

CASE STUDY 5.2: GIRLS' FRIENDSHIP ISSUES

The ongoing issues between Dina and a group of girls in her Year 9 form came to a head after an incident in an art lesson. When the teacher was busy helping other pupils, a group of girls began to lark about and to flick spots of paint at each other. What started as fun turned nasty when several girls targeted Dina at the same time and with large amounts of paint. Tearfully, Dina went to the teacher for protection and after the lesson the teacher referred the matter to Pat, the year head, because although she had dealt with the misbehaviour, clearly the incident was part of a larger issue about the relationships between the girls, which needed to be addressed.

Pat was trained in RJ and felt using this approach offered the best long-term likelihood of resolving the issue. RJ starts with the victim, so Pat spoke to Dina, who was still very upset about what had happened. For quite a while Dina had been included in this group of friends, but now she felt excluded and that the group of girls, several of whom were taller and heavier than Dina, were ganging up on her and that it was getting worse as they could see that she was afraid of them. It had started with name calling, but now there were incidents in class of which the art lesson was the worst Dina had experienced. The paint flicking had attracted attention but often teachers didn't notice and some of her books and class assignments had been taken or defaced so that she had had to replace them. Usually she had backed up her work but it wasted time and made her feel bad.

RJ involves getting the pupils together, to discuss and reflect on what has happened, but when she spoke to Dina about this, Dina did not want to be in a room with the whole group of girls and it was clear that she felt very threatened by this prospect. Pat asked if there was one girl that Dina would be prepared to meet and Dina thought about it and said Debbie, who was a member of the group, but not the leader. This at least got the process started so Pat set up a mini-conference with Dina and Debbie.

Pat started by reminding the girls of the rules of RJ. They must respect each other and the process. They must allow the person speaking to have his/her say and not interrupt. They must try to be truthful at all times. Pat finds that using this approach creates respect for the process and helps create a secure environment in which people are prepared to say what they think and feel.

Pat started by getting Dina to say what she felt was happening and how she felt about it. Dina described the incident and said that she was now very reluctant to be anywhere near them in a classroom and to put her bag down, and that it was affecting her social life because she didn't want to go out anywhere in case she met them. She was very worried that more people could become involved.

Debbie responded that she felt guilty after the incident in the art class because it had gone too far. She said:

> We shouldn't have done it. We like Dina but she takes things very seriously, and can be a 'goody goody', so we tease her, but I hadn't realized how much it was upsetting her and on Monday it went much too far. We weren't flicking paint at her to start with, we were just larking about, but she told us to stop and moved her work away to protect it, so we started to aim paint at her. Afterwards I felt bad. The school informed my parents that I was involved and they talked to me about it and said that it made them ashamed and this made me feel unhappy.

Pat asked Debbie what should be done to move the situation forward and Debbie said that she would talk to the others because they should apologize to Dina and they should stop teasing Dina because it was upsetting her.

Pat asked Debbie if she wanted to be friends with Dina, and Debbie said she did because really she liked Dina. Dina's response was also positive – she wanted to be friends with Debbie.

It was agreed that they would try to support each other in school.

Pat used a RJ contract form to record the outcome of the meeting and the actions that had been agreed. Both girls signed it and received a copy each. To end the meeting Pat asked the girls to shake hands.

She asked Dina to remain for a few minutes after the end and asked her how she felt about things now. 'It went better than I expected,' said Dina, 'and I'm pleased that Debbie wants to be friends with me.'

'We got a long way in that meeting,' said Pat, 'and I am very pleased. Now do you think we could have a larger RJ conference with the group?'

Dina, however, was not ready for this. She felt that she could not trust them to be honest when the whole group was there. 'What about meeting Natalie then', asked Pat, naming the group leader. 'Would you be prepared to do a mini-conference with her with me present?' Dina was quiet for a few minutes, and then she agreed to the meeting. 'If I do this, things could really get better, so I have to try,' she said. Pat expressed her pleasure at this response: 'I am so pleased that you could take such a mature approach.'

At the mini-conference with Natalie, it took a while to get either of the girls to talk in more than one word answers, but Pat continued to probe, to get them to open up, especially to see what had turned the gang leader against Dina, and Natalie finally responded to the question 'What's really going wrong – are there other issues we should talk about?' Natalie began to talk about things that other girls had said which gave the impression that Dina had been very critical of Natalie behind her back, and made her feel upset because Dina is well regarded and Natalie wanted her good opinion. Then she felt angry with Dina and looked for a way to get back at her. Exploring the issue made it clear that the problem was gossip, which had grown out of a very small incident – misinterpretation of something Dina had said. To join in with the others she had tried to make a joke but she isn't good at humour and other people had taken it seriously.

'I realize that I should not have simply accepted the gossip – I should have asked Dina,' said Natalie.

The question 'What do we do now to put things right?' was crucial to this session, and Natalie answered: 'I am going to stop targeting Dina, she hasn't done anything nasty to me. In future I will try to get the facts right. It is important to give someone a chance to explain.' 'I'm not going to try to do jokes in future, I'll just be me,' said Dina.

Pat recorded onto the contract:

> We'll try to get the facts right before we act.
> We'll try to understand other people's viewpoint and how they see situations.

They signed the contract and shook hands.

Afterwards Dina said she felt less anxious about being in lessons with Natalie and when Pat checked back a few weeks later, Dina said that it was better; they had stopped targeting her and though she was still wary of the group and very careful about what she said, Debbie was supporting her and they were becoming really good friends.

For discussion/reflection
- What are the issues involved in this case study?
- What makes RJ a useful tool to deal with the situation?
- How does it compare with situations with which you have had to deal?

Using an outside consultant
Case study 5.3 illustrates how one particular school addressed a bullying issue and the role played by the year head.

CASE STUDY 5.3: SCHOOL C

We began to notice a problem with a group of girls in Year 10. Individually they appeared pleasant girls, but as a group they appeared to have a negative impact on others in their form. Pupils claimed that they were intimidated and that the leader of the group, Cherrie, a girl with a strong personality, manipulated the others in the group and encouraged her 'friends' to spread unpleasant and largely untrue rumours about girls who were not in the group.

As the year head, I worked closely with the deputy head with responsibility for pastoral affairs. We found it difficult initially to pin it down and to get firm evidence. As usual the 'witnesses' were not prepared to come forward, so we had unsupported stories, but an increasing number of them. We found this very frustrating, so we focused on dealing with the situation. We tried the normal approaches that we used to deal with this kind of problem: encouraging students to talk to us, resolution-focused counselling, face-to-face mediation; but they didn't work and then the situation began to escalate as a couple of the girls had become the subject of offensive blogs, which were upsetting them and affecting their school work. It took them a while to tell us about this. The positive thing here was that at least the blogs gave us the evidence that there was a real problem which we could address.

I talked through the next steps with the deputy and we decided to take them off-site for a day. First we had to obtain their parents' consent, but this didn't prove a problem as all the parents, in their different ways, wanted the situation resolved and the girls liked the idea of having a day conference for girls as they felt that their concerns were being taken seriously. The deputy suggested getting an outside facilitator to lead the day would provide objectivity and more effective resources than home grown efforts, so we asked Kidscape to recommend us a bullying consultant.

The consultant worked through a range of activities with the girls starting with an icebreaker to get them working together. All the activities were designed to make the girls think and related easily to their issues. I found it very interesting as I didn't always see the point of an exercise when it started, and then as it developed, I began to understand the aim and how it fitted to the overall programme. I particularly liked an activity which gave individuals a range of options. They picked up cards, which led to other cards, and this showed the girls how choices which seemed innocuous could spiral into actions that they could not have predicted and how easy it is to become involved in unsavoury group activities. It really made them focus on the consequences of some of their actions.

There was a good activity which focused on dealing with character assassination, followed by a kind of balloon debate. Instead of speeches you picked cards to choose which characters to keep and which to throw out of the balloon. As the girls learnt more about their chosen characters, revelations about the characters made them rethink their choices and made them think about their choice of leaders.

The consultant used an activity I had heard about before but would have been hesitant to have used myself without training. This was called Queen Bee, and showed them how the Queen Bee dominated the group; it addressed the issue of Cherrie's dominance and I watched the way some of them began to look at her during this session. He started the afternoon with a role play in which one of the leading bullies (not Cherrie as that would have been too obvious) took the part of the bullies. Watching the participants shout abuse, I realized that very sensitive handling was needed to ensure that these activities didn't backfire, and just how skilled the consultant was. The role play led to real discussion where the girls began to talk about their issues and how they felt. He gave about an hour for this – time to explore fully but not too long.

There were some tears in this session. As the final short activity he asked them what the conference had really made them think about. Areas that they identified included: understanding that rumours are often untrue; the effects that their actions can have on other people; and thinking for yourself and not just blindly following a leader. When one girl voluntarily apologized for her actions, others followed suit and the consultant offered 'sorry cards' for them to use if they quietly wanted to apologize to someone in the group.

The day proved very cost effective for the school and the girls told us that they had found it a valuable experience; they felt that it had really cleared the air and enabled them to talk freely, which had been a major issue previously, and it had made them think about how they relate to others. We have monitored progress since the conference and the feedback is that relationships are much better and more open. There have been no significant incidents. We continued to work with those involved, e.g. to help Cherrie, who does have leadership potential, be less controlling. For example, we are now using coaching techniques to help individuals. Overall, we are very pleased at how the situation has really moved forward.

For discussion/reflection
- What are the issues in explored in Case study 5.3?
- What are the lessons of this case study for you as a pastoral leader? In this context, you might want to also consider Case study 5.5: Involving the students.

The case studies have illustrated a common dilemma for schools – how important it is for the students to see the action taken to deal with the bullying, yet how difficult it is to get students to come forward, particularly the witnesses. As Case study 5.1 indicated, students will talk to staff when they are confident that there will be a positive outcome. All too frequently victims fear that if the action is unsuccessful, their position will just become worse. For witnesses there is an understandable reluctance to become involved and the fear that they will become the next target. Schools have developed a variety of ways to encourage students to confide concerns. They range from the more technical, such as a confidential email or a dedicated a mobile phone line, to the basic – just providing a cardboard box where pupils can place confidential messages. You can never, of course, promise confidentiality, but a track record of addressing concerns swiftly and effectively when they are raised makes it more likely that individuals will be prepared to come forward. You need to be aware, however, that if you succeed and students come forward, it will initially raise your bullying statistics. It doesn't mean that the level of incidents has risen, rather that now people trust you enough to tell you it is happening.

CASE STUDY 5.4: SCHOOL D SUMMARIZES ITS STRATEGIES TO COMBAT BULLYING

We found that we needed to take a multi-faceted approach to dealing with bullying. In our school we:

- educate children about dynamics of bullying
- explore issues of power with the child
- recognize the importance of the peer groups and peer influences
- implement consequences for bullying behaviour to ensure bullying stops
- build positive leadership
- use referrals for professional interventions
- work with parents and children.

Research has shown that proactive approaches can significantly reduce the number of bullying incidents. It is also clear that no one approach used on its own is a blueprint for success. This was illustrated by Case study 5.4.

Involving the students

A lot of schools have found that involving the students in addressing the issues has more impact than when the strategies are devised and implemented by the staff. The school featured in the Case Study 5.5 uses this approach.

CASE STUDY 5.5: CONSULTING THE PUPILS

At our year heads' meeting, we had discussed a recent bullying incident and were anxious to prevent any more outbreaks of this kind, but felt that we were reacting after the event rather than being pro-active and needed to rethink how we addressed the whole issue of bullying. After a lot of discussion, we came to the conclusion that if we involved the pupils more, the measures that we took would be more relevant for them and might be more effective. As a first step we decided to involve them in redrafting the whole school anti-bullying policy, which has to be reviewed annually. Each year head led the initiative with his/her year group under the overall leadership of one of the assistant principals. We started by focusing tutor time sessions on defining what we meant by bullying, and what the aims and objectives of our policy should be. This also meant that we clarified what isn't bullying, so that we understood and agreed at what stage teasing or a friendship dispute became bullying.

We then consulted on what strategies we should use to deal with bullying. We held year council meetings to bring together the points that the individual forms had raised and finalize a document that was sent back to the forms for approval. My year group suggested that each year group should have its own anti-bullying policy, but they appreciated that we have to have one overarching document as is a statutory requirement to have a whole school policy. For this reason my year group, Year 10, decided to have a year anti-bullying charter to supplement the whole school policy and this is now displayed in each Year 10 classroom. A session of School Council was convened to look at the drafts for each year group and assimilate them into one whole school anti-bullying policy. Our final document was sent to a governors' meeting to be ratified and then published and placed on our website in November to coincide with anti-bullying week. The requirement to review the policy annually means that we have to revisit it regularly, and this helps to keep the anti-bullying initiative high profile and assists the pupils' ownership of the document.

During our consultations about the policy, the assistant principal suggested that we ask the students about how the learning environment could be made more bully-proof. One of the questions was: 'Where and when do you feel most vulnerable?' Some pupils identified some dark areas of the school where they felt unsafe, but the main problem area proved to be the school toilets. Some pupils, and it wasn't only girls, said that they really didn't like using them at all, mainly because 'gangs' of pupils could force them into a cubicle or peer under the doors to find them or 'tease' them. This made us focus on what we could do to improve the toilets. We have no major building programme at the moment, so it had to be affordable; nevertheless two of us went to have a look at the facilities and design of the new academy currently being built in the neighbouring LA.

As a result we got the toilet blocks redesigned so that the doors now go from floor to ceiling and no one can peep under the doors. We have also established surveillance cameras in these areas and a policeman established on the school premises does a regular sweep. We have tried to make the toilets generally smarter and were able to do some redesigning to remove corners where a pupil could be isolated. In each year group, the year head walked the school with a group of pupils looking at the dark areas and then talked to the pupils about what we could do to make them safer and lighter. They came up with some sensible suggestions, which we were able to adopt. Whereas we couldn't widen corridors, we could change the lighting system, so we did. Similarly, in response to comments from the pupils, we changed where the playground supervisors stood at break and lunchtime.

Not all of the ideas worked; a trial run of a one-way system proved it was more trouble than it was worth, but feedback from the students is that they liked being consulted, and really appreciated that we had tried to use their ideas and explained the problem if we couldn't implement something that they wanted. One girl actually said, 'Every time I use the toilets now, I think they are so much better and that this came about because the teachers asked us what we wanted'.

Using peer mentoring

One of the most effective strategies for schools to use against bullying is peer mentoring. This is because often pupils are more willing to confide in other pupils than in staff. It can be more effective than staff-led approaches, perhaps because it gives pupils more responsibility. It provides peer pressure against bullying.

Your school's particular circumstances could determine how you focus and organize the system. A case study describing how one school introduced peer mentoring can be found in Chapter 8, pp. 200–205.

The National Peer Mentoring Programme

The government has recently launched the National Peer Mentoring Programme. It builds on the Children's Plan, which highlights the importance of developing peer mentoring pre- and post 16.

This two-year initiative (2009–2011) is run by the Mentoring and Befriending Foundation (MBF) and makes it easier to for schools to access funding. The MBF provides the funding to create the infrastructure and the resources and support the training of the peer mentors. The initiative focuses on enabling young people to provide support and advice to each other in schools. It is designed to apply to all young people in pre- and post-16 education.

Through the initiative children and young people will:

- work with groups or individuals to resolve disputes through conflict resolution
- develop befriending schemes which encourage friendships for those children who otherwise might struggle to fit in or be accepted
- be trained to listen to problems and support their peers.

An additional aim is to target the disengaged young people in the community. A successful pilot scheme involved 180 schools and colleges and 3,600 students.

The Mentoring and Befriending Foundation (MBF)

The MBF has produced a National Peer Mentoring Pilot dissemination manual highlighting the good practice and methods used to successfully set up and sustain peer mentoring schemes. You can visit the MBF website (www.mandbf. org.uk). Contact Sarah Willey, National Contracts Manager, on 0161 787 3835 for further information on this manual, or Kirsty Shaw, Peer Mentoring Administrator, on 0161 787 8600.

Cyberbullying

Cyberbullying is the use of ICT, particularly mobile phones and the internet, deliberately to upset someone else. It is a form of bullying, but instead of the perpetrator carrying out the bullying in person, they use technology to do it. Most of it takes place outside school, which makes it difficult for you to deal with, but it affects the self-esteem and morale of the pupils for whose welfare and progress you are responsible.

Cyberbullying can include a wide range of unacceptable behaviours, including harassment, threats and insults and, as with face-to-face bullying, it is designed to cause distress and harm. Cyberbullying can also cause physical harm, as it includes 'happy slapping', in which the perpetrators take photographs or videos of a victim being assaulted. A variation called 'cyberbullying by proxy' has exposed victims to hate groups and adult predators, as well as making innocent parties appear to be the perpetrators of wrongdoing.

It is a growing problem. A number of studies have looked at the extent of, and trends in, cyberbullying. For example, research conducted as part of the DfE cyberbullying information campaign found that 34 per cent of 12-to 15-year-olds reported having been cyberbullied. To make matters worse, the research indicates a year-on-year increase in the numbers and it is not only your pupils who will be the sufferers. It takes place between children and between adults, but also across different age groups. Young people can target staff members or other adults through cyberbullying. Cases have occurred in which school staff are ridiculed, threatened, falsely accused and otherwise abused online. Qualitative evidence gathered by the National Association of Schoolmasters Union of Women Teachers (NASUWT) through a survey of teachers demonstrates that cyberbullying affects the working lives of staff and has a severe impact on staff motivation, job satisfaction and teaching practice.

How is it different from other forms of bullying?

In cyberbullying, the audience for the bullying can be very large and reached rapidly. This means that the degree and seriousness, as well as possible risks and repercussions, have to be evaluated differently from other types of bullying. If content is shared across mobile phones or posted online, it becomes difficult to control who might see it or have copies of it. Not being able to be certain that the event has been contained and will not recur/resurface may make it harder for the person being bullied to gain a sense of 'closure' over an event. A single incident can be experienced as multiple attacks. For example, a humiliating video posted to the web can be copied to many different sites. A single instance of bullying – the creation of a nasty website or the forwarding of a personal email – can have repeated and long-term consequences, as content that is taken off the internet can reappear or be circulated again.

What powers do schools have to deal with cyberbullying?
Teachers are not always clear what they are allowed to do in situations where the bullying is off-site or involves the pupil's mobile phones. The list below outlines the powers that schools currently have. Knowing what you are allowed to do when faced with cyberbullying issues and being able to clarify this for the staff on your team is an important first step. If you need more detail, follow-up on the references given at the end of this chapter.

- Head teachers have 'reasonable' power to regulate the conduct of pupils when they are off-site or not under the control or charge of staff members. This is particularly significant because cyberbullying, despite its effects on school life, is likely to take place out of school.
- Section 3.4 of the School Discipline and Pupil Behaviour Policies guidance provides more advice on when schools might regulate off-site behaviour.
- The Education and Inspections Act 2006 (EIA 2006) outlines some of the legal powers schools possess and provides a defence for school staff confiscating items from pupils, such as mobile phones being used to cause a disturbance in class or otherwise contravene the school behaviour/anti-bullying policy. (If you need more information on confiscation see section 3.8 of the School Discipline and Pupil Behaviour Policies guidance.)
- School staff may request a pupil reveal a message or show them other content on their phone for the purpose of establishing if bullying has occurred. Refusal to comply might lead to the imposition of a disciplinary penalty for failure to follow a reasonable instruction. Where the text or image is visible on the phone, staff can act on this. Where the school's behaviour policy expressly provides, staff may search through a phone if appropriate.
- Civil and criminal laws can apply in cases of harassment or threatening behaviour in cyberbullying, but leave this to your head teacher as it would be wise to take specific legal advice on this.

Whole school measures
- Ensure that a specific acceptable internet use policy is in place – although users are tracked, students need to be aware of appropriate and acceptable behaviour. It is also important that everyone is are aware of data protection issues, and how to respond to reports or

discovery of offensive messages or images. Ensuring that passwords are kept private is important, so that accounts are not accessed or misused by anyone else. *Safe to Learn* (DCSF, 2007) has an exemplar of an acceptable use policy.

- Government guidelines suggest that schools specifically address cyberbullying in their mandatory anti-bullying policies. Schools should also issue clear rules on the possession and use of mobile phones in school.
- Ensure that security systems are in place to prevent images and information about staff or pupils from being accessed improperly from outside school and keep internet blocking systems updated so that harmful sites are blocked. All e-communications used on the school site or as part of school activities off-site should be monitored.
- Taking a whole school community approach, ensuring that the issues are discussed and the school community shares an understanding of what cyberbullying is and what the consequences and sanctions will be, is crucial to preventing and dealing with cases effectively. Teachers, students and parents/carers need to have sufficient knowledge to deal with cyberbullying.
- Ensure that the curriculum teaches pupils about the risks of new communications technologies and how to use them safely.
- If you use peer mentors in dealing with bullying or have school counsellors, give them training on cyberbullying.
- Work with police and other partners on managing cyberbullying. Bring in specialist teams if available.

Where do you fit into this as a pastoral leader?
- You are likely to be the first point of reference for a distressed pupil or his/her parents.
- You will liaise regularly with the parents over progress.
- Your level of involvement in resolving the issue will depend on the seriousness of the incident and the level of your own expertise.
- You will need to monitor the regularity of incidents and should keep SLT informed of any that occur and what actions you are taking.
- If you have to handle serious or escalating incidents you should liaise closely with an SLT member. Case study 5.3 has an element of cyberbullying.
- You will have to apply the rules about confiscating mobile phones – this is why you have to know what your powers actually are.
- Make sure that you make the rationale of the school's approach clear so that it doesn't appear simply to restrict pupil freedoms. This will

help develop their understanding of the issue and also show that you have taken account of the pupil voice.

- You are likely to have to handle liaising with and bringing in the police or specialist teams to work with the pupils.
- You would need to organize the cyberbullying training for your peer mentors.
- You will have to keep the issue high profile in your year group by returning to it regularly in year assemblies, etc. to send out a consistent clear message that it is unacceptable.
- If you are involved in organizing the PSHE programme for your year group, include items about bullying, especially around Anti-Bullying Week in November when it is most high profile. This will help the students appreciate that you are aware and that help is available. If PSHE isn't within your pastoral responsibilities, liaise with the member of staff who deals with the programme so that you are up to speed with how it is being tackled for your year group. If an incident occurs, you may need to include additional items into your PSHE programme.
- Resources such as films about cyberbullying and the importance of being safe online are available. Contact some of the organizations listed below to get up-to-date resources.
- From time to time you may want to use pupils to carry out a survey in your year group, e.g. about school safety (see Case study 5.4).

Below is an exemplar of the kind of guidance that you will have to issue to the pupils to help them handle cyberbullying. You will probably also need to issue a sheet giving helplines that pupils could contact.

EXEMPLAR 5.3: CYBERBULLYING GUIDANCE PUT OUT TO PUPILS BY SCHOOL F

Contact names, phone numbers and emails often change so although some helplines and contacts are included here, always check the current contact details with the organization.

Cyberbullying help for pupils
Bullying is not your fault. It can be stopped and traced.

- Don't ignore the bullying. Tell someone you trust, such as a teacher or parent. Or you can call an advice line, such as one of those listed below.

Text/video messaging
- You can stop receiving text messages for a while by turning off incoming messages for a couple of days. To find out how to do this, visit www.wiredsafety.org
- If the bullying persists, you can change your phone number. Ask your mobile service provider (such as Orange, O_2, Vodafone or T-Mobile).
- Don't reply to abusive or worrying text or video messages. Your mobile service provider will have a number for you to ring or text to report phone bullying. Visit their website for details.
- Don't delete messages from cyberbullies. You don't have to read them, but you should keep them as evidence.
- Text harassment is a crime. If the calls are simply annoying, tell a teacher, parent or carer. If they are threatening or malicious and they persist, report them to the police, taking with you all the messages you've received.

Phone calls
- If you get an abusive or silent phone call, don't hang up immediately. Instead, put the phone down for a while. Then hang up or turn your phone off.
- Don't give out personal details such as your phone number to just anyone and never leave your phone lying around. When you answer your phone, just say 'hello', not your name.
- If your mobile shows the caller's number, don't answer it. Let it go to voicemail. Don't leave your name on your voicemail greeting.
- If you receive calls that scare or trouble you, make a note of the times and dates and report them to the police. If your mobile can record calls, take the recording too.

Mobile phone companies are taking steps to help tackle cyberbullying. Each phone company should have a number to ring to report phone bullying. For example:

- Tesco Mobile: Text 'bully' to 60000 to receive advice and support
- BT: 0800 666 700 or call 150 for personal advice
- O_2's Nuisance Call Bureau: email ncb@o2.com or call the customer service department on 0870 5214 000
- Vodafone RespondPlus service: visit www.vodafone.co.uk

Emails
- Never reply to unpleasant or unwanted emails.
- Keep the emails as evidence. Tell an adult about them.
- Ask an adult to contact the sender's internet service provider (ISP) by

sending an email to 'abuse@' followed by the host, e.g. abuse@hotmail.com

- Never reply to someone you don't know, even if there's an option to 'unsubscribe'. Replying simply tells them your email address is real.

Web bullying
- If the bullying is on a school website, tell a teacher or parent, just as you would if the bullying were face to face.

Chat rooms and instant messaging
- Never give out your name, address, phone number, school name or password online. Use a nickname when online. Don't give out photos of yourself.
- Don't accept emails or open files from people you don't know.
- Remember it might not just be people your own age in a chat room.
- Stick to public areas in chat rooms and get out if you feel uncomfortable.

Tell your parents or carers if you feel uncomfortable or worried about anything that happens in a chat room.

Helplines
Helplines are also available to call if you need to speak with someone.

- Childline offers a free 24-hour helpline for children and young people. Telephone 0800 1111. The Childline website is www.childline.org.uk
- Get Connected offers a free confidential helpline for young people (open 1:00 p.m. to 11:00 p.m. every day). Telephone 08088 084 994.
- Samaritans has a helpline for those in distress offering multi-channel support. Telephone 08457 90 90 90, email Jo@samaritans.org or SMS text 07725 90 90 90.

Supporting parents of children involved in bullying
You will be the member of staff who liaises with the parents of pupils in your year group involved in bullying. They will be concerned and anxious to support their child, but may not know how to do this. As well as telephone communications and in-school meetings, having some written guidance can be reassuring for the parents. Exemplar 5.4 is an extract from a leaflet sent out by one school.

EXEMPLAR: 5.4 SUPPORTING YOUR CHILD

Friends are very important to children and adolescents. They thrive when they have supportive friendships and may be lonely and unhappy when things go wrong. There are many reasons why a child may be picked on or be aggressive and unkind to others. Your children need you to help them learn how to make and keep friends, be a listening ear and to take appropriate action to help stop bullying.

How you can help
Encourage friendships
- Encourage your son/daughter to invite friends round.
- Help them find ways to make friends, such as joining things.
- Try not to criticize their friends.
- Encourage them to talk about any worries.
- Listen to their point of view without interrupting.

Notice signs of unhappiness such as
- Unwillingness to go to school
- 'Losing' money or other possessions
- Spending a lot of time alone
- Sudden changes in the people they spend time with/friendships.

Boost self-confidence and self-esteem
- Praise them even for small everyday things.
- Let them know that you enjoy their company.
- Show you are impressed and pleased when they do well.
- Be interested in what they think and do.

If your child is being bullied
- Make it clear that it is not their fault.
- Let them know it's good to tell you.
- Reassure them that you can help.
- Discuss ways to handle it.
- Talk to the school and make sure that you know what the school is doing about it.

If your child is bullying others
- Try to find out why.
- Let you know that you love them, though not the bullying behaviour.

- Talk about feelings not the detail of who did what.
- Help them to say sorry and mean it.
- Help them to accept the consequences of what they have done.

Whether your child is bullying or being bullied
- Show you care that they are unhappy.
- Don't try to handle things on your own – talk to the school and to other parents.
- Be confident about taking action – they need your help.
- Aim to change behaviour and feelings, not look for blame.

Using technology to prevent bullying or cyberbullying or to help the victims of it

ICT can be a tool to help you deal with bullying because it can supply you with prevention and detection methods to help you track and prove that there has been bullying. This has long been an area that caused major difficulties because so much about bullying was in an individual's perceptions and it could be difficult to prove. Tracking software, such as Securus, looks out for key words and phrases and takes screen shots of the relevant pages; it shows what was written. These pages provide a trail of evidence that could be used in confronting a bully or his/her family. Some of the key phrases, such as 'I'm going to . . .', may turn out to be false leads but the real value of having this software in place is that it acts as a deterrent because pupils know that the tracking device is in place and that if they have sent unpleasant messages this could be stored in the system and they could be caught.

Another way to use technology is to set up a pupil online forum, e.g. a Here2Listen site, where pupils can report bullying incidents, raise concerns and post messages or ask questions. The real value of this approach is that often the pupil wants you to know but is reluctant to be seen to come forward, and doesn't necessarily want you to take action. Telling someone brings a feeling of greater security. Speak Out Now is a software package that enables pupils to report bullying and to say what action they want the school to take. This is useful because pupils are often fearful of reporting an incident not just because this could increase the bullying but because bullying is so high profile that a minor incident could escalate out of proportion to what is actually happening. In this programme, when the pupil logs on, he/she is taken through a series of steps asking them to identify the perpetrator, give the names of any witnesses, categorize the type of bullying incident and which member of staff they would like to deal with it. They can say that they just want the member of staff to have a watching brief and monitors what is going on, or they can ask for intervention and specify at what level. The software can also prioritize incidents depending on the language the pupil has used to describe them. Incidents including physical abuse, e.g. hitting, would be prioritized for urgent action. Schools introducing this system indicate that it receives regular use. It also helps schools to chart the pattern of bullying incidents and indicates that most are low-level name calling, either in person or via texting or the internet. This doesn't mean it should be disregarded, rather that you can catch it early when your changes of dealing with it effectively are better and you can prevent it from escalating. It also means that the bully gets the message that you will act and the victim knows that support is forthcoming.

Software systems are as good as the people who use them, so they won't solve all the problems and sometimes the member of staff has to advise the pupil that monitoring is insufficient and that action needs to be taken; but without the software, schools could be much less aware of incidents. It appears to make pupils more prepared to speak. The initial telling someone is often the biggest step.

References and web links

Anti-Bullying Network: www.antibullying.net
  - A cyberbullying information sheet for teachers and others working with young people can be found at: www.antibullying.net/cyberbullying1.htm
Beat Bullying: www.beatbullying.org
  - This charity uses an online questionnaire about the children's lives in and out of school. The pupils' responses lead to prompts with advice or different courses of action and the results are forwarded to administrators who decide what action to take.
Childnet International: www.childnet-int.org
  - Childnet has as a range of resources for primary and secondary schools. The website also has a sample family agreement which can be printed out (see www.childnet-int.org/kia). Childnet has produced a summary of the DfE's guidance and a film for schools to use in addressing this issue, which are available at the Digizen website (www.digizen.org/cyberbullying).
Department for Children, Schools and Families (DCSF) (2007), *Safe to Learn: Embedding Anti-Bullying Work In Schools*, DSCF. Available at: www.teachernet.gov.uk/wholeschool/behaviour/tacklingbullying/safetolearn
  - This very useful pdf publication gives comprehensive guidance and a lot of useful resources. For example, its case studies section includes an exemplar of an acceptable use of the internet policy. You can download it or order copies online at www.teachernet.gov.uk/publications (search using the reference 'DCSF-00658-2007').
  - Copies of *Safe to Learn* can also be obtained from: DfE Publications, PO Box 5050, Sherwood Park, Annesley, Nottingham NG1. The DfE produces its resources in association with Childnet International.
Parentline Plus – Be someone to tell has developed a free anti-bullying pack for parents www.parentlineplus.org.uk and www.besomeonetotell.org.uk
Direct gov has a link on its website supporting parents to protect their children from

cyberbullying, e.g. keeping your child safe on computers and mobile phones, www.
direct.gov.uk

Kidscape: www.kidscape.org.uk
- For anti-bullying resources and training.

LA websites
- Some LAs provide sample internet safety policies that can be adapted according to need. For example, you can download an e-safety policy template for schools to use at www.bracknell-forest.gov.uk/e-safety.
- The following example policy provides a template for schools to edit and includes the rationale behind having an internet safety policy. Available at: www.ngfl.ac.uk/docs/Internet_policy.pdf

Securus: www.securus-software.com
- Securus develops e-safety monitoring software for schools.

Speak Out Now: www.speakoutnow.co.uk

TeacherNet: www.teachernet.gov.uk
- See TeacherNet's 'Useful websites and resources' page at www.teachernet.gov.uk/wholeschool/behaviour/tacklingbullying/cyberbullying/usefulsites

Teachers TV: www.teachers.tv
- Teachers TV has a number of programmes about bullying. See the menu for what is available as new programmes are regularly added.

CHAPTER 6

Dealing with pupil welfare

Schools (including independent and non-maintained schools) and further education institutions have a duty to safeguard and promote the welfare of pupils under the Education Act 2002. They should create and maintain a safe learning environment for children and young people, and identify where there are child welfare concerns and take action to address them, in partnership with other organizations where appropriate. As a pastoral leader you are one of the key people involved in enabling the school to carry out this task.

One of your main responsibilities as a pastoral leader is to deal with pupil welfare and provide support and guidance for the pupils in your year group or house. You are not social workers, but in practice you and your tutors do a lot of social work. This chapter explores the kind of problems which may arise and discusses how you should carry out this part of your job, which needs tact, sensitivity and the ability to remain objective. It focuses on your role in dealing with pupils directly. It also focuses on how you support and develop your tutors to handle this aspect of their role. The approaches described in this chapter can also be used to help you deal with adults, staff or parents who are experiencing problems.

Approaches to dealing with pupil welfare
Using a problem solving model
A lot of the problems will be about pupil progress, but in many cases,

friendship problems or home problems compound the issue. You have to unpick the problem before you can help the student to move forward.

Using a problem solving model can be an effective approach to helping pupils with difficult issues to resolve. It is also a useful tool for conflict management because it focuses on identifying and resolving the issue and can take the personalities out of the equation. Case study 6.1 illustrates how you can apply this model.

A PROBLEM SOLVING MODEL

1. Clarification
   — What is the problem?
   — Does it have component parts?
   — What are the current symptoms?
2. Analysis
   — Diagnose the problem.
   — Categorize the symptoms.
   — Suggest possible causes.
   — Consider the viewpoints of the different people involved.
3. Approaches
   — Generate ideas to solve the problem.
   — What are the possible strategies?
   — Who can help with the solution?
4. Action
   — What can be done in the short term?
   — What can be done in the long term?
   — Specify steps to deal with the problem.
   — Decide who is going to monitor progress.

Gaining the pupils' trust
Encouraging them to share the problem
You can only help pupils when you know what the problem is. A lot of what you do is to encourage pupils to talk to you and share their problem. The first essential is to be able to gain the trust of pupils, who need help in managing their school career because of home problems of problems connected with the classroom.

Guidelines for establishing trust
Trust builders include:

- **Honesty** – this is crucial to establishing trust and involves being authentic and honest; ensuring your words are matched by your actions; 'walking like one talks'; saying identical things to one's face and behind one's back; being straightforward versus 'playing games'.
- **Clarity of communication** – giving clear messages, both oral and written. The pupil needs to be clear about what has been agreed and what action will be taken.
- **Listening** – attending *actively* to what others say (see p. 143 for guidance on how to listen actively).
- **Open-mindedness** – not having made up your mind before the session; being willing to explore new possibilities and new experiences.
- **Honouring your commitment** – ensuring your words are matched by your actions; offering to help move work forward; confirming who will help what and when and following up to make sure that it happens. There is nothing worse than making a promise and failing to deliver. If this happens, the student will feel let down and won't trust you next time.
- **Positivity** – taking a positive and problem solving approach to dealing with a difficult situation. People need to feel positive and supported. The problem solving model is a collaborative approach to dealing with problems. The question, 'What can we do to move this situation forward?' uses 'we' rather than 'you'; this helps the pupil to feel that he/she is being supported and that you are working together.
- **Admitting mistakes** – not being too perfect and showing a willingness to admit to mistakes you've made and make amends rather than maintaining an image of perfection and arrogance and denying responsibility for mistakes or placing blame on others.
- **Sharing/empathy/disclosing** – being willing to share experiences that show the pupil that he/she is not the only one to experience a situation, or that you have made a similar mistake in the past but learnt from it and moved on. Don't overdo the empathy.
- **Valuing** – respecting the viewpoints, ideas and ideals of others; actually *hearing* what others say.
- **Involving others** – drawing out the opinions, feelings, ideas, skills of others and asking for their help and participation.
- **Technical competence** – being respected for doing the job well, being efficient and effective. If you lack the expertise for a particular aspect of the task, finding someone who has it.

How to help your tutors improve their communication skills

Often the tutor is the first person to become involved. Some tutors will be naturally much better and much more interested in doing this than others. The more caring tutors deserve the opportunity to develop and the others could possibly improve a bit with support. For this reason an important aspect of your role is to develop your tutors' skills in listening to pupils and giving the pupils the confidence to talk to them about a problem.

Stress the importance of listening sensitively to pupils, who want to talk or confide. Often people don't listen effectively – this can be because:

- They are unable to concentrate.
- They are too preoccupied with their own concerns – although they appear to be listening, they have turned off and mentally gone out.
- They are too focused on what they are going to say next.
- They are unclear about what they are listening to.
- They are confused by what the speaker is saying – can't follow the points being made or find the argument difficult.
- They are not really interested in what the speaker is telling them – the 'I wish they would get on with it' syndrome.

You may find it useful to offer the tutor team an INSET on developing their listening skills. It doesn't need to be lengthy, but it could pay dividends. You can do this either as your team meeting for the half term or the pastoral leaders can set up a voluntary twilight session for those tutors who are interested and bring in an external tutor to lead the session. The materials provided in this chapter, including the 'Checklist for effective listeners' and 'Steps to counselling' could be used as the basis for a session with your tutors, as well as providing guidance for you. You may also have to provide INSET about recognizing abuse (see Chapter 7) so that the signs are picked up and acted on quickly.

It is important that the pupil is given an opportunity to talk to someone to whom he/she can relate. Encourage your tutor team to listen sensitively if a pupil wants to talk to them. When a pupil begins to talk about his/her problem, whatever it is, the tutors will not know what might lie ahead. Your advice to your tutor team should be that they should not ask too many questions, or press for disclosures. What they should do is to give the pupil the space to talk, and help the child to feel safe and to feel the teacher will know what to do. They should not interrupt or disturb the flow. It is particularly important that if issues of child abuse emerge, an over-conscientious teacher does not put the subsequent investigation or a court hearing at risk by asking questions, which could put ideas into a child's mind. 'Did he tell you to touch him?' or 'Does your step-dad hit you often?' are clear examples of leading questions, whereas 'That's a nasty bruise, how did it happen?' is more open and provides an opportunity for the pupil to confide. It must be the child's story, with no grounds for anyone to claim afterwards that the child was coached into providing particular details in the story.

Guidelines for effective listening
Effective listeners:

- concentrate on the speaker
- follow not only the words but also the body language to help them understand what the speaker is really feeling or saying
- are alert to the nuances
- respond immediately but briefly using supportive noises, e.g. 'uh huh' (encouraging grunts!)
- repeat the words to check for accuracy
- ask questions to check for understanding
- keep comments short so that they don't interrupt the flow
- use simple and direct language to keep things as clear as possible
- reflect back and summarize to show they are following and check for understanding – this continuously evaluates the messages being delivered
- respond positively through their own body language: being attentive; leaning forward in the chair; showing interest; making regular but not over-intensive eye contact and short oral responses
- reinforces and clarifies messages – presents things in different ways to get them across and ensure they are understood and that the student knows what the follow-up will be.

Effective listening means
Listening with awareness
This allows you to gather information – essential when you are preparing to give feedback. It helps you to hear the speaker's perceived experiences and point of view. This adds to your knowledge about that person. When you listen with awareness, you show respect for others. Sometimes you will need to make some notes, but always make this clear first as it affects eye contact and can make you appear less involved. Explain this.

Showing involvement
Effective listeners are active listeners. Active attending allows you to hear, understand and interpret what is being said through hearing the emotions being expressed. Remember sometimes the speaker says one thing but means

another. It involves attending to body language – facial expressions, posture, use of hands and pitch of voice. An attentive listener shows empathy and judges the right time to speak. When you attend, you can also identify what is being left out and evaluate the hidden message.

Developing understanding through asking questions

Through questioning, you can develop your understanding of the main points that the pupil is putting forward. Questioning shows clearly that you are listening, but only if the question is appropriate. Questions should be supportive, sensitive and challenging. They help the speaker to develop their points further, re-examine and re-state their views.

Listening questions can be phrased in these ways:

'And then what happened?' (encourage)

'Can you give me an example?' (clarify)

'How did you feel when . . . ?' (explore)

'Have I got it right?' (understand)

Using 'body language' to demonstrate listening, including

- Appropriate eye contact
- Non-verbal prompts, which encourage the person to continue speaking, for example:
  — Nodding occasionally
  — Using appropriate facial expressions in response to the person's feelings rather than your own reactions to them
  — Tolerating silence to communicate patience
- Sitting at an angle or adjacent to rather than opposite the person
- Adopting appropriate stance, e.g. open rather than folded arms
- Avoiding distractions, such as tapping pencils, etc., making sure that you are not interrupted.

Providing the right level of support for your tutors is always a difficult issue, partly because of pressures of time and partly because you want to give them some independence in the role, but it is important to encourage your tutors to liaise with you and to consult you if there is a doubt about what the problem is. In fact it is very important that the tutor refers the problem upwards immediately a serious issue arises.

Guidelines for counselling pupils

Although a lot of schools are able to fund a trained specialist counsellor, either full-time or part-time, many cannot afford to do this and in your role as a pastoral leader you have to undertake quite a lot of 'counselling'. In real terms, much of what you do is not really counselling. There are different interpretations of counselling and you should be careful how you use the term. Much of what you do is simply listening – the pupil needs to tell someone about the situation that they are in and their feelings about it, which is why you need to hone the listening skills of those involved. A lot of it, however, is practical – pupils come to you for advice or guidance and because they want support.

If it is to be effective, counselling must be handled carefully and with sensitivity. Some guidelines for counselling are outlined below, but if you are interested in counselling, you may wish to do a substantial course to give you more of the theory and some opportunities to learn about counselling techniques. A lot of LAs run modules on counselling. These are usually a series of twilight sessions spaced over a period of around six weeks which include assignments and can count towards qualifications, for example for some Open University courses. Some universities also offer this kind of training, so if you want to develop this skill, which can be a valuable asset for a pastoral leader, find out what is available locally and how to get onto the course.

Mainly you counsel pupils, but sometimes counselling is needed for a member of your team, and occasionally you find yourself, usually informally, counselling parents along with their children.

Steps for counselling

1. Establish the need

Sometimes pupils come to you seeking help with a particular problem. More often, you or another member of staff notices that something is amiss. For example, the work of a talented pupil begins to deteriorate. Attendance can also be a symptom, particularly if a pupil is having difficulty on an academic course. Sometimes the form tutor picks up the problem, but asks you do deal with it. Quite often, a few of the friends of the pupil in distress come to see you because they want an adult to be aware of the problem or to seek help for their friend. You have to be sensitive to need. Sometimes, it is effective to ask 'Can I help?', but usually the pupil will initially try to conceal the fact that he/she has a problem. One's first instinct is to deny and claim that everything is all right, when clearly it is not, so you will have to probe for any information about the problem.

2. Set up the interview

Once the need is established, you have to provide the right opportunity to offer counselling. This involves making sure that sufficient time is set aside to enable the problem to be at least aired and to set a timetable for follow-up sessions. In practical terms, you need at least half an hour. Counselling only works in a private, calm, unhurried and undisturbed setting; it is up to you to create those conditions.

3. Encourage people to talk

Counselling is about getting people to open up and talk about their problems. Usually at the start they are defensive or find difficulty in talking. Often the person is not very articulate at the best of times, and isn't used to talking about issues that are personal. Sometimes you will feel that after the first sessions you have not made much progress. This does not mean that you have failed or that you should give up; you should persevere, but you will need to encourage the confidences and draw the person out, using all your sensitive listening skills. (See the guidance on listening given earlier in this chapter.)

Techniques for helping people to talk include

Offer reassurance, so that the person knows that you are not disapproving or critical. Examples of the kind of statement you could use are 'Yes, I quite understand why that's getting you down' or 'Yes, I do understand'.

Be non-threatening. Try to take a non-threatening approach, for example, 'I thought it might be a good idea if we had a chat . . .'.

Make the setting relaxed. Sit at a 90-degree angle to the person being counselled, or next to them. Never sit behind a desk when you are in a counselling situation. Find a room with easy chairs.

Give your undivided attention. Show that you are giving the pupil your full attention. Do not allow interruptions and maintain attention. Keeping eye contact is important for showing your attention and concern, but use this technique with care. Remember that eye contact is not used in some cultures.

Ask open-ended questions that make it easier for the pupil to open up to you and describe the problem. It also helps you get a feel of what the pupil thinks the issue is and what really matters to the pupil. Examples of this technique include: 'How do you feel about that?' 'What bothers you most?' 'When do you find that you get most angry?'

Check the words first. Repeat back what the person has said to check that you have heard correctly before you move on to interpret what you have heard.

Listen carefully. Demonstrate that you have heard what the pupil has said, by rephrasing and summarizing what has been said. Examples of this technique are 'Just let me see if I have understood . . .', 'So you are saying that . . .' and 'Have I got it right, you are saying that . . .'.

Don't say too much yourself. This is the pupil's opportunity to talk, not yours. Sometimes in order to draw someone else out, it can be very useful to share your own experiences. Use empathy, but don't be self-indulgent. Allow a silence to continue and resist the temptation to speak for the person being counselled. Encourage the person to talk by making listening noises such as 'uh huh' or 'hummm'.

4. Help people think through their problems

Having discovered what the problem is, the next step in counselling is to help the person accept responsibility for his/her own problem and to work out his/her own solution. It is his/her problem, not yours, and in the end he/she has to solve it. For this reason it is important that you do not offer ready-made solutions. Giving your solution to the problem is unlikely to help, so resist the temptation.

Your aim is to be friendly and encouraging, and, above all, neutral. As well as the listening techniques outlined above, you can use other approaches, such as:

Sharing

This involves describing, in an open and honest way, a similar experience that has happened to you and how you felt about it. Use this technique sparingly, be concise, and avoid taking over the conversation. Beware of imputing to the person being counselled feelings that are yours rather than his/hers.

Admit your own fallibility

This is another form of sharing. Make comments like 'I've often made the same mistake . . .' and 'I must admit, I find that difficult too . . .'.

Be non-judgmental

Offer relevant advice or suggestions, but do not express your views or criticisms. 'If you wish, we could allow you to do your homework in the library after school . . .', 'You could discuss this with . . .'

Ask questions

Ask questions to solicit ideas and establish alternative ways to solve the problem, e.g. 'So what do you think the options are?', 'How can you avoid, getting into that situation?', 'How can you improve the situation?'.

Always turn it back

The person being counselled controls the agenda, not you. If you have to make a suggestion, phrase it tentatively or use a question rather than a firm suggestion. Examples are 'I suppose one option could be . . .' or 'Have you considered this line of action?'. The main point to remember is to keep asking open-ended questions, as this will help the person being counselled to think through to his/her own solutions.

5. Let people find their own solutions

The final stage of a counselling session or series of sessions is to try to arrive at a solution to a problem. Remember, the aim is that the person arrives at his/her own solution, even if this is not the one that you personally favour. Once the person has reached this point:

- Accept the chosen solution, even if you have misgivings. Your aim is to help and encourage, so be careful to support any solution which emerges from the session.
- Agree an action plan, and if possible, a review date. This helps the person to be clear about what he/she is going to do, how he/she is going to do it and by when.
- Make it clear that you would be happy to talk to the person again, not just for the review, but if he/she needs another session to talk, especially if further problems develop.
- Generally the only notes made during a counselling session are agreements, e.g. the action plan. Making notes distracts from attentive listening and can be threatening for the person being counselled.
- Do not promise confidentiality. This does not mean that you would normally betray a pupil's confidence, but there are some particularly sensitive areas, such as child abuse, in which you cannot keep a pupil's confidence. Usually in these cases, the pupil has come to you because he/she wants someone to know and this will be discussed in the sessions.

6. After the session

You must think carefully about how you handle dealing with the person after the interview. This matters, because for counselling to succeed you have to suspend any professional authority relationship you have with the person being counselled. It is important to restore the professional relationship immediately as, for example, in the period after counselling he/she may test you out and behave in a way which results in you having to apply sanctions.

Your aim after the session/s is to remain supportive in a low-key way. Resist the temptation to check progress too frequently; this puts pressure on the person and is interference. The occasional caring enquiry is fine and is usually appreciated.

Holding the cuddly toy

A technique used sometimes in counselling or coaching is to use a soft toy, e.g. a teddy bear, which the person being counselled holds. Holding the toy represents their ownership of the session and reminds you not to take over.

An exemplar of a comprehensive whole school counselling policy is included below. It comes from a school which has a school based counsellor and shows how the school uses counselling. It gives some useful definitions and clarifications, e.g. of confidentiality, which you could use with your team to develop their understanding of how counselling operates.

EXEMPLAR 6.1: THREE SECTIONS OF A SCHOOL'S COUNSELLING POLICY

Extract 1: What is counselling? A definition

Counselling is a way of helping people through talking and listening. The person being counselled is encouraged to express his/her feelings about the problem, so that they can understand their situation better and find ways of coping or of moving forward. A counselling situation involves both parties respecting clearly agreed boundaries and commitment to privacy and confidentiality.

Counselling . . .
- offers a regular space and time to talk or think about worries or difficulties
- helps young people explore their feelings and look at how they might want things to be different by talking and using a range of activities
- may be about developmental issues, resolving problems, improving relationships, making choices, coping with changes, gaining insight and understanding, growing as a person
- is carried out by a trained, fully qualified counsellor.

Counselling and pastoral support

All students at our school can access a range of pastoral support, characterized by good listening and use of counselling skills.

Some students may need additional help from the Inclusion Team.

School counselling is a targeted service, following identification of need by staff, parents, guardians, social workers or the students themselves.

School based counselling is a distinct service; it is an additional source of specialist help available on school premises and in school time.

Who will benefit?

Counselling often means unpicking what has gone wrong in the past or seems to be going wrong now, so that the student can move forward. This list is not exhaustive, but it may prompt you to consider a student who may benefit from counselling when:

- parents are going through divorce or separation and the student is showing changes in behaviour or indications of stress
- there are known family relationship problems
- there is evidence of stress or change in behaviour such as becoming withdrawn or disruptive
- there is a death of someone in the family, or friend – even when the student seems to be coping
- there is knowledge or suspicion of some form of abuse or domestic violence
- there are difficulties with friendships, bullying or teasing
- a student, new to the school, is having difficulty settling or integrating into the school or the form
- they are angry, erratic or show mood swings or depression
- there are drug, alcohol or eating problems or evidence of self-harming
- there is a sexual identity issue, racial discrimination or pressure to conform to cultural expectations
- there are health or disability issues
- you or colleagues regularly feel angry or exasperated with a student.

Counselling can also be an early intervention strategy to prevent deterioration in emotional well-being, behaviour and attitude. It can enhance the student's self-esteem and ability to cope more effectively in school. Young people with longstanding behaviour issues are not as easily helped as at the preventative stage and students who are referred later on may find it too difficult to engage in the counselling process.

Extract 2: Confidentiality, referrals and parental consent
Confidentiality
Confidentiality is essential to the counselling process:

- to enable the young person to develop a trusting relationship with the counsellor
- to allow the young person to open up and share feelings without fear of blame or reprisal
- to allow the young person to speak freely about issues concerning them
- to encourage others to come forward for counselling.

A young person's right to privacy and confidentiality is legally established in the Human Rights Act 1998, Article 8.

Problems in maintaining confidentiality are unlikely to occur if there is mutual trust, goodwill and respect between counsellor, school, staff and parents.

The young person is free to talk to anyone about their counselling sessions if they wish, but should not be directly questioned by school staff.

The counsellor will not pass on any detailed accounts of sessions, but may communicate periodically with the SENCO and the school pastoral staff about general progress, with the child's permission.

For the young person to feel supported between counselling sessions, they may wish a trusted member of staff to know they are receiving counselling.

Sometimes, it may be necessary to liaise with or refer the young person to another agency for further help. But this should only happen with the young person's express permission unless it is subject to child protection and mental health concerns.

In schools where a counsellor is an employee of the school, head teachers have the right to make decisions about sharing information and confidentiality. This needs to be done in a reasonable way and in the best interest of the student. It is also subject to the Data Protection Act 1998 and the duty of confidentiality inherent in any counselling service.

An individual's wishes about confidentiality may be overridden by a paramount duty to protect a child's welfare. (A child is defined as anyone under the age of 18 by the Children Act 1989.)

Breaching confidentiality
At the outset, the counsellor will make it clear to the young person that they may need to breach confidentiality (i e tell someone and seek help). This may happen when the young person or any other person is at risk of significant harm.

The counsellor will discuss this with the young person again if the need arises, and, if the child is 'Gillick competent', try to gain their consent to disclosing concerns. Where possible the counsellor will keep them informed and involve them in this process. Counsellors will be familiar with, and work within, school child protection procedures and know how to contact the member of staff designated as the school's Child Protection Officer. Even without the student's consent, it may be necessary to disclose information they have revealed. Young people who are considered Gillick competent can have access to counselling without their parents' permission or against their parents' wishes (see 'Parental consent' below).

In the case of a young person threatening suicide or serious self-harm, there is a general acceptance of the need for intervention even when this involves breaking confidentiality.

More minor concerns will remain confidential unless the young person wants them shared, to seek further help.

The counsellor is **not** required to pass on information about a young person breaking a school rule or committing an offence, unless it could be deemed that by doing so the counsellor was aiding and abetting a crime (e.g. a young person dealing drugs in school).

Referrals

Students can only benefit if they want counselling. Counselling is voluntary.

Referrals may be made by teachers, parents, the school nurse, other colleagues or the young person.

It takes courage for a child to accept an offer of counselling, and may feel like failure rather than an opportunity to get help.

If you are unsure about referring, consult the counsellor, SENCO, the year leader or a member of the SLT about the nature of the student's difficulties.

The **link member of staff** who can act as a channel for referrals and liaise with the counsellor is the SENCO.

The role of the link member of staff is important, enabling the counsellor to be most effective in-school. The link member of staff, through induction and liaison, will ensure that the counsellor becomes a recognized and valued part of the school community. The counsellor and link person will work together to make sure the service is understood and appropriately used. The school counsellor is also given opportunities to talk about their work, e.g. form times and PSHE lessons.

Parental consent

Young people may be offered one or two initial exploratory sessions with a counsellor before committing themselves, and before any involvement with parents.

Some students may be happy for parents to be approached for consent for them to have ongoing counselling.

Sometimes a parent may withhold consent or the student may be very distressed and unwilling for the school to approach the parents. In these cases, counselling can still go ahead if the counsellor assesses the young person as Gillick competent to consent in their own right.

If a student is unwilling to involve their parents and is assessed to be competent, the student may give their own written consent for counselling. No specific age is stated in legal guidance, it depends on their capacity to understand the issues involved.

Young person's agreement

Assessment of competence based on the Gillick principle depends on:

- the maturity of the young person
- the young person having sufficient intelligence and understanding to enable them to understand what is being proposed, i.e. counselling
- the young person having sufficient intelligence and understanding of the consequences of his or her actions.

The school counsellor, with the link member of staff for counselling or head teacher, will make this assessment.

This principle derives from the Fraser Guidelines – the findings of Lord Fraser in the case of Gillick versus W. Norfolk heard by the House of Lords in 1985.

Extract 3: How we organize counselling

The process

Following a referral, the school counsellor will make initial contact and offer an appointment to the young person.

The initial session provides an opportunity for the student to learn more about counselling. They will be told that it is voluntary and confidential (with a few exceptions, which will be explained), start to gain trust in the counsellor, and talk a bit about their situation. The counsellor will also start to engage the student and make an initial assessment, which will inform future work

The student can enter into an agreement to meet the counsellor regularly, initially for up to six sessions (half a term). The sessions usually last 30 minutes.

How long does counselling continue?
Once counselling begins, if a person has missed two or more sessions without a clear reason, such as sickness, the link member of staff will follow-up with the young person.

Sometimes it will be appropriate to extend the number of sessions and this needs to be discussed with the young person before the sixth session.

Stopping counselling sessions is usually agreed between the counsellor and the young person. The reasons for this may be that the sessions are not beneficial or that the maximum benefit has been achieved for the time being.

It may sometimes be necessary to liaise with or refer the young person to another agency for further help. This will be done with the young person's express permission, subject to child protection or mental health concerns. The school counsellor, SENCO or the designated teacher for Child Protection will establish links with appropriate contacts in other agencies locally.

Facilities
The counsellor needs uninterrupted access to a reasonably quiet, comfortable room. Ideally, the room should be furnished in a way that differentiates it from a classroom or office. The counsellor also needs a secure, lockable place to keep case records and the use of a telephone in privacy.

Appointments
It is important that systems are as discreet as possible, and that the minimum numbers of staff are aware that a student is receiving counselling on a need-to-know basis. They may only be aware that a student is receiving counselling, not why.

The SLT for Inclusion and specific members of the Inclusion team plus the SENCO, and the year leader for each year group, will know which students are receiving counselling.

The school counsellor will provide an appointment slip to the student concerned. AT KS4 in particular, the school counsellor aims as much as possible to vary the counselling slots given to students who are seen over a long period of time so as to avoid the student regularly missing the same lesson.

The school counsellor will need to notify the subject teacher of a student's absence. Permission slips are available for this.

It will be helpful if the counsellor receives advance notice of a student being absent from school, so that unused sessions can be used for assessments or other counselling work.

Records
It is appropriate for the SENCO to keep a record of:
- Students referred to the counsellor
- Parental consent sought or obtained
- The number of sessions attended up to the end of counselling
- Any further action.

The school counsellor will also keep 'process notes' for the duration of their work with the student.

Evaluation
The school counsellor audits the service to provide feedback to senior management, pastoral staff and the counselling service, detailing numbers of appointments by year groups, gender and presenting problem, and a record of the student's counselling sessions is kept in the pastoral folder and SEN folder. This information can be used to highlight trends or areas of concern to influence policy.

As a pilot at the end of the current school academic year, the school counsellor and SENCO invited Year 10 students who had used the counselling service to complete and return an anonymous evaluation form. These evaluations will be used to improve the counselling service. The pilot evaluation form is likely to be adapted and amended over time, following feedback.

NB: Any staff that are aware of specific students who are receiving counselling are well placed to notice how a student responds to counselling and the longer-term outcomes. It is important to recognize that in the early stages particularly, as a student starts to talk about their feelings, there may be an adverse reaction, with things appearing to get worse before they get better.

Range of provision
- The counsellor offers a client based service for students and staff.
- The counsellor uses both sites Tuesday, Thursday and Friday.
- Staff can make contact with the counsellor for personal appointments. If sessions are regular, staff may see the counsellor at lunchtimes or after school. If sessions are required during free lessons, the cover officer is informed and permission is sought from the Head Teacher for release from cover for that lesson.

- Students can make contact with the counsellor for self-referral. A list of students being seen is given to the SENCO weekly and the information on students who have a regular slot are passed on to LPLs at least once a term.
- Student referrals by staff or parents are given in writing to the counsellor, Year Leader or SENCO.
- The counsellor sees students before school from 8.15 a.m., then two students during each lesson.
- Some students are seen by the counsellor once a fortnight. Each student is given a permission slip by the counsellor, which they keep for information for teachers, supply teachers and student supervisors.
- The counsellor has frequent informal 1:1 staff consultations.
- Lunchtime sessions are used to meet staff, emergency sessions and for Year 12 peer counselling training. Supervision and professional development for other counsellors and/or mentors are also provided.
- The counsellor has supervision fortnightly and has a weekly meeting with the SENCO.
- Statistical evaluations are issued every six months to the SENCO.
- Registration time is used for emergency sessions and promoting students' good health and well-being by covering areas such as anti-bullying, sex education and Year 9 anti-bullying training and supervision.
- The counsellor is present on examination results days during August.
- Some staff training days are used for group work with year leaders and non-teaching assistant year leaders.
- The counsellor has UKCP registration and attends relevant courses as part of his/her continual professional development.

EXEMPLAR 6.2: SAMPLE TEACHER AND STUDENT PERMISSION FORMS

Teacher reminder form
Reminder Slip Staff: . . . .   Subject: . . . .
The following student has an appointment with the school counsellor, lasting 30 minutes, on: . . . .
at: . . . .
week: . . . .

Name: . . . . Form: . . . .
We expect this appointment slot to continue for at least half a term.
Thank you for your support.

Signed:. . . . . School Counsellor
Signed:. . . . . SENCO

Student's permission slip
This is to remind:
Name: . . . . Form: . . . .
That you have an appointment with the school counsellor
Your appointment is on: . . . .
at: . . . . **to:** . . . .
Please aim to be prompt.

Please show this slip to your subject teacher before you go to your appointment.

Thank you (signed)

Case studies

The case studies which follow are worked through to help you benchmark your practice, but they can also be used without the solutions, as problems that you could discuss with your team as part of their development. The second case study is set out with questions you can use.

In Case study 6.1 the year head applies a problem solving approach to dealing with pupil welfare. It also illustrates the importance of communication skills in teasing out what the real problem is, and using a counselling approach to help the student take ownership of the problem.

CASE STUDY 6.1: USING A PROBLEM SOLVING APPROACH TO SUPPORT AN 'UNPOPULAR' PUPIL

Amita is an able pupil and hitherto very successful academically. Her parents are supportive and very ambitious for her. She comes to see you and tells you that she is experiencing a problem. Quite often her exercise books and work files mysteriously disappear, and if they appear again, they have been mistreated. Amita has to spend a lot of her time rewriting her notes or reconstructing her files. Even though much of her work is kept on her home computer, and absolutely everything now is backed up more than once, anything which she brings to school or does in class is at risk. She comes armed with a letter from her parents who claim that it is happening because she is an Asian pupil and that she is experiencing racism.

Diagnose the problem and break it down into its component parts
Your first task is to unpick the problem. Having work taken or destroyed is certainly a symptom that there is a problem, but is the underlying problem really racism or does it mask other issues? Your first task is to check whether Amita is the only student experiencing this problem or whether it is a symptom of a bigger outbreak. When you ask a sample of able students, including some Asian pupils, whether any of their work is disappearing or being defaced, their answers make it clear that they don't have a problem; currently Amita is the only student to have her work targeted in this way. The tutor tells you that it is not the first time this has happened, and she has spoken to the form when things get particularly bad, and finds this has a short term effect on safeguarding Amita's belongings, but she regularly suffers taunting and name calling. This makes you begin to wonder if there are elements of bullying in this problem.

Probing below the surface issues
To find out more you talk to some of the more mature and responsible members of her form. They tell you that she is under pressure, however, because she is unpopular with other students, including other able pupils. She has no 'street cred'. They say that Amita is her own worst enemy because she is both arrogant and selfish in her dealings with others. They also say that the majority of the form thinks that Amita is 'sad'. The tutor adds that when it comes to group work, Amita is rejected unless the subject teacher insists on her joining a particular group and she has had to ask the teachers to do nominated groups with this form. She also tells you that she thinks the situation is deteriorating; some of her teachers have mentioned that Amita has started to react by attempting to be a nuisance in class. This is not making her more popular with others, but is affecting her work and progress. The form tutor says that had you not approached her, she would have come to see you for guidance in how to deal with Amita's problems.

- Unpicking the problem has shown you that the underlying problem is not racism – other bright Asian students are not experiencing the same problem as Amita.
- There is a sub-issue that at least one member of the form is prepared to deface or take another student's work. Intellectual jealousy may be a component part of the problem; Amita is unpopular with other able pupils.
- The underlying problem/main issue appears to be Amita's own inability to interact successfully with her classmates.

With whom do you need to liaise?
- Liaise with the form tutor on an ongoing basis as she has already been dealing with this problem and picks up on new incidents faster than you can. You need to decide and clarify how the responsibility will be shared as you don't want to undermine the tutor.
- It can be helpful to use another year head as a sounding board. They may have had to deal with a similar issue in their year group and can tell you what strategies worked for them.
- If things get worse, you should inform your pastoral line manager so that any strategies you use have official sanction. It is also very useful to have someone in a senior position to use as a sounding board or to provide advice.
- You may also need outside advice, e.g. from the school or local counselling or psychological service, to support Amita. Guidance on liaising with external agencies can be found in Chapter 7.
- Consult and liaise with Amita's parents. Make it clear to them what you have discovered, so that they understand what the problem is really about, what you intend to do to help their daughter, and that you will keep them informed of progress. This will test your communication skills as they are likely to be reluctant to believe that their daughter is the main source of her own problem.

Generate approaches for moving the problem forward
The main strategy
- You need to use your interpersonal skills, especially your listening skills, to get Amita to talk freely and accept that she has a problem.
- Expect Amita to use blocking devices aimed at preventing you from knowing what the real situation is.
- Initially she is likely to deny that she has a problem. Typical negative responses are: 'What problem?' or 'I haven't got a problem!'
- Similarly anticipate the 'YP' syndrome – 'It's not my problem, it's *your problem*'. This response puts the blame for the situation on others.
- You have to use the techniques described earlier in this chapter to get past the blocking devices and establish that there are genuine issues. Use the evidence that you have to reinforce that you know more about the situation than she is telling you and that you have a good idea what the position really is. How you deliver this message it is more important than what you say. Experience tends to build up your expertise in saying difficult things to vulnerable people.
- Focus Amita on her classmates' perception of her attitudes and

behaviour. The issue is that they perceive her as arrogant. The arrogance may be a mask for insecurity or it may be real, but it is her manner when she speaks to and interacts with others that so irritates the members of her form.

- If you can get her to accept this, you have made a major move forward in dealing with the problem. She may still be looking to you for solutions, but she has accepted that she has a problem.
- Helping someone to change their behaviour is never easy. You are using a problem solving approach and a bit of counselling, but you may want to use professional counsellors to work with Amita, both because of their professional expertise and on time grounds.
- As time goes on, you hope that more of the suggestions about how to move forward come from Amita as she begins to take the initiative in managing the interactions with the form more positively. It is unlikely that her essential self-centredness can be entirely removed, but she can moderate her behaviour so that she doesn't disregard other people's needs or understands that they have a right to their point of view.

Other strategies to reinforce support
You ask the form tutor to:

- reinforce the strategies being used with Amita
- reiterate that taking and defacing other people's property is unacceptable and that she would be monitoring this
- continue to investigate because there is at least one person in this form who takes and defaces other people's property – often 'moles' within the form will tell you who it is.

You have established that Amita doesn't want to be a loner and would like to have some friends, so you ask one or two of the more mature sensible girls in the form to 'befriend' Amita for the next half term or so to help her integrate more.

You ask Amita's parents to try to reinforce at home the strategies being used at school but not to nag her and to do this as unobtrusively as possible.

Monitoring arrangements
The situation will need monitoring, so you ask the tutor to monitor the situation and to report back to you on a regular basis.

CASE STUDY 6.2: ACADEMIC PRESSURE

You are the head of Year 10 and you become aware that Claire has lost weight this term, and is looking generally anxious. You consult the tutor, but she says that Claire is her usual hardworking self, perhaps a bit quieter than usual, though she is never exuberant. No one, says the tutor, has mentioned any particular problems. It is always difficult to get Claire to confide, so you are not surprised that she has not asked for help. You ask the tutor to put out a round-robin to Claire's subject teachers as a check on her progress and to give you a lever into any discussion. The round-robin reveals that the teachers are rather concerned about Claire. They cannot fault her effort. Her work is detailed and always beautifully presented. She has been in top sets all the way up the school and identified as a potentially good GCSE candidate.

Now, as her GCSE courses get under way, the teachers are beginning to suspect that her results are gained by effort and learning by heart what she has been told in class by the teachers or other pupils. There is no real spark and written assignments lack depth and sometimes indicate a real lack of understanding. If they speak to Claire, she insists that she will try harder and do better next time.

When you speak to Claire, at first she denies there is a problem, but when you talk about her results in recent tests, she becomes very tearful. She is unhappy because she is not succeeding, and because her peers and her teachers can see that she is not doing well. She is terrified of how her parents will react to her report. Claire is the oldest child and the family is very proud of her achievements so far. There is the additional complication that her mother is the head of a local primary school and everyone knows her. Claire tells you that her mother is keen that she should win a place at Oxford or Cambridge. Claire does not know what more she can do to improve. She is working until at least midnight every night.

For discussion/reflection
If you want to work on this case study, here are some questions to focus your discussion or reflection:

- What are the symptoms of the problem?
- What is the main problem here and are there some sub-issues or component parts?

- How do you help Claire to deal with her problem?
- Who can help?
- What targets would it be sensible to set for Claire to help her improve?

There are also some management issues for you as year head. The subject teachers responded to the round-robin but no subject teacher had approached the tutor or you to share his/her concerns about Claire. How can you improve liaison between subject teachers and the pastoral team in order that this kind of information reaches you sooner?

Supporting Claire

- You have to work with Claire to help her feel better about her situation and know that there can be a way through.
- You want her to achieve the best she can, so you have to consult her teachers to see if there are ways to help her improve her understanding in subjects where she is finding the concepts difficult. Make sure that any targets set are achievable, as confidence and self-esteem are very important here.
- You have to get her to agree that the problem has to be shared with her parents – the best route is for her to talk to them, but it is likely to have to be you.
- You have to involve her parents. The weight loss could be a way into raising the problem with them. Check first if they have noticed it. Your aim is to get them to understand that Claire is really upset about disappointing them and that this is affecting her health.
- You may well have to do battle with their preconceptions about her academic ability. They won't want to believe you. They may initially decide that coaching is the answer, so try to prevent them putting yet more pressure on Claire.
- You want them to ensure that she stops working so late and gets enough sleep. If she is worried and depressed, this will affect her ability to sleep and to achieve in class. She needs to know that they still love her even if she doesn't go to Cambridge.
- Check how bright the younger siblings are – could one of them achieve the mother's ambitions, or is the school going to be dealing with this scenario again in a couple of years?
- Explore her strengths and flag these up to her parents; there are plenty of other universities besides Cambridge and careers that could bring her success in the future. A visit to the careers service could give her direction and hope.

- Monitor the situation and get the school nurse to keep an eye on Claire.

CASE STUDY 6.3: TAKING A COACHING APPROACH TO SUPPORTING A PUPIL

Kieran had a history of getting into trouble. He was considered by his teachers to be an able boy with the potential to do well, but currently he was underachieving. He took little trouble with his school work, was likely to do badly in his GCSEs and according to his teachers he was either sullen or on occasions distinctly 'stroppy'. I had talked to his parents on a number of occasions, but they said that they had tried to talk to him but he didn't listen to them either; in fact he seemed determined to do the opposite of anything they said or asked him to do, and they were at their wits' end to know what to do.

The situation was complicated by the fact that Kieran's younger sister had died in an accident a few years ago, so his parents didn't like to push Kieran too far. They asked me yet again to talk to him. I had tried talking to Kieran in an encouraging way about how not throwing away his chances and getting his qualifications, but it seemed to make no impact, but I had another go. I tried to be as positive as possible, but it probably sounded to him as if yet another adult was nagging him and I could see that he had mentally turned off. He was tolerating me, but not really listening to me and I couldn't get a dialogue going.

In the end I said rather desperately: 'If you could do absolutely what you wanted, what would you like to do or be?' He suddenly focused and looked at me for the first time and said:

> I'd really like to be a social worker. I met a lot of them when my sister died. Most of them meant well but weren't much good. I'd like to be able to do more for people than they did for me and I'd like to get high enough in the system to do something about it.

I was taken aback, but clearly he had thought about what he really wanted, so I probed a bit. Since he knew what he wanted the outcome to be, I asked what he had done so far to set him on his way to being a social worker, and he started to tell me how he had found out what the qualifications were, where you could study, etc. I realized that Kieran was very aware of what he needed to become a social worker – he had done the research – yet he was not working in class and was unlikely to get the GCSEs that were the first key step to success. His maths was particularly weak. So I asked what was holding him back, and he talked about how the teachers didn't seem to expect him to do much and he had got into the habit of not working for them and that now he wasn't sure that he could succeed. I pushed him a bit further about what he could do to overcome these obstacle, and he said, 'I suppose it's really down to me, I could behave a bit differently in class'. When asked what this would mean, he said, 'Work harder and do my homework'.

I summarized where we had reached, and then asked him what other things did he need to do to achieve his aim, and he thought for a bit and came up with three things: support from his parents; stay on at school; and get some help with about his maths. I asked, 'What could he do now right now to move himself forward', and he said, 'Eat supper with my parents, clear my things from the table and talk to them about my ambition'. I asked him if it would it be helpful for him to write down his action points, and he thought about this and said it would help him to keep to what he had said he'd do.

The following day I had a phone call from a very weepy mother, to thank me.

I had some follow-up sessions with Kieran, but I had learnt from this experience not to tell him things. I had to give him responsibility for making his own future.

For reflection/discussion
- What are the lessons of this case study?

Key points about coaching
- Coaching works from the present, it doesn't unpick the past.
- It encourages the coachee to talk – much of the time you are silent.
- It using probing questions to help the coachee identify and clarify the goals and help him/her work out how to move forward.
- It gives the responsibility to the coachee.
- It does not offer advice.

CASE STUDY 6.4: SUPPORTING PUPILS WHO ARE CARERS

Charlotte's mother is an invalid. She has Crohn's disease – a digestive tract disorder – and heart and kidney problems. Charlotte has to help a lot at home and the situation has got worse over time. The family informed the school when Charlotte started in Year 7. Sometimes she was late because she has to give her mother her pills in the morning, and if her mother is really unwell, Charlotte has to get the doctor and wait until the doctor has come. Occasionally this has affected her attendance, but the school understood about the situation.

Now, however, the marriage has recently broken up, and her mother has become too dependent on Charlotte. The absences are always covered by a note, but are becoming much too frequent and are beginning to affect Charlotte's progress. Her mother is preoccupied with her own problems and does not seem to understand. It is not school policy for year heads to make home visits, so it is clearly time to bring in the EWO to visit the family and check the situation at home. While the EWO should deal with the attendance, there are ways you can support Charlotte at school.

How to spot a young carer
- There is a pattern of absence – they often miss school for a couple of days at a time.
- They may be late – rushing into school at the last moment or regularly late to registration.
- Homework isn't completed or given in.
- There is underachievement and/or erratic performance.
- They look tired, worried or preoccupied.
- There is inattentiveness – poor concentration in lessons.
- They are withdrawn and reserved.
- They have a mature outlook for his/her age.
- They are reluctant to turn off their mobile phone during lesson – on-call.
- They have difficulty in attending any after-school extra-curricular activities.
- Parent/s don't attend parents' evenings.

Supporting young carers in school
- Raise the level of awareness of your tutors (research indicates that

more than 75 per cent of young carers go unnoticed).

- Give this checklist to your form tutors so that if they notice some of these signs they can follow-up with the student and do an initial check what the problem is.
- Remind them to speak to the young person private, not in front of their peers during form time.
- Advise them to try to find out what the problem is and what the school can do to help them.
- Be flexible about lateness and use of mobiles and make sure that relevant teachers and support staff know this is the case.
- Always get the student's permission to inform others of their home situation.
- Provide facilities for the pupil do homework for part of the lunch hour – often the school has a lunchtime homework club.
- Carers can be bullied by their peers because they may look uncared for or because of their parents' or siblings disabilities. Get your tutors to watch out for this and take immediate action.
- Tweak your SEAL/PSHE programme to promote tolerance of disability and mental health and include the issue of having to care for your parents. You may have to revisit anti-bullying. You can download ideas for lessons at KS3 or KS4.
- Look for opportunities for them to have some relaxation and fun.
- Find out where the nearest young carers support group or project is. Visiting the Young Carers website (www.youngcarers.net) could get you started.

Recent DfE guidance has recommended that schools develop a policy on young carers and have a designated member of staff to look after their needs.

Dealing with bereavement

At any time a high proportion of schools are dealing with bereavement. A child in your year group might lose a parent or sibling or close friend, or a pupil may die either through illness or an accident. The death of a pupil is painful both for the pupil's friends and difficult for the year group as a whole to manage. Many staff members feel anxious about supporting a bereaved pupil in school or addressing bereavement and loss in the curriculum. You may have to provide support or organize training to give them the confidence and skills to respond appropriately to the diverse needs of children and their families. As the year head you have to help the pupils and your tutors to cope with this situation and liaise with the pupil's family. Some guidelines are provided below and there are resources, training and support to help you in this sensitive work.

What are your responsibilities and what can you do?

- Check the school's bereavement policy for guidance – if there isn't one then it makes sense for a group of year heads to draft one for future use. A sample bereavement policy can be found on the next page for you to adapt to fit your needs.
- If the school has nominated one of the pastoral team as the key bereavement worker who will liaise with and support the family if a bereavement occurs, liaise with this person.
- Liaise also with the relevant year leader/s if the pupil has siblings in the school.
- Check whether any of the tutors involved have recently suffered a personal bereavement – if it is too close they may not be able to deal with it for others. If it is sufficiently in the past, it may make them perceptive and able to use empathy well with distressed members of the year group.
- Fear about saying the wrong thing often inhibits people from talking about the issue, so you may need to support and work with your tutors.
- If a child in the form has died, his/her friends are likely to be devastated and will want someone to talk to. Make sure that some-one appropriate, most likely you or a trained counsellor, makes time for them.
- When you talk to pupils use straightforward language. Avoid euphemisms, e.g. 'Katrina has gone to sleep'. With younger pupils this can be confusing; for older pupils, it doesn't help them face and deal with the reality of what has happened. Always acknowledge that someone has died.
- It is important to give enough information without overwhelming a young person. Sometimes with traumatic death, especially suicide or murder, it may help to provide information in stages. If the pupils are not given enough information by the adults around them, they may fill in the gaps themselves and they may get things wrong.
- Children, including teenagers, often feel that they could have done something differently that may have prevented a death. (This also happens with divorce.) A natural part of teenagers' development is to overemphasize their role in things. This may intensify their feelings of guilt and they need reassurance and explanations about why they

are not to blame. They may need referring to counselling or the child bereavement service for this.

- Don't rush the grieving process. You may need to revisit it with your year group or the group of close friends the following year. Acceptance of loss takes a long time.
- Expect anger, which often accompanies grief – give pupils access to time out space if they need to be alone or opportunities to discuss feelings.
- Allow for individual differences both in feelings and in the expression of feelings. There is not one way to grieve.
- Provide access to counselling on or off the school premises. Do this sensitively. The pupil won't want others to know. This may involve you in making referrals to child bereavement services.
- Use PSHE as a forum for discussion. There are plenty of resources available to help you and your tutors, some of which are listed at the end of this chapter. Advise the tutors that in the short term they may need to deviate from the prepared programme or lesson plan so that they can discuss difficult emotions that arise.
- You will probably be involved in organizing some form of memorial service. Consult both the family and the pupils about the format of this and explain the views of each group to the other so that they understand the rationale for what is chosen.

EXEMPLAR 6.3: A SAMPLE BEREAVEMENT POLICY

Aims

Middleham High School aims to meet the needs of all of its children and staff. When home circumstances are changed because of a death in the family and all around is 'different', our school aims to be a place that both child and family can rely on, and gain some much needed support. If the death is of a child or member of staff, the whole school community will work together and with outside agencies as appropriate, to support each other.

Procedures

Within school we work in partnership with parents. When children join the school, we find out as much as possible about every child, to tailor the academic, social and emotional teaching in school to match their needs. Parents should make teachers aware of any previous changes that might have profoundly affected their child (divorce, bereavement, moving, new babies, etc.). If there has been bereavement, information on what the child was told (in terms of religious beliefs, etc.) should be sought, in order that the school does not say anything that could confuse or upset the child or family.

When school is informed of bereavement or loss the following action should be considered:

- The family should be contacted for appropriate support. (See the pastoral administrator for addresses and relevant telephone helplines.)
- The family should be asked how much and what the child already knows and how they have been involved.
- It should be explained to the family how the school can be involved to support the child and family.
- The importance of 'included care' will be explained, i.e. both parties assessing and reporting changes in behaviour. (Eating and sleeping patterns may change or behaviour in school may deteriorate or the child becomes withdrawn.)
- Involve relevant support, e.g. the school nurse, the school counsellor or outside agencies as appropriate, e.g. CAMHS, Working Together, behaviour and education support teams (BESTs), Forget-Me-Not counselling.
- When the school is informed of the death of a child or member of staff, the following action should be considered:
  — Discussion should take place with the family and their wishes taken into account before decisions are taken on how and what to tell the children in school.
  — Counselling should be available if necessary, e.g. in cases of sudden or violent death (outside agencies should be involved with this, e.g. BESTs or Forget-Me-Not counselling).
  — The school may be closed, or as many people as possible released to attend funeral or memorial services should it be appropriate and they wish to do so.
- Staff and children should be supported throughout the grieving period; anyone displaying signs of stress should be offered appropriate support.

Managing the relationship with the family

- Effective communication between school and home is vitally important. Without it ultimately both parties will fail the child or any siblings. Contacts with the family need to be quick off the mark and sensitively handled.
- Some families have spiritual or religious beliefs about death.

If talking about these matters, it is important to respect both the pupil's and their family's views, recognizing that these could be different, e.g. don't send flowers if this isn't the custom in the particular religion. Some faiths bury their dead very fast, others take much longer. Be aware of when the family is going to need to take children out of school for the funeral and what the religious practices are.

- You may have to act as mediator between the pupil and his/her parents. There may be tension in the family around the death. Often there is anger at the loss and sometimes family members blame each other. For example, a surviving parent may blame a child because there had been arguments about the child's behaviour in the period immediately before the death of one parent occurred, or the child witnessed angry family scenes before the death and blames the surviving parent. In extreme cases you may have to seek outside agency support for the family.

Listening to the pupil voice

Involve the pupils. They need to talk about what has happened and what it means to them. What you do should be led by the pupils' wishes, so listen to what they say and act on it. Be flexible in how you organize the PHSE activities. Here are some points made by senior pupils during PSHE discussion about how they would like to be treated:

- 'Tell other teachers, especially supply teachers, about my loss. I may not wish to talk to them about it, and don't want to keep having to tell people, but I do need them to know. Keep this on record.'
- 'Talk to me about what has happened. I may need more information, advice and education about loss.'
- 'Make arrangements that will help me. I may need miss work or find it difficult to concentrate so I want the school to arrange for me to get extra help with my work so I don't get behind, especially before exams.'
- 'Realize that it is difficult for me and that I have a lot on my plate. Try not to put the spotlight on me too much. I will participate when I can.'
- 'Help me to cope by treating me the same as everyone else, yet let me have time out if I need it.'
- 'Let me know about groups for children and young people who are also coping with loss and change.'

- 'Ask me how I am feeling. It may not be obvious. Don't do this in front of the whole class.'
- 'Give me a note that allows me permission to leave class briefly, without having to explain myself if I feel overwhelmed.'
- 'Understand that I will not "get over it" or "put it behind me" but with time I will learn to cope with all the changes.'
- 'Give me extra encouragement for all the things I am managing to do and keep me in mind.'
- 'Find a way of getting my attention back in class, without others noticing and making me embarrassed. Wait until I am ready to talk.'
- 'Remember that I am still the same person, but that I am feeling a bit upset and lost at the moment.'
- 'Help me to think ahead rather than to dwell in the past – at the right moment, encourage me and help me make future plans.'
- 'Don't forget me – I might slip a bit back a bit and need some more support a few months later or even a year later. Check tactfully how I am doing.'

Some memorial ideas
- Create a memorial book – involve the form in organizing it.
- Put up message boards or a part of the school learning platform where children can write messages – it is important for them to be able to express their feelings, but this way you can monitor the sites that they use.
- Have a ceremony: a candlelit ceremony can create a reflective environment.
- Plant a tree or flower area with a ceremony of dedication and a memorial plaque.

References and web links
Counselling
British Association for Counselling and Psychology (BACP), BACP's code of ethical practice (2010), *Ethical Framework For Good Practice in Counselling and Psychotherapy*, Lutterworth, BACP. Available online at: www.bacp.co.uk/ethical_framework

Bereavement
Child Bereavement Charity: www.childbereavement.org.uk
Childhood Bereavement Network: www.childhoodbereavementnetwork.org.uk
- This website has very useful up-to-date downloadable resources including two PowerPoint presentations and a workbook, *Teenage Grief: Professional Development Materials*. The resources were developed by Leeds Animation Workshop (www.leedsanimation.org.uk) from whom you can also order a DVD called *Teenage Grief*.

- The Childhood Bereavement Network is hosted by the National Children's Bureau, registered charity no. 258825, and is located at 8 Wakley Street, London EC1V 7QE. Tel: 020 7843 6309; Fax: 020 7837 1439; Email: cbn@ncb.org.uk

ChildLine: 0800 1111 – help for children and young people (www.childline.org.uk).

Grief Encounter: www.griefencounter.org.uk

National Children's Bureau: www.ncb.org.uk

NSPCC's resources can be found at: www.nspcc.org.uk

Coaching

Whitmore, Sir John (2002, 3rd edn), *Coaching for Performance*, London, Nicholas Brealey.

Young Carers: www.youngcarers.net

CHAPTER 7

Liaising with external agencies

Working with a range of agencies

Your responsibility for pupil welfare (see Chapter 6) involves you in a considerable amount of liaison with external agencies. For example, you may have to negotiate and liaise with social workers, who operate the Children's Act from within a social services department, education welfare officers, who respond to absence, the Local Safeguarding Children Board (LSCB), which has overarching responsibility for dealing with child protection issues, and educational psychologists, who make assessments of special educational need. This chapter explores this aspect of your role and provides detailed case studies against which you can benchmark your own practice or that of your school.

CASE STUDY 7.1: THE SUPPORT NETWORK OPERATING IN ONE SCHOOL

Liaison with non-teaching pastoral support staff, the SENCO and the various agencies who work with the school is now a major part of my role. Our school has several learning mentors, a school health worker who also manages our links with Child and Adolescent Health Services (CAMHS) and makes referrals to the various additional agencies; a part-time school based social worker who we fund jointly with another school in the borough and works half the week in each school; a non-teaching support worker who is the first point of contact for absence, texting/phoning parents and liaising with the EWO; and an SSP officer is based on the premises. The team meets weekly to coordinate approaches to how we deal with issues or support individual pupils. It is this coordinated approach that I find most useful because response is much faster and more focused than in the past and we are not treading on each other's toes.

CASE STUDY 7.2: A MULTI-FACETED APPROACH

When Mark came into the school he was already on the child protection register. This was because his mother was severely SEN. She had both learning and emotional problems. She was supportive but basically couldn't cope, and Mark and his younger brother had problems at home throughout their time in school. To support Mark, we found we had to deal with several agencies and put in place a whole range of strategies.

Liaising with Marks' primary school was our starting point as we needed to get as much information as possible. They supplied us with a lot of useful information about the family background and what had taken place at previous case conferences.

On an ongoing basis we had to liaise with a whole series of social workers who supported Mark's family. They visited the family regularly and supported it, but a problem for us was that the personnel kept changing, and Mark found difficulty in relating to new social workers.

Our CATs tests administered at the start of Year 7 showed Mark to be of average ability, but he couldn't cope in mainstream classes, so he was placed in our Learning Support Unit, and I liaised regularly with the head of learning support about his progress.

To support him emotionally we referred him to counselling. Referral is arranged through the Inclusion/SEN department. At that time we had a full-time counsellor in school, who worked with him. We no longer have that facility, so when we returned to counselling for Mark in KS4, we used the LA counselling service.

Mark had difficulty communicating his problems, and would miss counselling sessions for no apparent reason. This interrupted the continuity, so the counsellor referred the problem back to us. As the counselling seemed to have stalled, we sought another way to help him communicate. Mark had hardly known his father, so providing a male role model could be beneficial. We used the LA Mentors group, which provides adult mentors and role models, and found him a mentor from the local Afro-Caribbean community, who could relate to the issues that Mark had to face. This worked better than counselling, but of course many of Mark's problems were not of his own making, so there were ups and downs.

When, in Year 9, we reached option choice for Key Stage 4, we tried to plan Mark's timetable to focus on practical vocational courses designed to equip him with skills to help him and make him employable. His mother didn't attend the taster evening that explained the courses to parents and careers, so we asked the School-Home Support unit, which operates in our area, and had a worker part-time in our school to link with home to help Mark and his mother understand the choices and manage this stage. We found School-Home Support the most effective, non-threatening way to liaise with the home.

When Mark reached Key Stage 4, he hit more family and adolescence problems and his attendance deteriorated. As the truancy was becoming serious, we had to use the Education Welfare Officer (EWO) to chase the truancy issues, and do home visits, we tried to liaise between the EWO and social services. We nominated Mark for practical summer courses run by the LA. The family accepted the offer, but Mark's attendance was erratic.

As Mark's behaviour became more challenging, we used a mixture of mentoring and counselling. Although Mark's progress through school was not a major success story, we did manage to avoid having to exclude him. He finished Year 11 and, at the leavers' event, he said he appreciated that we had tried to help him.

The lessons of this case study

- The ups and downs that a troubled pupil may face during his/her school career.
- How many different individuals and organizations may be involved in supporting one pupil.

- Changes in personnel create problems both for the pupil and for you – it can be like starting again.
- How time consuming it is – if you have three or four pupils like this in your year group, it can occupy a lot of your time.

Making effective use of the education welfare officer (EWO) and the School Home Support Service

When to use the EWO

Your school's data management system means that accessing information on attendance and punctuality should not be difficult for you. The increased level of administrative support makes it likely that sending the standard attendance or punctuality letter home will be the responsibility of a pastoral support or administrative officer, but you still have responsibility for the pupil's overall performance and need to monitor the situation. It is vitally important because research has indicated that absence has more effect on a pupil's progress than any other single factor. In some areas the culture of attendance, especially in Key Stage 4, is not well developed. Pupil absence steadily increases in the last two years of compulsory education (see Case studies 7.2 and 7.3), and all too frequently the parents condone the absences. It is very difficult indeed to do much about attendance in Year 11, but generally, if problems develop, your main external support is the EWO. The title varies, but basically the work of an EWO concerns pupil attendance.

The role of the EWO is no longer negotiable between schools and the LA. It is governed by service agreements, drawn up in advance with clear targets and time allocations. In some areas, however, it is very difficult to fill these posts, which are not well paid, so sometimes a long time goes by in which there is no EWO available. In most cases the EWO is attached to the school and visits regularly, sometimes weekly, to check absences and agree to follow up in cases which cause concern. This is very useful, because if cases are followed up in the early stages it is sometimes possible to prevent them from developing into residual truancy. Using the EWO extends and supports your own work with the family. Case study 7.3 illustrates the kind of situation in which you would use the EWO.

CASE STUDY 7.3: ESCALATING ABSENCES

Shaun is a bright boy, but he was never a highly motivated pupil. His progress thorough Key Stage 3 never kept up with expectations. Now he is in Year 10, starting on diploma courses, but his attendance is getting worse. When you look at the attendance data for his form, you notice that there have been a series of absences, usually a day at a time, and the notes are not keeping pace with the absences. You suspect that Shaun is forging some of the notes and that he is beginning to truant. You have phoned home, but either no one is in, or your inquiries are met with evasions. You are not sure of the extent to which Shaun's mother is colluding with Shaun to cover his truancy.

In this type of situation, the EWO is your best means of following up the absence and improving Shaun's attendance.

Using the School-Home Support (SHS) service

The London based School Home Liaison was initiated as a project by the London Diocesan Board for Schools in 1995, with the aim of developing ways of reducing exclusions from school. Later it merged with SHS, which originated in the North of England. SHS is another way that you can support pupils. It is a national charity and its services are currently available in York, the East Riding, North Yorkshire, Bradford, Darlington Nottingham and London; it is expanding, however. The organization has specialists in:

- Attendance – complementing the work of EWOs and contributing to reducing truancy
- Transition from primary school, providing individual support and Year 7 friendship groups
- Curriculum support – providing learning mentors
- Running in-school or after-school drop-in groups or growing self-esteem groups
- Working with families – where the families have a poor experience of education
- Supporting recent arrivals in Britain – SHS community support workers help Polish and Turkish children integrate into school life.

SHS also operates a welfare fund to help families in financial hardship buy school uniforms and to finance school trips.

SHS workers are based in schools and work with all phases. The school pays the worker's salary and a package of support and training. Often they are taken on initially to improve attendance but the role expands because attendance is often the tip of the iceberg and the symptom of other problems. A visit from a SHS officer can be less confrontational than the EWO or a teacher turning up on the doorstep. Parents don't regard the SHS worker as a member of the establishment so they are more willing to talk to them. Using this kind of service can save a lot of time and free up year heads to focus on their role as progress managers. It has also proved very effective, especially in dealing with truancy. Case studies 7.4 and 7.5 illustrate the type of support the SHS workers provide.

CASE STUDY 7.4: SUPPORTING A PUPIL WITH ANGER MANAGEMENT PROBLEMS

On the occasions when he was present, Steve was very disruptive in lessons. He had anger management problems and other pupils knew how to wind him up so that he would erupt. When this happened, Steve would walk out of school and not come back for a couple of days. His mother was regularly called into school after an incident, but although she was supportive, she could not help, and the situation was getting worse rather than better. When the school appointed a SHS officer, Steve was referred to her, and she worked on regular basis with Steve to help him, especially on anger management, so that he can control his reactions more. Over time, Steve became noticeably happier in class; he is much more able to ignore the teasing or taunting. He hasn't walked out of a lesson for six months, and is actually doing his homework, whereas in the past, he would often rip it up.

CASE STUDY 7.5: DIFFICULTY IN SETTLING INTO YEAR 7

Within a few weeks of starting secondary school, Jasmine began to skip school. All her friends at primary school had gone to different schools and she found it very difficult to make new friends. She later told the SHS officer:

> I felt lost, particularly in the playtimes when I was just walking around on my own, and began to have panic attacks and have trouble breathing which brought my asthma on. It made me really ill. I had stomach cramp as well and was physically sick. After two or three weeks I couldn't stand it anymore and I just stopped coming in.

The SHS worker had good counselling skills and got Jasmine to talk to her, and liaised between her and the year head to arrange a special temporary timetable, so that initially Jasmine came in for a few lessons, the ones she enjoyed most, and over half a term this built up to a full timetable again. She also worked with Jasmine through the Year 7 friendship support group to help her make friends in the year group. The school's monitoring indicates that Jasmine has maintained her attendance and she is not on her own in the playground at break times. Feedback from Jasmine indicates that she now feels much better about the school.

To find out more visit www.schoolhomesupport.org.uk or contact SHS at Unit 6 Bow Exchange, 5 Yeo Street, London E3 3QP. Tel: 020 7538 3479; Fax: 020 7537 4361.

Dealing with mental health issues: liaising with Child and Adolescent Mental Health Services (CAMHS)

Expect to have to identify and deal with some mental health issues. Your responsibility is to notice the symptoms – excessive weight loss, cutting, bruises, unexplained absences, too many notes to avoid PE, etc. The school is culpable if it misses these. Then your duty is to refer the problem to the next level of professional care and try to ensure that the student receives the right professional support. Most year heads are not trained counsellors or qualified mental health practitioners, so you should not try to deal with it personally. You may have to persevere, however, to get the pupils the support that he/she needs.

There is more in-school support than in the past to help you identify the symptoms of a mental health issue. For example, each school now should have a school nurse, who may be your first port of call when you notice a health related problem, or who may pick up a problem and alert you to it. You will expect to do some initial pastoral support/counselling, which will help to clarify whether and what kind of additional support is needed, but you are not a professional and there are services within your LA who are trained to deal with these issues. There will probably be some regional variation in how they operate, so if you are new in post, your SLT member with pastoral responsibilities should be able to provide you with information that you need for contacting the relevant external agencies and guidance about the process. The LA website can also be a helpful source of information. There should be an area commissioner and a CAMHS strategy and you can access their action plan highlighting what is happening now and future plans.

Case study 7.6 illustrates the range of external agencies who are involved in dealing with a mental health issue and the process that you may have to go through. It also focuses on your duties in supporting the others affected by the central problem.

CASE STUDY 7.6: DEALING WITH ANOREXIA

The school nurse has a word with you because she has noticed that Marisa, one of your Year 7 pupils, is very thin, and has established that she is dieting because she thinks she is too fat and is unhappy about how her body looks. You have a word with Marisa's tutor so that she knows about the situation, and you ask her to keep an eye on Marisa. The tutor tells you that some of Marisa's teachers have mentioned that she has become inattentive in class recently. This surprised the tutor as Marisa is regarded as a very conscientious student. She explains that she had spoken to Marissa, and asked her if anything was wrong, but Marisa insisted that everything was OK and she had promised to improve her concentration.

You speak to Marisa, and your discussion with her establishes that the nurse has been right to alert you – her worries about her weight are affecting her ability to focus on her lessons, so you raise the issue with her parents, who have noticed a weight loss and, with their agreement, arrange a session for Marisa with the primary mental health worker (PMHW).

You also tweak the year PSHE programme to include sessions on nutrition. Your role is to deal with the day-to-day support to pupils and their families and to identify issues that may need further, more specialist, attention and to clarify the next step for the parents.

If seeing the PMHW doesn't work, then the PMHW should refer Marisa on to the next stage, which is seeing a clinical psychologist or community mental health nurse. Expect to have to wait some time before Marisa can have an appointment, so monitor the situation closely and liaise with her parents, who are understandably anxious about the situation. They have noticed that Marisa is trying to hide the fact that she is going out to be sick after meals, so bulimia appears to be an issue. You may need to advise them that nagging Marisa to eat is likely to be counterproductive and make her secretive. The family will need advice about how to put down clear boundaries for good nutrition in a healthy and positive way.

The sessions with the clinical psychologist will include cognitive behavioural therapy. If the psychologist doesn't explain what this means to Marisa's parents, you may need to do so, or to reiterate it because they were too anxious to take it in. You would need to explain to them that the psychologist will work with Marisa to explore issues such as beliefs about eating, nutrition, growing up and the effects on your body, sexuality and self-esteem.

If this fails to alleviate the situation, then the next step is to refer Marisa to a specialist outpatient centre dealing with eating disorders. Family and individual therapy may also need to be arranged. There are similar specialist outpatient centres for other types of mental health issues. Hopefully by this stage things are starting to improve.

If Marisa still doesn't eat and becomes dangerously thin, then she will need specialist inpatient services for more intensive therapy. Teaching will have to be arranged for Marisa while she is in the hospital, and you will have to liaise with the hospital education unit about what work Marisa should do, so that she isn't behind with her studies when she returns to school. You will need to take in account that the unit will have general teachers rather than subject specialists and because of the small numbers and fluctuating groups they have to teach mixed age groups. The advantage for Marisa is that they are used to dealing with pupils who have emotional issues which come between them and their studies, and they are often imaginative about how they deliver the topics, so it is very much in her interest for you give the hospital's teacher and TAs the fullest information that you can.

You may also have to support Marisa's friends and classmates, who will be anxious and concerned about what is happening to their friend, and to check that Marisa is not the only pupil in the form with eating problems – sometimes, particularly with cutting and self-harm, you get copycat issues. These children need the opportunity to talk thorough their feelings and any reassurance you can give them. Talking about Marisa can get pupils to open up about their own problems about moving into adolescence.

Form time/PSHE may need to be used to explore these issues and you are likely to have to help the tutor with this or lead it yourself. Their tutor could also use some form time for members of the form who are friendly with Marisa to write her cards or letters so that she knows that people at school care about her progress and haven't forgotten her.

Once Marisa begins to recover, she can go home, and return to school, but she will need to be carefully monitored in case she relapses. You will be responsible for managing her re-entry to school, keeping an eye on her progress and liaising with the tutor, the external agencies and her parents. Arranging with the school nurse to check her weight and talk to her regularly and let you know if there are any problems should ensure that nothing will be missed because you are busy with other things.

Attending a case conference

There will be a plenty of occasions when you will have to represent the school at case conferences convened to bring together a range of agencies to support a child experiencing difficulties at school or at home or more usually both and to make decisions regarding the child's future.

A checklist for attending a case conference
Before the meeting
- Make sure that your information on the pupil is as is up to date and accurate.
- Check attendance: Do the absences form a pattern? Have they been covered by a note? Are the notes precise about the reason for absence or a bit vague? Are all the signatures genuine?
- Check recent academic progress – most of this will be on whatever pupil achievement tracker software program your schools uses, but you may need to supplement it with a round-robin to staff.
- Check behaviour: Your pupil behaviour programme should be able to provide a list of incidents and occasions on which you had to communicate with the home.
- If malnourishment or health is an issue, you may need to consult the school nurse for her opinion and get a concise report for you to use at the meeting.
- Always let the tutor know that there is to be a case conference even if you cannot explain the full circumstances, either because you don't know them or for reasons of confidentiality. Consult the tutor as he/she may know the student better than you do and should be able to contribute to building up a picture of how the child is managing in school.
- Inform your line manager. Technically you need permission to attend the meeting and if you are a teaching year head, you may need cover for some lessons. Sometimes it is simply too difficult for the school to release you to attend. Usually in these cases a member of the SLT attends. Sometimes the serious nature of the case means that the school's designated senior person has to attend. (See Case study 7.7, which describes a situation where child abuse is involved.) If this

happens you should provide comprehensive briefing for the person. Make it as clear as possible as the SLT member won't know the pupil as well as you.

At the meeting
- First and foremost, you are representing the school at a conference which will make some immediate decisions about the pupil.
- One of your roles is to listen. You are present to learn how the different parties, parents, social workers, etc. view the situation.
- You are there to provide information about the pupil's progress, behaviour and attendance at school, so that the social workers can build up an overall picture of what is happening.
- You are entitled to raise points which concern you, for example if you have concerns that the absence notes that you are receiving are not genuine, or you think that the child is pressurizing a vulnerable parent into writing the notes.
- When expressing the points you want to make, you should clarify what you actually know as fact and what is simply hypothesis based on past experience or speculation.
- You may be asked your view on possible outcomes based on your experience of dealing with the child or the parents. For example, should the child be given counselling through the school's own counselling scheme or would it be better for him/her child to have counselling that takes place off the premises?
- Sometimes, if the school appears the oasis of peace in a child's troubled existence and moving the child away from home would mean a change of schools, you might want the group to consider the negative effect of moving the child to a new school at the same time as out of the home, or to ask for arrangements which don't necessitate a change of school.
- You may be asked what the school can do to support a particular option, e.g. whether counselling can be provided through the school or whether the pupil can attend breakfast or homework club, etc.

After the meeting
- You should make clear concise notes on what has been discussed and decided at this meeting and you should place this information on the pupil's file.
- You have to provide information about the case conference to a number of people.
- For a start, you must report back to your senior managers the main

points of the conference and what decisions were made in regard to the pupil.

- You should also brief the tutor, so that he/she is aware of any new arrangements made for the child and any possible implications.
- Liaise with any other people who may be involved, such as non-teaching administrative assistants. If, for example, attendance has emerged as an issue, it will need to be monitored carefully.
- If there are health issues, the school nurse may need to know what has been decided and to monitor progress for you.
- You have to make any necessary arrangements, e.g. arrangements may need to be put in place for the pupil to see the school counsellor or to go out of school for counselling sessions or to see a CAMHS officer.
- Once counselling has started, it is between the pupil and the counsellor, and you should not interfere unless an incident arises of which the counsellor should be aware.

Dealing with incidents of child abuse

Clarifying abuse

A child may be subjected to a combination of different kinds of abuse. The main duty of teachers, particularly form tutors, who see the students on a daily basis is to notice that something is wrong and report it to you or the designated senior person. It is important that your tutors understand that there are different types of abuse and that they notice the main signs and symptoms, which could mean that a child is suffering one or more forms of abuse. The checklist of the main categories of child abuse and list of the main symptoms below can be used to help your tutors develop their awareness.

It is also possible that a child may show no obvious outward signs and try to hide what is happening from everyone, so stress that vigilance is an important part of the tutor's role.

THE MAIN CATEGORIES OF CHILD ABUSE

This definition of child abuse was drafted by a school using L.A. guidelines. More technical definitions can be found on the internet, for example in Wikipedia at www.wikipedia.org/wiki/child_abuse

A definition of abuse

Injury, neglect or harm, either physical, emotional or sexual, which is caused to a child by his/her parents or carer, either by deliberate acts or by failure to protect them.

Main categories of abuse

Physical injury

This includes bruises, lacerations, burns, fractures, eye injuries, etc. All children are liable to cuts and bruises from time to time and it can be difficult to distinguish between accidental injuries and abuse. This makes teachers very wary of suggesting that a child may be suffering abuse. If you do notice bruising or other injuries, keep an eye on the frequency that the injuries occur and whether they are always to the same parts of the body. Notice also if the marks look like the outline of an instrument such as a stick or brush, or the bruising is on fleshy areas such as the upper thighs or arms, or the child has burn/scorch marks on, for example, hands or feet.

Neglect/failure to thrive

You may notice that a member of your tutor group is poorly clothed, dirty or frequently hungry when he/she arrives at school. The procedure in the case of possible neglect is different from other incidents of abuse. The logical person to whom to mention this is the school nurse, who will be able to apply objective criteria such as growth milestones, or the head of year, who can liaise with the EWO, who carries out home visits in the course of her duties. Sometimes these pupils are already on the child protection register for this reason.

Emotional abuse

Unless a pupil confides in you directly, you are unlikely to be able to identify emotional abuse; rather you may find that a pupil has very low self-esteem but you do not know why this is the case. Sometimes this causes the pupil to behave badly and be difficult to teach, at other times it has the effect of making the child overanxious to please because he/she is afraid of displeasing adults. Such pupils may also be very clingy and want a lot of your time and attention. Occasionally, for example in a PSHE lesson, they may speak of what they are experiencing at home.

Sexual abuse

Sexual abuse includes touching, penetration and other sexual acts, and requiring children to behave sexually, act as a source of adult sexual stimulation or participate in experiences which are inappropriate for children. It can also include exposure to pornography, and usually involves 'grooming', i.e. preparation for the abuse, rather than being a spur-of-the-moment incident. Signs of sexual abuse range from a general mistrust of adults to gross physical injury or pain in the genital area.

At risk of abuse

The concept of 'dangerousness', identifying whether a child is at risk, is actually the key issue in determining whether a child should be placed on the child protection register. A child's confidences may lead you to think that he/she is at risk. You have to inform a senior member of staff, who will consult the professionals whose job it is to do a risk analysis.

Child abuse: signs and symptoms

Although the signs listed below do not necessarily indicate that a child has been abused, they may help adults recognize that something is wrong. The possibility of abuse should be investigated if a child shows a number of these symptoms, or any of them to a marked degree. What is really essential is that the tutors are vigilant for any signs of distress, or changes in the behaviour or attitude of the pupils in their tutor group. The child may not be exhibiting symptoms of child abuse at all – something quite different may be wrong. What really matters is that the child's signals are met with a response.

Physical abuse

- Unexplained recurrent injuries or burns
- Improbable excuses or refusal to explain injuries
- Wearing clothes to cover injuries, even in hot weather
- Refusal to undress for gym
- Bald patches
- Chronic running away
- Fear of medical help or examination
- Self-destructive tendencies
- Aggression towards others
- Fear of physical contact – shrinking back if touched
- Admitting that they are punished, but the punishment is excessive (such as a child being beaten every night to 'make him study')
- Fear of suspected abuser being contacted.

Neglect/Failure to thrive

- Constant hunger
- Poor personal hygiene
- Constant tiredness
- Poor state of clothing
- Emaciation
- Untreated medical problems
- No social relationships

- Compulsive scavenging
- Destructive tendencies.

Emotional abuse

- Physical, mental and emotional development lags
- Sudden speech disorders
- Continual self-depreciation ('I'm stupid/ugly/worthless', etc.)
- Overreaction to mistakes
- Extreme fear of any new situation
- Inappropriate response to pain ('I deserve this')
- Neurotic behaviour (rocking, hair twisting, self-mutilation)
- Extremes of passivity or aggression.

Sexual Abuse

- Being overly affectionate or knowledgeable in a sexual way inappropriate to the child's age
- Medical problems such as chronic itching, pain in the genitals, venereal diseases
- Other extreme reactions, such as depression, self-mutilation, suicide attempts, running away, overdoses, anorexia
- Personality changes such as becoming insecure or clinging
- Regressing to younger behaviour patterns such as thumb sucking or bringing out discarded cuddly toys
- Sudden loss of appetite or compulsive eating
- Being isolated or withdrawn
- Inability to concentrate
- Lack of trust or fear of someone they know well, such as not wanting to be alone with a babysitter or child minder
- Starting to wet the bed again, or wet him/herself in school nightmares
- Become worried about clothing being removed
- Suddenly drawing sexually explicit pictures
- Trying to be 'ultra-good' or perfect, overreacting to criticism.

CASE STUDY 7.7: RECOGNIZING CHILD ABUSE

The case comes to your attention when Zara, a Year 8 pupil, is found by the police in the early hours of the morning with a bag containing clothes and personal belongings, wandering around in the town centre, near the railway station. When questioned at the nearest police station, she said that she had been planning to go to London to find her auntie, and that she was afraid to go home, because her mother worked nights and her step-father keeps 'hurting' her. When Zara is examined, there are clear signs of recent sexual activity and a lot of bruising.

Zara is taken into temporary care and the social services department convenes a case conference to help the Local Safeguarding Children Board (LSCB) make an assessment of the case. The deputy head, who is the school's designated person for child protection, asks you to provide the information she needs for her report on Zara's recent behaviour and progress at school. She also wants your take on the situation.

You review what you know about Zara, who is a very quiet pupil and who hasn't come to your attention because she has never been in trouble – there are no incidents on her file. You do not know her well and her mother tends not to come to progress evenings or to ask for alternative appointments. You check Zara's reports and find comments that indicate that some of her teachers suspect that she has the potential to do better. For example, her English teacher remarks that Zara's occasional contributions to discussions are pertinent and perceptive, but consistently her teachers mention her lack of motivation and rather short concentration span. Your round-robin to staff asking for up-to-date information about her progress doesn't add much. Apparently Zara has been even more detached in class than usual. She has not been very responsive to the teachers' efforts to get her to work harder and increasingly tends not to give in her homework.

In the hope of learning more, you have a word with some sensible members of the form and Zara's tutor, who needs to be put in the picture anyway, and you become concerned at what you learn.

Her classmates tell you that Zara is very much a loner, but say that recently she'd looked unhappy. One or two of them had tried to talk to Zara to find out what was wrong, but she had rebuffed their efforts and they'd given up. She had to their knowledge never mentioned a boyfriend and, from her behaviour, they were pretty sure that she didn't have one. They didn't think to tell anyone their concerns.

The tutor tells you that Zara, who gives the impression of living in a world of her own, and who discourages his enquiries about herself, has been even more withdrawn recently, except in one PSHE discussion on family relationships, in which she had a real outburst attacking the whole idea of family and then, when asked to explain her views, clammed up completely and wouldn't speak any more. After the lesson, the tutor tried to follow this up by talking to Zara, but the girl wouldn't open up to him. The tutor didn't follow this up, as Zara never wants to talk to teachers and he didn't want to push her. The tutor added that he has noticed that instead of dashing off immediately when school ended, Zara has been hanging around the playground, especially the car park. He had had to tell her to go home a couple of times. He had been thinking of mentioning it to you as he thought it a bit odd.

As a result of this incident, the year heads requested that the school provide some training to help them train up their tutors to recognize possible abuse in future and so that they would know what to do if a potential abuse issue should occur.

The lessons of this case study

- Teachers are not expected to be experts in child protection issues. As the checklist above makes clear, the teacher cannot be expected to know whether this is a child abuse issue or something else. What really matters is that the child's signals are noticed and meet with a response.
- The school should have set procedures for handling cases of suspected abuse, consistent with the LSCB (established in 2004 as a result of the Victoria Climbie case, which exposed the various agencies as not coordinating sufficiently to provide protection) and LA guidelines. It is statutory to have a policy for dealing with child abuse, and it should be published in the school prospectus. The tutors should be aware of the school's statutory child protection policy and know what it says. In a notorious case in the 1990s, which led to the Hunt Report of 1994, the teachers were not only unaware of the policy's contents; no one knew where it was.
- If you need to provide awareness raising training for your team, liaise with the school's designated senior person as providing this kind of training comes within his/her job description. You may also find that it would pay dividends to open the session to any new staff or those who need to refresh or update their awareness.
- Stress that it is vitally important that they report any possible problem. It is better to be safe than sorry. If they tell you, then you should report it to the school's designated senior person, but

they could go direct, so they also need to know who the school's designated senior person is.

- Ask them to let you know that they have reported a possible issue, so that you are not left out of the loop and are aware of what is happening to a child in your year group. This is also important because you are likely to be the person who has to deal with things on a day-to-day basis.

The designated senior person

The school has to have someone senior designated to deal with child abuse issues. The designated senior person should be a senior member of the school's leadership team who is given the lead responsibility for dealing with child protection issues, providing advice and support to other staff, liaising with the LA, and working with other agencies. The designated person need not be a teacher but must have the status and authority within the school management structure to carry out the duties of the post, including committing resources to child protection matters and, where appropriate, directing other staff. In many schools a single designated person will be sufficient, but a deputy should be available to act in the designated person's absence. In large establishments, or those with a large number of child protection concerns, it may be necessary to have a number of deputies to deal with allegations made against members of staff. The designated senior person's responsibilities include:

- Referring cases of suspected abuse or allegations to the relevant investigating agencies.
- Having a working knowledge of how the LSCB operates, the conduct of a child protection case conference, and attending and contributing to these effectively when required to do so.
- Acting as a source of support, advice and expertise within the educational establishment when deciding whether to make a referral by liaising with relevant agencies.
- Liaising with head teacher/principal (where the role is not carried out by the head teacher) to inform him/her of any issues and ongoing investigations and ensure there is always cover for this role.

Guidance for when a child confides in a teacher

In Case study 7.7, the LSCB was dealing with the problem and asked the school for supporting evidence. It is much more problematic when a child confides in you or a member of staff and the staff needs clear guidance about what they should do or say. Case study 7.8 illustrates some of the problems.

CASE STUDY 7.8: HANDLING A POTENTIAL CHILD ABUSE SITUATION

Lucy was a bright but quiet, rather reserved girl. No problems had emerged in her first two years in the school and you did not know her very well. Then, in Year 9, her English teacher came to see you, because Lucy had apparently described her home situation in an essay. She claimed that her parents were getting on very badly, that there were constant rows at home and that her father had begun to drink heavily and kept threatening to kill himself. She also claimed that he had tried to commit suicide before, and that she was desperately worried that he might do it again. Her account was very powerfully written and sounded genuine, so the teacher was worried. When you check with Lucy's tutor, she tells you that she is becoming concerned about Lucy as she looked very pale and tired and had become much more withdrawn, often sitting on her own. Other teachers were reporting that she had become 'difficult'. She had always been quiet, but now at times she would be quite uncooperative.

You talk to her about her story and she insists that what she had written was accurate and that it is getting worse at home. She is clearly very troubled and worried about any prospect of your talking to her parents – it would make it worse, her dad would be angry. Not to talk to the parents of course is a very usual plea, just as the essay is a plea for help. The issue is what is it really all about?

This is the time to refer the problem to a senior member of staff, so you approach the deputy head teacher, who has responsibility for child protection, and he suggests that he contact LSCB for advice. This is a sensible strategy as it will safeguard you and also show that the school is acting responsibly. You cannot afford to make mistakes and it needs professionals to deal with it. The problem is that on a daily basis you are the first point of reference. Prompt liaison with the relevant external agencies is a crucial strategy for the school. He consults the LSCB and they advise you to talk to the parents as soon as possible and to tell them what you had been told and share your concerns about Lucy's emotional well-being and the impact it was having on her school life.

As often happens when a problem of this sort comes to light, it escalates rapidly. A meeting is arranged with the parents, but before it could take place the PE teacher comes to see you and reports that Lucy has scars on her arms and legs. When you get the school nurse to look at them, she reports that Lucy was beginning to self-harm and in class the incidents of uncooperative behaviour are also escalating.

Lucy's parents listen to what you have to say but they insist there are no problems at home and totally deny all aspects of Lucy's story. Both sound very concerned. Her father, an architect, appears shocked; her mother anxious, but very reasonable. She offers suggestions, which explain away everything you said. To you it sounds like she was making excuses and you wonder if she is covering up a situation that she can't manage. For example, she immediately blamed it all on Lucy's lively imagination. She said that Lucy wants to be a writer and has always made up stories. She also attributed it to adolescence, saying it had made Lucy 'more moody'. They hadn't noticed the self-harming but they had noticed that Lucy now wears long-sleeved clothes. Her mother claims the cutting is copycat, because there other girls in this class with self-esteem issues who self-harm.

It was agreed that Lucy would see the school counsellor, and that an appointment would be made for her with CAMHS. The school would all keep in close contact and you say you will do your best to support her through this difficult period. The deputy asks you to liaise with the external agencies on a day-to-day basis, but to keep him in the loop.

You find it hard to reconcile Lucy's stories with these apparently normal parents, but you do find it difficult to believe that she was just making up the whole story. Something has to be going wrong, but you can't tell what the issue really is. Her reaction is to accuse you of not believing her and to add things to her story, which now becomes much worse. She finds ways to be near you and to seek your attention. For example, she starts to travel home on the train that you take and walks through the carriage to sit near you. You try to vary your times of travelling home, but report this development to CAMHS and are told to continue to monitor the situation and to liaise with them.

Lucy then appears in school with bruises on her arms, legs and face. They could be accidental – but are they? You check with her mother, but each time you are told about accidents: Lucy had a fall while skating; or she wasn't wearing her glasses and walked into a cupboard. You are concerned because it is happening too often, but is it Lucy seeking attention or is it physical abuse? Lucy starts to ask you to get her taken into care – she doesn't want to be at home and is very anxious. Again you pass this on to social services and ask that a suitable professional, a CAMHS officer or a social worker, talks to her to establish what is going on. When one set of bruises definitely looks like it had been caused by someone gripping her arms hard, you again contacted social services, who come into school to talk to Lucy. Lucy now claims that her father caused the bruises and that her mother knew about it but was covering for him. As a result Lucy is taken into temporary foster care, but all the agencies think that she was still withholding important information, and that it was unclear what was really going on.

You often find her outside your office at the end of the day wanting to talk to you. She begins to hint about sexual abuse, and tells you about how she keeps dreaming that her father had come into her bedroom when she was a child and how she feels shame about what happened. You report this immediately to the deputy, who is the school's designated senior person, as possible child abuse issues must be reported immediately and the LSCB involved. Before they can come in and talk to Lucy, one of Lucy's friends comes to see you. She is very worried about Lucy, who has confided to her that her father had repeatedly, over a period of years, sexually abused her. She says she has promised Lucy not to tell anyone, even her parents, but she can't keep this promise and wants you to do something to help Lucy. You explain that she has done the right thing, that there can be no confidentiality, and that referring the accusation will enable Lucy to get help.

The deputy promptly rings the LSCB, who sends in a child protection officer. She explains to Lucy what would be involved if she was going to take this further. As Lucy vacillates over whether she wants the police involved, she says that her mother has left her father. Later Lucy tells you that she's living with her mother now, and that things are 'OK'. Soon after this, Lucy and her mother move away and Lucy moved schools.

The lessons of this case study
- What stands out from this is how difficult it is to know whether a pupil is telling you the truth and that rarely are you being told the whole story, especially at the beginning.
- A plea for help is often made through something innocuous in itself – a picture drawn in art, a situation in drama, an essay or a story told in PSHE.
- Staff should be encouraged to liaise with the year head if a piece of

work done in class includes disturbing content. Basically, the student wants someone to know, and to do something – that is why he/she has told the story.

- The child increasingly talks about the problem to others and adds details and information reaches you via friends.
- Look for supporting evidence – physical signs and changes in behaviour as well. This is where the checklist comes in. Having this evidence can make a real difference to being able to help a child.
- Only sexual abuse is passed straight on to specialist child services. With physical or emotional abuse or neglect, the usual advice is to try and liaise with the family.
- Once the first story is told, expect it to keep changing and that the situation is likely to escalate as more and more signs of a problem emerge and more details come out.
- The child (the term 'child' is used for all pupils under the age of 18) will try to draw you or the tutor into the situation and get you on his/her side. The child may appear quite manipulative and this can affect whether you think you are being told the truth. It is not for you or the teachers to make this judgement. A teacher is not the relevant professional so the problem should be referred as quickly as possible to the senior designated member of staff, who will refer it to and liaise with the relevant agency.
- You will have to handle situation on a day-to-day basis, but also keep liaising with the relevant agency. This agency may change, e.g. from CAMHS, which deals with metal health issues, to the LSCB, which deals with child protection, as the story develops. This is time consuming for you and you may need to train up the administrative assistants to make initial contacts.
- You have to work with parents who often find the situation very difficult to accept or manage or who might be guilty parties. You have to be non-judgmental and objective. This can be a difficult line for you to walk.
- You may never find out what the true situation is. In this case, even the professionals involved, the social worker, CAMHS, and the police child protection officer when he became involved, did not know whether to believe her.

Handling this kind of situation can be very difficult for your tutors because their role is to build positive and supportive relationships with the children and their families. They will be anxious not to jeopardize the relationship unless absolutely necessary, so they will hesitate before making referrals, in case 'they make the wrong call'. They won't want to damage the trust with the pupil and their families or make assumptions about them, and will fear that intervening with insufficient evidence may add to the child's problem. You need to make it clear to your tutors that it is extremely important that they are not too trusting and unquestioning about the signs and symptoms of abuse, and that while it is not their responsibility to investigate suspected abuse, they do have a duty to report any concerns to you, and any safeguarding issues to the school's designated child protection officer.

It is important is to provide clear guidance for your tutors about what to do if a child confides in them. For this reason, an exemplar checklist to use with your tutors is provided below. Reissue the checklist annually as people will lose it or forget its contents.

If a child tells you about abuse

- Find a quiet place to talk and enable the conversation to take place without interruptions.
- Stay calm and be reassuring.
- Listen, but do not press for information. Tell the child that you are glad that the child is telling you about the matter.
- Yours is a listening role, do not interrupt the child if he or she is freely recalling significant events.
- If questions are needed to clarify understanding, they should be framed in an open manner in order not to lead the child in any way. This could be important in any later court proceedings.
- Do not give undertakings of absolute confidentiality.
- You must report orally to the designated senior person immediately.
- Make a note of the discussion as soon as is reasonably practicable (but within 24 hours) to pass on to the designated senior person. The note should record the time, date, place and people who were present as well as what was said.
- Remember, your note of the discussion may need to be used in any subsequent court proceedings.
- Your responsibility in terms of referring concerns ends at this point, but you may have a future role in terms of supporting or monitoring the child, contributing to an assessment or implementing child protection plans.

Safer School Partnerships (SSP)

Your role may include liaison with your SSP officer. The development of SSP indicates a radical change in schools' relationship with their local police service. Although some schools always had a good relationship with their local community policeman, whom they used to deliver aspects of their PSHE programme, a lot of schools, especially inner-city schools, traditionally were very wary of having police on the premises, viewing this as too 'big brother-ish' and exasperating the hostile attitudes towards the police held by many pupils. The perception is now very different. Indeed the SSP initiative now contributes towards implementing the Every Child Matters agenda. One head's recent comment sums this up:

> I said I would leave if I had to have a police officer in my school. Now I would say it is one of the most successful initiatives we have intro-duced. If I hadn't seen it happen in my own school, I wouldn't have believed it.

Launched in 2002 as a response to the Street Crime Initiative and piloted by the DCSF collaboratively with the Youth Justice Board (YJB), SSP's original aim was to establish 100 partnerships, but the scheme took off and continues to expand. The 2009 Steer Report recommends that all schools implement it and have an attached police officer. Schools and police forces are beginning to realize the possible benefits of this type of close partner-ship working. Together, they can identify, support and work with children and young people at risk of victimization, offending or social exclusion. The focus of SSP is early intervention and prevention. The schemes encourage the police, children and young people to build good relationships, trust and mutual respect. Police officers working in partnership with schools under this scheme continue their operational policing approach, but the aim is to do so in a way that fulfils a prevention and deterrence role, and supports victims of crime. Where the partnerships are most effective they are seen as an integral part of local neighbourhood policing and *not* merely as a police officer attached to a school.

At present this approach can take different forms depending on funding, the views of the school and the local policing strategy in respect of schools. Current arrangements include:

- A fully operational police officer based full-time in a school working closely with a member of the school's senior management team, project worker and administrator.
- Police officers seconded to behaviour and education support teams (BESTs) and working with this multi-agency partnership in a secondary school and its feeder primary schools.
- Police officers, both full-time and part-time, mainly providing reactive support to a cluster of schools in SSP style of policing.
- Police officers or police community support officers (PCSOs) based

with the neighbourhood policing team, working part-time in a problem solving as well as educational role.

Where the scheme is effective, the benefits include:

- Help with attendance and truancy issues – attendance tends to improve
- Help in dealing with bullying – pupils see that it is dealt with swiftly and the incidence decreases
- Police have greater powers of search than teachers or head teachers, etc. and can find evidence
- More positive relationships between police and students due to its problem solving, preventative approach
- Helping schools to develop a range of strategies for dealing with situations that may otherwise threaten safety and well-being – fewer incidents on the premises.

References and web links

Child and Adolescent Mental Health Services (CAMHS): wwww.dcsf.gov.uk/everychildmatters/healthandwellbeing/mentalhealthissues/camhs/camhs/

CAMHS network: www.camh.org.uk

Local Safeguarding Children Boards: www.dcsf.gov.uk/everychildmatters/safeguardingandsocialcare/safeguardingchildren/localsafeguardingchildrenboards/lscb/

National Society for the Prevention of Cruelty to Children (SPCC)'s website and helpline: 0800 1111 provides resources, refresher notes and training tools for child protection: www.nspcc.org.uk

Safer School Partnerships: guidance booklet (pdf) and information available at: www.teachernet.gov.uk/wholeschool/behaviour/sspg

School-Home Support (SHS): visit www.schoolhomesupport.org.uk or contact SHS at Unit 6 Bow Exchange, 5 Yeo Street, London E3 3QP. Tel: 020 7538 3479; Fax: 020 7537 4361.

The Youth Justice Board's website also provides information about the SSP: www.yjb.gov.uk/en-gb/yjs/prevention

CHAPTER 8

Your role in managing extra-curricular activities

When we deal with the issue of underachievement, we usually think about classroom initiatives such as seeing things from the learners' perspective through a multi-sensory approach (learning styles); boy-friendly texts; matching the activities to the needs and abilities of the learners, etc. This is one of the reasons why your tutors find difficulty in appreciating that they do have an important role in supporting raising achievement. The roll out of the SEAL programme in both primary and secondary schools has now focused schools much more on addressing the social and emotional issues, which can affect behaviour. Although much of the SEAL initiative is delivered through assemblies and through subjects such as PSHE, there is also a place to support the development of students' social skills outside the classroom, especially around the school, where a lot of pupil interaction takes place, and through extra-curricular activities.

This chapter features initiatives outside the classroom that schools have developed and implemented to help the students deal with issues of growing up with difficult family circumstances. No blueprint works for every school so different approaches to dealing with the same issue are featured. Often the projects will be part of the school's Extended Schools Initiative. Some of these activities will be whole school programmes; others will be your responsibility to organize. How they are organized and by whom will vary from school to school. In the case studies featured in this chapter, however, the year heads identified the need and took a leading role in organizing and implementing the initiatives. For this reason, the second part of this chapter features your role as a project manager and explores what you need to do in order to lead and manage change effectively.

Outside the classroom: introducing initiatives to support students' development

Peer support schemes

Peer support schemes are regarded as valuable means of fostering pupils' emotional development and their social skills. The kind of scheme you need will vary according to the circumstances of your school. In some schools the mentors are always the more senior pupils, in others the mentors for Year 7 might be Year 8 or 9 pupils. How they are selected and their role can also vary.

Case study 8.1 is an example of a school which used support from the Mentoring and Befriending Foundation's National Peer Mentoring Programme (see Chapter 5) to set up a scheme to support the transition to secondary school for its Year 7 pupils.

CASE STUDY 8.1: SUPPORTING YEAR 7'S TRANSITION TO SECONDARY SCHOOL

We operate a rolling programme in which year heads move up with their groups. It was four years since I'd last been head of Year 7, but this time round I was much more conscious of their difficulties in settling into secondary school. I discussed it with the tutors, and we felt we needed to find out what the pupils felt, so the tutors talked to their forms in PSHE time, and then I put it on the agenda for year council, where it provoked a lively and sensible discussion. They asked for buddies to help them settle in.

Our school is very large, with over 1,500 pupils. A lot of them said that they felt dislocated and lost both geographically and personally when they arrived, particularly if they had been at very small primary schools. Sometimes the whole primary school was only 150 pupils. A lot of them mentioned friendship issues, difficulty in finding friends, or that the 'friends' who came from their old primary school no longer wanted to be with them, so they felt lonely or left out. They said they would like support from older pupils, who would be available and attached to them. They thought that sixth formers would be too removed and too intimidating but that they would be able to relate to pupils from Years 8 to 11.

We discussed it at a year heads' meeting and decided that, subject to the head's approval, we'd run a pilot. I was keen to see it up and running, so I offered to be the project coordinator for the first two years. When I went to see the head, she was very willing to support the project because she saw it as supporting the Every Child Matters (ECM) agenda and our SEAL initiative. She particularly saw it as providing practical opportunities for pupils to have responsibility and to develop their skills. She told me about the National Peer Mentoring Programme (NPM) and got the ECM deputy, who was experienced in making bids, to find out how we could be included and access funding. We liked the idea of being involved in the NPM because, as well as the funding element, it provided us with a network of other schools we could consult and a framework that we could use.

At the beginning of spring term we used an assembly to introduce the scheme and ask for volunteers and were pleased when a lot of pupils applied. As part of the practical experience, we held interviews, which most of them passed. Those who didn't succeed this time were given constructive feedback and could reapply. Then we used the second part of term to provide the training and begin to develop the mentors in their role. We put in place an initial training day and follow-up sessions to support handling one-to-one sessions. Once the scheme started regular training and support would be available for them. We talked through the issue of missing curriculum time for training; there were of course a few grumbles, but most staff could see that it was developmental and soon we began to notice that the motivation, and in some cases the self-organization, of the students involved in mentoring tended to improve.

In the summer term the mentors visited Year 6 pupils in their primary schools and talked to the pupils who would be coming to us. We identified the most potentially vulnerable Year 7s and matched them one to one with a mentor. Others would be identified after arrival and referred by the head of year as the need arose. The format had to be flexible to meet demand and needs. Details of the scheme were included in the Year 7 induction pack so they knew right from the start that help was available. To encourage them to use the scheme the mentors designed and performed a role play scenario in a year assembly; it featured mentoring helping an unhappy pupil deal with a difficult situation. Then the form tutors followed up with PSHE activities including posters and worksheets which sparked discussion on settling in issues.

Each mentor has a duty day once a week. When they are on duty, the mentors wear a kind of uniform – T-shirts in summer and warm 'hoodies' in winter – with 'Mentor' written in bright colours across the front. There was a lot of discussion about the labelling; I thought that a badge would be better, but I wanted the mentors to make key decisions and they wanted the top to be labelled and brightly coloured. They were right; it works and the mentors wear it with pride. They all have a mentor file. It contains mentor code of conduct, a contract and a confidentiality agreement which both parties sign. There is also a logbook which mentees can use to record their thoughts and feelings and in which mentors can reflect on the issues discussed, guidance offered or the skills used. Being in the NPM initiative meant that we didn't have to develop these documents from first principles. We have good resources, including worksheets focused on the kind of issues, e.g. friendships or being left out, that they may have to deal with, which they can use to focus discussions. After a one-to-one session, which tends to average an hour to an hour and a half, they fill out a session review sheet about the main issues discussed. It quickly became clear that some matters could be resolved quickly with just one or two sessions, but that others would take much longer. As one mentor said, 'I know I'm succeeding when the mentee still wants to talk to me, but doesn't need weekly sessions'. Of the original 20 children identified as potentially vulnerable in the first year the scheme ran, only five were still being seen weekly by the spring half term, but a number of other children had been referred.

The mentors know that if they need advice or guidance the coordinator is available. After four weeks if the issue hasn't been resolved, the coordinator checks the state of play and offers advice on how to move forward. They learnt quickly when to refer someone. As one mentor told me: 'I know that there are plenty of resources to help me deal with issues like name calling, but if there is physical bullying, then I'd consult you immediately.' A Year 11 mentor said very perceptively: 'We also had to learn that sometimes a mentor–mentee relationship doesn't work, but it doesn't mean I've failed or that the scheme's no good, but that someone else might be a better mentor for this person or that there's a need to approach things differently.' Bullying issues are sometimes referred to what we call the Mediation Group; this comprises two mentors, the mentee/victim and the 'bully', and together they try to resolve the issue.

An important feature was to provide the Year 7s with a safe haven until they found their feet, so a Peer Mentoring Room was established. They can go there at lunchtime, eat their lunch and talk or play games with their mentor. The funding helped us provide games and make the room attractive. We taught the mentors some games as part of their training. The games are useful as part of social development and also to get unhappy children talking. We didn't want to prevent the children using the room from having school lunch as for some this is their main meal of the day, so they are allowed to collect it and bring it with them, but must return plates, etc. It is part of the mentor's duties to see that the room is left clean and tidy.

The mentors also act as role models for younger children. If it's quiet in the mentoring room, the mentor goes out to the playground and plays games with younger children. This is useful as many of the children and a lot of our lunchtime supervisors did not know any games. The mentors are trained to spot and handle some potential conflict situations and often prevent friendship issues from deteriorating into bullying. They also stop some children from being picked on by tougher individuals or groups.

Marketing makes a big difference. We try to keep the scheme high profile and accessible. The first half term of the Year 7 programme has a module about peer mentoring. Posters are displayed around the school as a constant reminder with clear information about the scheme and they are changed regularly. We run poster competitions to provide us with a supply. We have a post box that children can leave messages in and the mentors in their bright uniform are very visible at lunchtime. The half-termly newsletter to parents always includes information about the scheme and there is a section on the school's learning platform, including an email that pupils can access. The parents also talk to other parents about the scheme. We have had very positive feedback from individual parents about the impact of the programme on their child. Regularly I'm told, 'She is much happier now' or 'Before he wouldn't talk about school, now he does', and I felt overwhelmed when one set of parents said: 'We didn't expect a big secondary school to pick up on problems so fast and provide this level of care.'

We recruit regularly for new mentors because we have come to value the skills and personal qualities it helps our pupils to develop. Mentors tell me the scheme has:

- developed their confidence
- increased their understanding of how easily small problems escalate and the need to tackle these early
- increased their willingness to take responsibility or deal with difficult situations
- developed their listening skills and the ability to speak to another person about their situation
- developed their empathy – the sympathetic understanding of another person's position.

They also say that it makes them feel really good to see a positive change in their mentees.

We didn't anticipate some of the good effects. For example, staff tell me that mentors who had problems themselves in the past now tend to behave much better in class and that they are generally more attentive which has had a good impact on their progress, and parents also comment on the fact that their children behave more responsibly and talk to them more about school matters.

There have also been positive outcomes for mentees:

- They appear to develop more of the coping skills.
- Many say that it has helped them to gain confidence and feel stronger.
- They talk of feeling reassured to have someone around to whom they can turn and who will listen sympathetically.
- Some say they appreciate having a ready-made friend – they don't feel left out any longer.
- Friendship problems are largely sorted out by the mentors and take up much less of my time than in the past.
- 'I don't dread coming to school now' – feedback from one mentee.
- Providing a buddy/mentor nipped some potential school-refusal in the bud and has positively affected Year 7 attendance.

I have learnt:

- to give the mentors as much ownership and responsibility as possible – they respond very positively to this
- that the role of coordinator is pivotal – I am now training up a

non-teaching pastoral officer to take over from me
- to keep the initiative high profile
- that once the key features were in place, the initiative developed its own momentum
- flexibility and accessibility are crucial to maintaining effectiveness.

For reflection/discussion
Think about/discuss:
- the ways that the school used the pupil voice
- the positive effects on the students of being a peer councillor or mentor
- how this approach can be applied to many areas of the school
- where this approach could be used in your own school/how it compares to the scheme used in your school.

Organizing lunchtime activities

CASE STUDY 8.2: ORGANIZING THE HOMEWORK CLUB

The club was set up as a lunchtime activity because many of our pupils find it difficult to do their homework at home. We also wanted to put in some support for their learning and utilize some of the expertise that our TAs had to offer. My Year 8 club was allocated Olga, the TA attached to the maths department. She is Russian and her degree was actually in engineering, so she brought a wealth of expertise to the scheme. I deal with all the organizational issues and technically I'm in charge, but the TA works with the children. I pop in during the session to check things are OK, but really I'm not needed.

Olga has a good knowledge of the maths curriculum and very high expectations. She started to do questions from GCSE question papers with my Year 8 pupils. I didn't realize this until I got the letters from a number of parents praising her work with their children and stating how much progress they were making as a result of attending the club. They stressed that they really like the way that she treats them as serious students and encourages success. For example, she worked regularly at lunchtime with Laura, a girl with particularly low confidence in maths. This had made her very reluctant to work independently and she was often late handing in assignments. When Laura got her two most recent assignments completed on time and gained good grades in both, her mother emailed me to me to say how pleased she was.

I also watched Olga work with two African girls who had only recently joined the school. They had EAL issues, but one spoke a bit more English and had more self-confidence than the other. Olga used the more able student to 'teach' the other in her mother tongue. This approach worked very well; the second child improved and it made me realize you can provide help using the child's mother tongue via other native speakers. I liked the way Olga gave responsibility and treated both with respect as learners.

This case study illustrates
- the kind of interventions that you regularly make to support learning
- that you don't have to do everything yourself – the year head made the arrangements and supervised, but the club was taken by a TA
- how much the school gained by giving the TA the opportunity to use her expertise.

The homework club was good experience for the TA and led to her being put on the specialist HLTA programme.

Leading extra-curricular support groups
It is often useful to look at two different ways of approaching a problem. Case studies 8.3 and 8.4 both address the issue of the need for an extra-curricular group to support pupils in developing their social and coping skills and help build their ability to deal with the problems that they have to face.

CASE STUDY 8.3: THE YEAR 9 BOYS' SUPPORT GROUP

My wife teaches at a local primary school where they run a Boys-to-Men initiative, which provides boys with mentors, and she was talking quite a lot about it at home. It made me think, because all the criteria her school used applied to many of my Year 9 boys and, at least in Key Stage 3, we now use a lot of primary techniques and are finding that they are work- ing for us, so I decided to set up a boys' mentoring group. My thinking was that we'd lose nothing if I ran a pilot, and if it succeeded, the boys involved in it would benefit and it could become part of the ongoing support strategies I use to help the boys build self-esteem.

A lot of our pupils come from a part of the town that is described in reports as 'deprived', with significant long-term unemployment. Our data analysis also flagged up that a lot of the boys on our 'Cause for Concern' list are from single parent families. Looking at the individuals identified in this way, a regular feature was that they were uncommunicative and often appeared withdrawn; several were regarded as uncooperative.

My wife also talked about the work done at her school by a voluntary group with reserved and passive children to help them develop their social skills. They set up an after-school club for a group of these pupils, which ran for a term and which used group activities including a form of circle time to encourage the children to talk and share. Some of their confidence to talk came from the fact that the carefully selected group did not include the disruptive or very dominant children. She said that what was interesting was that the school's evaluation of the project found that once the children had started to develop these social and interpersonal skills, they did not go backwards once the project ended; they kept the skills. I wanted to organize something for the boys which would combine both elements of the primary initiatives. Although the finding was that the earlier you start the better, I felt that even in Year 9 there could be some clear benefits. Providing a support group, which included mentoring for these boys, could significantly help them deal with their problems.

I identified an initial pilot group, deliberately keeping the group numbers small, and then began the talks with their parents. Convincing the parents was crucial not only to getting the initiative off the ground, but to its chances of success. I had to make it clear that the boys were not in trouble but that it was an opportunity for them, and that we were not passing judgement on the parents, but providing additional support through mentoring, so that this could be a good career opportunity for them. I used non-teaching parent liaison officers to liaise with the harder-to-reach parents. All the parents reacted favourably; in fact several said that they were grateful that the school was trying to help their boys, so I went to the head and asked for a small grant from the extended schools budget to cover costs for the group, and to provide some refreshments and the occasional activity outside school.

The first two or three weeks were the hardest; they came, but they treated it as a bit of a laugh and I wondered if I would have done better to get a youth worker to lead the group. I persevered and just went on with the activities and hoped. Then, a few weeks into the term, one boy suddenly opened up and this led others to speak about their own experiences. I have since done some training to help me develop better activities, which relate to them and help to get them talking sooner. That first moment, when Tyrone told us that his father didn't want to see him and how that made him feel was a real breakthrough. Initially it was met with profound silence, but then other boys began to talk about their relationships with their fathers and to offer Tyrone advice.

You never know when a boy is going to share something that really matters to him. You notice a boy listening intently to a particular story, but he may not speak himself until a few weeks later. It is as if they have things trapped inside them that suddenly burst out. Something will spark them off. An example is that suddenly one boy began to talk about the way he felt when his parents split up and then another boy came in to share his feelings about his father's new family. A really good moment was when Stephen, who hadn't seen his father for months, told us that his father had rung him and said he wanted to see him. Stephen talked about how this made him feel and several of the others boys then shared similar experiences and feelings.

As it became clear that it was safe to talk in the group and that no one would laugh at them or ridicule them and the details would go no further, the boys became increasingly more willing to talk. Errol told me that knowing that other members of the group have been though the same things and understand what he was feeling really makes a difference. I have worked really hard to make the boys feel safe in the group. This gives them the confidence to share. It is clearly therapeutic for the boys to have a venue in which they can talk like this. Quite often there are tears. Seeing a boy with a reputation for being tough break down and become emotional has a strong and positive effect on others.

The meetings last for an hour and always include tea and some refreshments, but at the last meeting before Christmas I used the grant to provide a meal, so that session had a party spirit. We organized an outing for them – a residential weekend – and I liaised with the youth service to set up a camping opportunity for the group in the summer holiday. All of these proved very popular with the boys. There is also access to the psychological services if issues arise. It is mainly used as a support for me because I don't pretend to be a psychologist, but it was useful to be able to consult them when Tony shared his problem about anger management with the group.

Most of the time Tony is very quiet and represses his emotions, but then the anger builds up and he can't control it. This has led to incidents in lessons which ended in confrontations with the teacher or other boys, or in Tony walking out. When this happened often he did not return for several days. Being a member of the group means that he shares his feelings before he reaches the anger trigger point, and he has come to realize that once he has said how he is feeling, he starts to feel better. After we had discussed this in the group, he asked for additional help and I sought the psychologists' guidance about providing this.

Finding the mentors took a while. I asked around, seeking volunteers from the governors and parents association,and one of the governors asked at the local chamber of commerce. Gradually we are building up a group of reliable mentors from a range of backgrounds, who come in regularly to see their mentee. Good intentions were all very well, but failure to turn up is counterproductive. This was important because so much of the sharing had been about the problems in their relationship with their fathers or how they felt when their father had let them down.

Initially the trial run was to be for a term, but the boys asked for it to continue and it made sense to do so, particularly as I wanted to evaluate the impact it was making. Monitoring the attendance data showed a stark improvement in attendance. The number of times where group members were recorded as being involved in behaviour incidents in which they wouldn't cooperate in class went right down and has stayed down, and there appears to have been an impact on achievement. Feedback from the teaching staff, which is confirmed by comments from the boys themselves, is that in several cases their motivation has improved, with an impact on their level of achievement. Two of them are going into much higher sets in Year 10 than would have been anticipated at the beginning of the year. I can't unpick what is down to the mentoring and what comes from the support group experience, but suspect it is the combined opportunity that has made the difference.

A small group project focused on enabling boys to share what they are feeling clearly has a positive effect. Part of its success is that it enables them to develop relationships with pupils in similar situations to their own but without being in a neighbourhood gang. It is cheap in terms of money, so it is easy for a school to afford, but demands a lot of the staff involved. My Year 9 group want it to continue into Year 10, and although it was originally meant to be a short term initiative, the consensus is that it would be beneficial to do so. This created an issue about starting another group and it became clear to me that with two year groups involved, I could not do it all myself. Running the group had been time consuming and hard work but extremely rewarding, but now it needed to involve other year leaders as this kind of opportunity would need to be integrated into our extended school programme for other year groups.

Case study 8.4 describes how a school took a different approach and developed an inexpensive extra-curricular activity to help the social development of its Year 7 pupils.

CASE STUDY 8.4: THE YEAR 7 AFTER SCHOOL CLUB

When I became head of Year 7 after taking my previous year group all through the school to Year 11, it was like starting again and I was very conscious that the level of pupils who came from very challenging circumstances had increased. Our school is an inner-city specialist technology college in an area which had never been prosperous and which had been badly affected by the recession. We have a large number of pupils with behavioural difficulties and many with turbulent home circumstances, and our records indicated that the level of confrontations had been increasing both inside and outside the classroom. We were introducing the SEAL initiative, and one objective for us is to help the pupils develop their social skills, to help them handle situations better.

When we discussed the problem at my year meeting, one of the team suggested a regular extra-curricular session for Year 7 pupils, with some fun activities and opportunities for sharing, perhaps through some circle time. Another team member suggested it could be run by Year 12 and 13 pupils as this would be developmental for them and cheap for us. The team found the idea very attractive as it was simple, and seemed to have a lot of advantages. They were keen to introduce it as soon as possible. They could see clearly that over time there could be a lot of benefits for the school and its pupils. I was particularly pleased because the team was involving itself in planning for the year group. This meant it wasn't my scheme – it was their scheme.

At this stage I went to see the assistant head with pastoral responsibility and discussed the whole project with her because it needed SLT approval before it went any further and I'd need a budget. She was very interested and supportive, which gave me a good sounding board to talk through how viable some of the ideas would be in practice. At her suggestion we put it on the agenda for the next year heads' meeting so that other year heads knew what was being proposed for Year 7 and could think whether they wanted to do something similar in their year groups now or in the future. She also suggested that I liaise with the assistant principal in charge of extended schools as this area might be able to contribute to the funding – if not this year, then in future years. We also liaised with the head of sixth form as I needed her approval before I could start to recruit sixth formers to be club leaders.

At the meeting with the assistant principal I raised the problem of having insufficient meeting time for the planning group to do the job. There were a lot of issues to resolve, but we were only due one meeting in the half term. She suggested that we used a bit of the INSET budget and started the year meeting in the last period of the day. It was manageable as it wouldn't need much cover and it was a one-off. It would give us two hours and she offered to get some refreshments provided from the INSET budget. This approach would indicate to the team that their input was valued and supported. This was a very helpful offer, and I immediately accepted it.

The team gave a lot of thought to how the plan should be implemented. It was very important that it worked successfully, and that it was an enjoyable experience for leaders as well as the Year 7 pupils. This would ensure the supply of volunteers and we wanted their enthusiasm to impact on the Year 7s. They decided that the first year would be a pilot, a learning experience for everyone, and that we would review and adapt the scheme after the first year.

There was a lot of discussion about how the pupils should be selected for the scheme. The team's desire to make it a voluntary activity conflicted with the need to target particular pupils. I decided to use the information they received from the primary schools, which was on our database, to identify a target group and that the opportunity should be offered to all the pupils so identified. This gave both a nominated and a voluntary element to the scheme. During the year, the data built up on the pupils and work with the external agencies could lead to more pupils being added to the list.

When we discussed it at the year heads' meeting, the head of Year 9 suggested that the local psychological service should also be consulted and offered the opportunity to participate in the programme, and to invite them to my next year team planning meeting. People felt it was a good idea at least to inform the service of the school's initiative and ask for advice/suggestions and guidance. I took this suggestion back to my team, who approved of the idea, so I contacted the psychological service. In the event the psychological service liked the scheme very much. One of them came to our next planning meeting and they were particularly helpful in providing guidance about which pupils would benefit most from being offered the opportunity. At their suggestion the planning group also liaised with social services because joined up thinking in using the support services would be cost effective and benefit the pupils. They also made some helpful suggestions about how the scheme could be monitored.

The guidance from the psychological service led the team to structure a scheme that offered a different group the opportunity each term. Ten or twelve pupils at the most could be targeted at one time and would form a club. Next year, if the scheme worked well, two groups could run at the same time. It was felt that it was wiser to run one group well this year rather than to do too much before the expertise had developed.

The team decided that the leaders should work in pairs or threes so that they did not have to take too much responsibility and were part of a team. It was felt that the Year 12 and 13 pupils would need definite training to carry out the task. This meant that we had to think about how we could provide this without holding up the progress of the initiative. Most of the team wanted the project to get started as soon as possible. Then someone suggested that we target the members of the sixth form childcare course because this activity could form part of the practical work that they did for their course and contribute to certification. Both sides could benefit from the arrangement.

There was a lot of discussion about the need to have an adult on the premises. It was pointed out that for the first hour or so after school, which was when the club would operate, there was invariably someone working in the staff room and that legally this would be adequate. There are also other extended school activities. There was a feeling, however, that for the first year we should provide more back up for the sixth formers and I volunteered to be available every third session that the club would operate, if they would volunteer to work on a rota basis in the staff room at the other times the club was operating. This would give the Year 12 and 13 leaders security without any overt staff interference. To my delight, Sonia, who originally suggested that we needed the club, volunteered at once and others followed her lead; there were sufficient volunteers from the team to do one slot each to cover the term.

Facilities were not a problem as we're a new-build school, with ample space. One of the large year rooms could be made available on a regular basis and the field or a large hall could be booked occasionally.

The pupils would be given the opportunity to name the clubs and some choice about the activities included in the programme. This would con-tribute to the pupils' ownership of the initiative. The budget enabled us to provide some refreshments and squash, biscuits and crisps would be provided to ensure that the pupils were not hungry and to make the activity a pleasant experience. An outing would also be included in the ten-week programme, and the school would have to budget for this and make arrangements for any transport.

Arrangements would have to be made to ensure that there were no problems about the pupils' journey home. We are an inner-city school, so most pupils use public transport or walk, but the letter to parents included a question about how the pupil would get home after the course and individual arrangements were made.

Parental consent was essential before a pupil could be included in the programme, so letters were sent to all the parents and a session for parents to explain the scheme was arranged before the initiative started. The invitation was also put on the events section of our web-site. Attendance at parents' meetings was always an issue for the school, and for this reason much thought was given to how to entice the par-ents into school to attend the meeting. Year 7 parents are usually more enthused than other year groups, and for the pilot we did not need a huge take-up. If the scheme proved popular and successful, getting the parents to attend next time would be easier. The school could also use some pictures of the club in operation as promotional leaflets for next time.

The meeting was made into a social event, including coffee and an opportunity to meet the form tutors and to hear about the scheme. Quite a lot of parents attended and showed interest, especially when they realized that they would not have to pay anything. A few phoned in or emailed me to say that although they could not attend for various reasons they were interested in this opportunity for their son/daughter and could they be kept informed. In one case the EWO liaised and got the form signed. As long as the parent had made contact and signed the consent form, the pupil could participate. Once it was underway, a section of the Year 7 part of school's learning platform always featured the club, with the programme, pictures and items by participants to give parents a flavour of its activities.

Acting as club leaders proved highly popular with our Year 12 and 13 students. Although sixth formers following the childcare course had been targeted, others came to see me to say they would like to be involved. It became competitive and leaders were chosen both for what they could contribute and what they could gain, and teams were made up with a mixture of strengths. A good link formed with the local university where a teacher training course helped the school to provide training for our volunteer leaders, and monitoring was built in for the leaders to provide the assessment needed to help them earn credits. The college also helped us to devise the written tasks and assignments, which the group leaders would have to complete to earn their credits.

We had to tell the Year 7 pupils that the occasional adult would have to come to monitor the group leaders so that they could receive accreditation for this practical element of their studies. For the Year 7 pupils, although they said they understood, this was the least popular element, as it was felt to be intrusive. We are still working on how to reconcile this need for the sixth formers with the need of the Year 7 pupils to bond only with the leaders.

Initially the college and psychological services helped us to develop a range of activities for the clubs, but over time others have been introduced, and existing activities are developed and adapted to meet needs. Circle time is always a feature of the session. At first there was some scorn, as pupils remembered this as a primary school activity, but rapidly it became a central part of the routine, usually held in the second half of the session. It encouraged pupils to speak in a non-threatening environment, to listen to others and to share experiences. The leaders' training helps them to cope when emotionally demanding experiences are shared. Sometimes this can lead on to the pupils seeing the counselling service; more often, once they have shared with other pupils, pupils are able to talk to their year leaders about their problems.

There was initially some concern that a ten-week scheme was insufficient and that the social skills developed during this time would be lost when the pupil left the group. In fact the school has found that unlike some of the intensive reading schemes, which have to be sustained if the pupil is to retain the skill, social skills are retained.

Pupils enjoyed it a lot and wanted it to continue after the ten weeks. They came to tell me how much they missed it. I had to explain very clearly that other pupils also had to be given a similar opportunity and the tutors reinforced what I had said. We decided that there was a need to provide something more so we offered a reunion social at the end of the year for all pupils who had taken part in the clubs, and this was very popular as it gave the pupils something to look forward to. The scheme has now operated for two years and we have increased the opportunities by running two parallel groups in each term.

It is difficult to evaluate the impact precisely but the staff noticed fewer fights in Year 7 and fewer pupils reported being bullied. Teachers also reported better interaction in class discussion and generally more positive relationships than in some previous year groups. This standard was maintained when the pupils entered Year 8, and the school feels that the pupils have learnt better coping skills as well as generally improving their social skills. At the end of the second year of the scheme, we plan to ask the college to carry out an evaluation for them and to modify the scheme in the light of the findings.

We are now looking at how they can extend the scheme to enable the whole of Year 7 to participate. We also now include in our Year 7 PSHE programme a session in which the pupils are clearly told about the extra-curricular sports and other opportunities available to them as Year 8 pupils. Year 8 pupils are the speakers in this session and we regard it as an important educational experience for them.

For reflection/discussion
- Compare the two case studies. What are the main similarities and differences?

- How can the experiences of these schools be adapted to help the pupils in your own school?
- Schemes in which Year 12 and 13 pupils help younger pupils with their reading have also worked well in as number of schools. Some of these schemes can relate to the demands of their diploma or other sixth form courses. Are there other ways that Years 12 and 13 could help younger pupils?

Implications for team building

In Case study 8.4, the year team became the planning group for the initiative. This was done during team meetings. It was a good team building activity because working together on the project gave the team a common purpose and helped the team to bond. It illustrates how working together on a project is one of the best ways that you can involve and develop your team. It wasn't burdensome for them because they were not going to be the team leaders. Because they were so involved some team members volunteered to be in school to act as support for the first term's sessions. The year leader, however, led by example as he stayed three times while the rest of the team stayed once, and made sure that he had enough volunteers that no one had to stay more than once.

A support group checklist

- Planning pays dividends – think carefully about the membership of the group.
- The participants need to be in a similar position with a lot of common factors for empathy.
- Keep the group numbers small.
- You need the support of SLT and a budget – get both of these before you start.
- Think about possible sources of funding – consult the relevant assistant head as a starting point.
- Getting the support of the parents is essential – think about how you communicate the initiative to parents.
- Decide whether you want the group to be ongoing or a one-off experience.
- Research indicates that half a term is the minimum time span to achieve results; 10 or 12 weeks works well.
- Group leaders will need to be trained and supported.
- It is likely to take time before participants are confident to talk.
- Give the participants as much ownership as possible – include choices in the programme. Get feedback from the group individually

and collectively about their experience – what worked for them, what they might want to see in the future.

- Liaising with the LA psychological service is good practice and an insurance policy for you – external agencies such as the psychological service or the youth service might also provide ideas and support.
- Track what is happening in the classroom to the students participating in the group.
- Always evaluate what the impact has been on attendance, level of incidents, behaviour, etc. though you may not always be able to disentangle the impact of other projects going on at the same time.

Your role as a project manager

The case studies in this chapter illustrate your role in leading initiatives and occasions in which you have had to act as a project manager.

Change is a transformation process from one situation or position to another:

- The present situation is where we are now.
- Between the two situations a change or transformation takes place.
- The desired future situation is where we want to be at the end of the transition.
- A transitional period is the time during which the change takes place.

As the leader of change or project manager your role could include
- Creating the idea or vision of the change
- Devising the strategies to achieve the change
- Planning the timetable for the change
- Selling the change to the team or other stakeholders
- Leading the execution/implementation of the change
- Troubleshooting – dealing with problems that arise
- Shooting at a moving target, i.e. the goalposts have changed during the innovation
- Monitoring progress
- Evaluating the impact.

In recent years:

- Change has become constant.
- The pace of change has accelerated and shows no signs of slowing down.
- Much change is externally imposed, often as part of a political agenda.

- More than one change may take place at a time – this creates a complex situation for the manager to handle.
- There may be sub-changes in a complex pattern of change.
- People have become weary and disenchanted with 'innovation overkill'.

Overcoming difficulties and harnessing the success factors
Barriers to change
Don't expect things to run smoothly – expect to have to overcome some problems. Barriers to change often include:

Resources, especially financial problems
If the initiative is not funded this limits opportunities or prevents you from starting it when you choose. You can usually overcome financial constraints by using creative thinking, but don't expect this to be easy. You will notice that in several of the cases the project leader had to find ways to get the initiative funded.

Political
Political barriers might include the limits that teaching unions place on what you can do. For example, you can't hold the meetings you need to create the new culture. This can make implementing change particularly diffi-cult. Don't confront this kind of problem as you do not have the power to deal with it. Usually it is short term. You have to work round the problem. Sometimes, as in Case study 8.4, the school will help you by covering your team for an INSET session – don't expect to get more than an hour or two by this means.

External factors
Things usually take longer than you anticipate and illness, adverse weather conditions or other factors can affect attendance at essential meetings, the starting date or the rate of progress. This can be beyond your control. What really matters is keeping the project high profile and maintaining the momentum.

Attitudes
Negative attitudes are a major barrier to change. It takes time and effort to turn a negative attitude into a positive one, but it can be done. Understanding why people feel negative and staying positive yourself helps you to manage the situation.

Some fundamental reasons why people resist change

Most of the barriers to change are short term problems, but you need to be aware of them and think about strategies to overcome them. Reasons why people resist change can be categorized as follows:

- **Rational**: The change may appear to be unnecessary, not thought through or in conflict with core values.
- **Personal/political**: Individuals may be concerned about the effect of change on their role, their possible loss of influence or status, or whether they have the knowledge and skills to carry out the change.
- **Emotional**: The individual may be resistant to change in general, anxious over their ability to cope with the particular change, or fragile because of previous negative experience.
- **Entrenched culture** – summarized as: 'We don't do it that way here.' To handle this effectively you need to recognize the emotional issues involved for example in surrendering classroom control in the workforce reforms or in changing approaches to teaching that have been used for a decade or more.
- **Problem in letting go**: This particularly affects delegation or role change, and was a major issue affecting restructuring, particularly changes in the year head role. Often people try to continue to do their old job even though their title and status has changed. It tends to be because they are unsure of the requirements of the new role, feel deskilled and lack confidence.
- **Doing more work while you implement new cultures**: For example, learning to supervise the teaching or administrative assistants to ensure that they understand what is required and are efficient.

For these reasons change requires
- Sympathetic, encouraging and understanding attitudes on the part of leaders and managers
- Clear direction
- Firm decisions and responses
- Honest answers – not pretending or hiding problems.

Your own attitude and the leadership that you give will make a huge difference to your success.

Leading an initiative – what are the success factors?

Case study 8.4 describes how a year head led and managed an extra-curricular project. It illustrates some of the key factors which bring success:

- Your own commitment, energy and enthusiasm is crucial; it is easier when you are personally enthused.
- The project was not top-down; it arose out of an idea from a team member.
- The team were convinced of the need for change.
- Support of the SLT is important as it might ensure that you get resources and keeps the initiative high profile
- Careful planning is required; frequently people want to get started now and rush into implementation, leaving too many issues unresolved.
- Have achievable targets – clear procedures and small steps made the change achievable.
- Having the first run as a pilot made it flexible.
- Good liaison and communication will keep a lot of stakeholders in the loop.
- The project was not too burdensome – part of planning time was an INSET and using sixth formers meant that the tutor team did not have to run the after-school scheme themselves.
- The year head led by example, e.g. offered to stay for three after-school sessions if team members would do one session.
- Effective negotiating skills are vital – the year head liaised well with the SLT and psychological service and negotiated resources and support for the initiative.
- Give ownership to the team and credit where it is due – it was clear to all throughout that the idea came from the team and that they are the focus group for the scheme.

Some case studies have described schemes that arose from the pupils' suggestions and a couple of the case studies used students as peer councillors or group leaders. Involving the students in planning and leading initiatives that will benefit them often has positive effects on their social development and can have a knock-on effect on their studies.

Seeing that the students enjoy and are benefiting from an initiative can change the attitude of staff from negative to more positive. This usually happens after the initiative has started.

Using Force Field Analysis to help you plan

Force Field Analysis is a way of clarifying the route towards an objective and involves six steps:

1. Outline the management problem as you see it now. Outline the key elements of the problem.

2. Identify the 'ideal situation' you would like to achieve. Put this in the middle of the diagram.
3. Identify all the potential driving forces. These are all those elements which are working for you in the process of moving towards the ideal situation that you have identified. Try to assess the relative strength of these driving forces.
4. Identify all the potential resisting forces. You need not go into too much detail at this stage – indeed you might 'brainstorm' to identify the driving forces. Working with someone else can help you be objective about the strength of a particular force and identify more forces. The driving and resisting forces can be shown on a diagram. An example is given below (Figure 8.1). The strength of the force is indicated by the length of the line on the diagram. These are the elements which work against change, and in particular against change towards your ideal situation.
5. Examine the resisting forces in more detail. Which ones matter most? The longer arrows show the stronger forces. What can be done to reduce or eliminate the resisting forces?

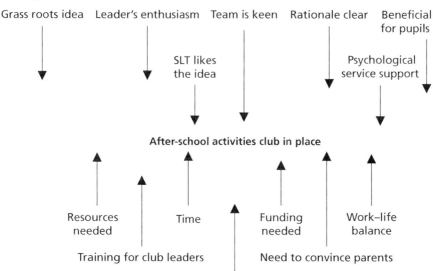

Figure 8.1 *Force Field Analysis of Case study 8.4 at an early stage*

6. Examine the driving forces in more detail. Which are the ones that are going to give you the most momentum towards your ideal situation? What can be done to maximize the effect of these driving forces?

The picture in Figure 8.1 is encouraging. Although the number of arrows is evenly balanced, notice that most of the resisting arrows are actually short term issues. You can normally do something to deal with these. For example, once you have provided the training for your club leaders, the problem has been resolved. Many of the resisting forces are about obtaining resources. Often initiatives are under-resourced. This makes leading the initiative harder for you, but usually it doesn't prevent you from doing it. You have to think creatively about what you can do.

The most serious resisting force was the need to get the parents on board. Often people become more willing to adopt a new approach when they can see the benefits – they can see what is in it for them. A strong driving force which helps you convince the parents here is that there are clear benefits for their children. To do this, you needed good communication skills.

Change has two elements – content and process. Often the project leader concentrates on the content but forgets the need to manage the process. Case study 8.3 illustrates this point because the content needed to be planned carefully, but potentially it was very good; how the project was led and managed, particularly the skill needed to gain support from a range of stakeholders, made all the difference to its success.

The team leaders in these case studies demonstrated their ability to lead and manage the process. They exhibited many of the characteristics of people who are good at handling change.

Characteristics of people who are good at handling change
- They have clear goals – they know what they want to achieve and don't lose sight of these goals.
- They communicate well – rationale, expectations, time frame, issues are all clearly spelt out to all stakeholders.
- They don't pretend everything will go like clockwork – they are prepared to spend time exploring the implications, concerns and issues – nothing is swept under the carpet.
- They have energy, determination, flexibility and perseverance – there will always be setbacks to overcome.
- They can negotiate and influence key players.
- They are prepared to see the proposed changes from the point of view of others involved and acknowledge their concerns as real concerns.

- They are proactive – they see opportunities and are able to seize them.
- They involve people so that ownership is shared.
- They protect people's security as far as possible, e.g. by breaking down the change into a series of achievable steps.
- They recognize and give credit where it is due and try to make change personally rewarding for people.

Web links

Mentoring and Befriending Foundation: www.mandbf.org.uk
- The MBF has produced a Peer Mentoring Pilot dissemination manual highlighting the good practice and methods used to successfully set up and sustain peer mentoring schemes. Contact Sarah Willey, National Contracts Manager on 0161 787 3835 for further information on this manual, or Kirsty Shaw, Peer Mentoring Administrator, on 0161 787 8600.

Peer mentoring: www.mandbf.org.uk

CHAPTER 9

Using data to raise achievement

What are the implications of strategic use of ICT to the pastoral leader's role?

CASE STUDY 9.1: STRATEGIC USE OF ICT IN MANAGING BEHAVIOUR

School A describes its experience

We are using the software package right across the school and find it very useful. We agonized for some time over whether to design our own or buy a commercial package, but in the end we decided that it made sense at this stage to start with a commercial package and to see what it did, the extent to which it suited our needs, and what we learned from it before attempting to design our own.

The SLT, behaviour managers, curriculum subject leaders and tutors all have access to it. Our staff are encouraged to record incidents when they happen and say what action they have taken. Tutors can log in and see the list of incidents specific to their tutor group. Tutors are encouraged to review this list on a daily basis and this helps them monitor and respond to the behaviour of their own tutor group. At the end of each month, data is available to profile the behaviour of each tutor group; the behaviour managers then use a variety of reports to inform their discussions of individual students' behaviour.

Subject leaders are able to profile behaviour specific to their department/ faculty area. This has enabled them to see what negative behaviours only or mainly occur in their subject or are teacher specific and to check perceptions of student behaviour across their department. From this, they are beginning to work on addressing the problems they have found and supporting the staff where a need has been identified. This makes a valuable contribution to ensuring that the behaviour policy is being consistently practised.

It became a very useful tool both for our behaviour managers, who are year leaders, and for our Key Stage managers. It provides them with graphs profiling the behaviour of the year group and the behaviour managers have used these in assemblies or year council meetings to involve the pupils in addressing the issues. Year behaviour managers have also used them for sessions with parents. The visual impact of the graphs is proving very effective and stimulates positive discussions. The behaviour managers also use the data to set targets for the pupils and use the record sheets with parents. The behaviour profiles can trigger report cards to set behaviour improvement targets based on their particular behaviour issues. The software can also demonstrate that behaviour is deteriorating or improving over time so we can feedback and discuss with staff, pupils and parents what progress is being made and what the next step should be. The behaviour managers contribute to the relevant section of the school's SEF and now they have the evidence that they need.

We are now working to link our behaviour software to our academic software, so that behaviour and progress can be clearly matched.

For reflection/discussion
- How does this case study compare to what is happening in your own school?
- What are the implications for a pastoral leader?

Where do you fit into this picture?
Many schools have an assessment manager, who is usually a member of the SLT and not always a teacher, in overall charge of the system. The data is usually imputed by a data manager as this is a time consuming occupation and needs technical expertise. The Key Stage or year leader is expected to deal

with the implications of the data relevant to his/her section of the school.

Although you have a very important role in analysing and using the information provided, there are considerable differences in what data is made available to you as year leader and in what format.

There is no consistent picture:

- Some pastoral leaders are still only receiving printouts and the data remains with the school's assessment manger. Basically it has been filtered for you, which limits your control over the data. This makes it difficult for you to manage the data as you can't analyse it through using the sort facility on the spreadsheet.
- The majority of pastoral leaders, however, are provided with computer access to particular software. This means that the school expects you to be able to manage and analyse the data relevant to your year group.

A major part of your role as the director of the pupil's studies is to be able to interpret the data and to use the information it provides about a pupil's potential or progress to support the pupil in his/her studies.

- You are expected to be able to access and track the progress of individuals within your section of the school so that you can see whether they are making the progress anticipated for them and whether an intervention is needed.
- The tracking process should help you identify underachievement, so that it can be rectified through the provision of booster strategies.
- You are expected to be able to monitor and compare the progress and achievement of different groups of pupils according to ethnicity, gender, SEN or EAL and within these categories, and to take appropriate action to ensure the pupil's equal opportunities and that the school meets the current inclusion agenda.
- As well as achievement, you can monitor what value-added the school is providing for individuals or particular groups of learners.
- You will be expected to identify differences in pupil achievement in different subjects if progress is better than anticipated and identity areas in which learners are gifted or talented and need extension provision.
- Your tracking and data analysis should enable you to make predictions about how the student is likely to achieve by the end of Key Stage 3, Key Stage 4 or post-16 studies.
- You are expected to use what you have learnt from your analysis of the pupil data to take appropriate action and liaise with the

relevant coordinators to provide an appropriate personalized learning programme for the individual.

- Your analysis of pupil data provides the SLT with information that they use for the SEF and for the school's strategic planning. In this way you contribute to planning for school improvement.

Case studies illustrating how year leaders carry out this part of their job can be found later in this chapter.

What data do you have to monitor?

Your school is likely to have software which covers the administrative aspect of your role, e.g. the register and pupil details, and to enable you to collect information on the current high profile areas of focus, i.e. attendance and punctuality, behaviour and achievement. A list of main ways you can use the data is given below, but you could monitor more widely, e.g. what extra-curricular activities does the student undertake? This would give you a more complete picture and help you create a strong personalized learning programme for the learner.

Administrative data

- Enables you to correlate all the information you have on an individual or class of pupils for administrative purposes
- Makes collecting the information you need to give the SLT for statutory returns and providing information to the LA easier
- Generates lists of your registration groups, with all the necessary pupils details, and can sub-sort
- Enables you to access the student's individual timetable, homework and course work deadlines lists, all of which helps you monitor the learner's subject programme
- Makes pupil transfer between schools easier.

Attendance data

- Enables you to create defined fields to record different kinds of absence – patterns emerge which can be used to flag up issues to tutors, parents or the EWO
- Enables you to can act faster, e.g. a.m. or p.m. roll call can be done electronically and information immediately processed or communicated to the EWO or parents
- Enables you to register pupils anywhere – the classroom or other areas – using a laptop or e-portal
- Enables monitoring of punctuality and absence from particular lessons.

Behaviour data
- You can monitor incidents for regularity and type.
- You can monitor an individual pupil's behaviour.
- You can generate incident reports for use with staff or parents.
- You can generate and monitor pupil behaviour report cards.
- You can generate graphs, etc. for use with staff, governors and parents.

Assessment data
- Enables you to track pupils from entry to exit: secondary pupils, from CATs testing on arrival in Year 7, through to the end of sixth form; systems now also exist to track the progress of special school pupils
- Helps you set more accurate targets and make appropriate interventions to support a pupil's progress
- Generates reports, usually with a bank of statements to enable consistency of reporting
- Enables monitoring of the rate of progress of any individual child and gives a much clearer picture of an individual's attainment and rate of progress than in the past
- Enables you to focus on the progress of particular groups and make comparisons or benchmark
- Provides a range of value-added data so you can see what difference the school or the Key Stage has made for pupils
- Enables you to compare the performance of different subjects
- Provides an integrated system so you can look at the effect of attendance or behaviour on performance.

How confident are you at using the data?
Data management is an ever-expanding aspect of your responsibilities. Using it effectively is crucial to school improvement. Schools are, however, at very different stages of development. Your school may be a market leader at the cutting edge of technology, but many schools are not. A recent informal survey by one supplier among its local authority support teams elicited the estimate that only a quarter of schools were using their MIS/SMIS packages to the full. Even more arresting was the same survey's estimate of how many head teachers were fully confident in using their MIS for school improvement. The answer was somewhere between 0 and 5 per cent. Both figures are for all schools, but it was reckoned that primaries came out worse than secondary schools.

How to develop your expertise

If you have been recently appointed as a year leader and are not familiar with the school's software, don't understand the terminology, or are simply not confident in using the system, then the best way to move forward is to ask for some training as a priority. There are a number of ways through which you could develop your expertise:

- To get a quick overview of what is happening it is usually worth checking TeacherNet for a summary. This will help you keep up to speed.
- You could go on a commercial course. This is the most expensive route for the school. It can be very useful and there are some excellent trainers, but it can be hit or miss because training is designed for groups and will not be specifically targeted for your personal or school's needs.
- A lot of schools bring in a trainer from their software provider, which means that it is focused on the school's own system. It is most likely to be organized for a group of year leaders. Its advantage is that it provides targeted training. The package that the school has bought may also allow for additional support or adjustments to the system to provide new fields to take account of changing demands.
- The school could bring in the LA assessment support team over half a term to provide an in-house training unit to familiarize the year or section leaders with the key questions that they need answers to and how to analyse the data to find the answers. This kind of support is very useful because it helps you understand value-added or how to interpret RAISEonline.
- Another option is to use in-school expertise with the training and ongoing support provided by an ICT technician or administrator, often the person who inputs the data. This can be the most useful alternative because as well as getting one-to-one initial training, you can refer to and discuss problems as they arise.
- Keep up to date with new developments in Assessment for Learning (AfL) by using the relevant websites. You can download the most recent AfL guidance free from the DfE Standards Site's assessment guidance, and also check your examination board's website to see what they offer.

Assessing Pupil Progress (APP): an overview

APP is the most recent development in AfL. Its objective is to provide a common framework for assessment. After a pilot scheme involving over

100 schools, it is now being rolled out for all curriculum subjects. It is based on evidence-based periodic assessments of how children are doing at school and forms part of the move away from the over-reliance on testing, which has been a feature of school life over the past decades, and looks likely to become a key plank of the AfL strand of personalized learning.

Teachers are used to day-to-day assessment (the interactions, communications and observations used to reflect on learning) forming a major part of AfL. They are also used to Assessment of Learning – the testing at ends of modules or Key Stages by teachers or national testing thorough Standard Attainment (SATs) Tests. The new feature of AfL is periodic assessment, which should give teachers and students a far broader view of progress.

APP uses national standards so it gives comparable information and, very importantly, it can lead to improvements to teachers' curriculum planning. Reviewing the evidence can help teachers determine how well pupils are doing as a whole, see where there are gaps in students' learning, and also gain insights which directly inform future planning, teaching, and learning during the academic year.

APP provides you with a range of diagnostic information to support AfL and to help you to make reliable periodic judgements about how pupils are doing related to national standards. The standards files help you get a clear sense of what achievement looks like, and aims to support teachers in reaching consistent judgements about national curriculum levels. It aims to provide teachers with detailed information about the pupils selected and enables teachers to generalize about other pupils who are working at a similar level or have comparable characteristics.

Potential advantages of APP include:

- It sharpens teachers' abilities to ask questions as they become familiar with the assessment criteria and observe more carefully what pupils are doing in lessons.
- It helps them to distinguish the different things they are looking for when carrying out assessment.
- It provides rigour and a measure of standardization to teacher assessments, and that in turn provides a continuous series of 'checkpoints' for measuring student progress against their targets.
- The assessment information can be used to coordinate intervention to tackle potential underachievement across the range of subjects.
- It helps teachers to look across the whole subject and ask themselves what the pupil does well and what they need to concentrate on.
- It can be used by departments as a diagnostic tool for formative

assessment and for setting individual improvement targets for a student's work.

- It can help parents to understand at what level their children are working, and what progress they are making. They don't really understand levels; it is much easier for them to understand a grid of what the pupil has achieved and what they have yet to do.
- It involves pupils more directly in their own learning and they can see what progress they have made – it enables them to become more reflective about their own work and more independent.

CASE STUDY 8.2: INTRODUCING APP

I am an English teacher as well as year leader for Year 9. Initially, when SATs ended at Key Stage 3, a lot of the teachers went on 'teaching to the SATs' as they didn't know what else to do. Then we became involved in the pilot for APP and this has helped us to move on and think very differently about how we organize assessment. Sarah, the head of the English department did the QCA training, then she gave us some initial training, after which we learnt by doing, i.e. using APP with our English classes. We had to learn to set assessment focuses (AFs) across each level and to use the assessment guideline sheets, which are grids on which we record our findings.

At the beginning we feared it would be paper-heavy, but actually it's OK. Sarah organized us so that we worked in pairs and could compare our findings. This helped us to develop our understanding. At first we were very dependent on the standards files. They are annotated examples of pupils' work at each level against national standards. We kept looking at them all the time and checking to see that we were right. Now APP is a regular part of our professional practice. We have moderation meetings regularly. They help us be consistent and in setting targets.

I found being involved in the initiative useful in my role as a pastoral leader as I understand the changes in how assessment was operating and could monitor the impact on the pupils. The pupils are even more conservative than staff about change, so it took time for them to get used to it, but now when I discuss it with my Year 9s in our academic review sessions, they tell me that they understand the criteria and can see the progress that they are making. Several of them said that in the past levels didn't mean a lot to them, but they find the grid is much easier to understand. I find target setting with them in my role as year head more focused than in the past and they talk more confidently about what progress they have made.

Benefits of using an integrated data system
- The way your school's system manipulates the data will help you make more informed decisions.
- It can help you take an overview as you will have better and more accurate information for assessing the progress of any individual or a particular subset of students.
- You can see at a glance where you are and call up any information that you want.
- Examining the evidence can shed a new light on things.
- It gives you specific evidence – you will be able to see accurate information about pupils immediately, and in more than one area – this will help you build up an informed picture and identify areas of underperformance or particular problems.
- Being able to bring information about attendance, behaviour and pupil achievement together means you have a more complete picture. It becomes easier to identify causes of underperformance and deal with the underlying issue rather than targeting the symptoms.
- Being able to track a pupil's progress enables you to set realistic targets and adapt them to enable personalized learning.
- It makes early intervention easier and can make a real difference to a child's progress over time.
- It improves your communication with parents and other stake-holders, because the information you want is to hand and clearly presented.
- It also speeds up communication because parents can access their child's data on the learning platform and can feel more informed and involved.
- It reduces the mountain of paper and streamlines administration.
- Increasingly, paper is no longer accepted, so having MIS enables you to meet statutory requirements, e.g. to submit teacher assessments at Key Stage 3 you have to use a common transfer file (CFT) and School to School (s2s) data transfer to send the teacher assessment data in the core subjects, and at Key Stage 3 you also have to send foundation subjects.

- It enables sharing of ideas and good practice.
- It improves your communication with parents and other stakeholders because the information you want is to hand and clearly presented.

Target setting

The most significant way in which your role as a pastoral manager has developed is that you, as the director of the pupil's learning programme, have to be able to use the information to make projections about what the pupil could achieve. You have to be able to help the student set targets, which will help him/her raise his/her attainment. Ideally your help enables the pupil to exceed those targets. You also have responsibility, either personally or through your use of your tutor team, for monitoring the student's progress towards the targets.

'Target setting' is one of the current buzz words. If it is to benefit the student and contribute to the raising of achievement, you need to be clear about:

- what target setting means
- how the targets will be recorded
- how both the teachers and the students will find the time to do it
- how progress will be monitored.

Target setting is about the defining the logical next step for the student to achieve.

Types of target
SMART targets
All targets must be *Specific, Measurable, Achievable, Resourced, Time related*.

Simply saying to a pupil, 'Try to improve your work' is not helpful, whereas in comments like 'Mary, your target is to finish the next piece of work on time' or 'Ian, if you label your diagrams, you will get more marks for them. This is something you should remember to do in the next assignment . . .' the target is specific, achievable and time related. It is easy for the teacher to check that the pupil has met the target.

Outcome and process targets

Examples of outcome targets	Examples of process targets
Raise proportion of students scoring above 85% on NFER reading test to 90%.	Implement new, more regular, assessment and early intervention.
Improve attendance rates to a minimum of 94%.	Provide daily clerical assistance time for phoning homes of absent students.
Raise average grade in science by 0.5 grade in the next two years.	Develop more effective teaching strategies in KS4.
Raise proportion of boys achieving A/B grades in French at GCSE by 7%–10%.	Experiment with single gender teacher at KS4.
Raise proportion of students achieving Level 6 or better in the KS3 science test by 10%.	Develop and introduce new materials to extend the most able students in science.

Target zones

Zone	
The historic zone	Continuing as 'We have always done, maintaining the status quo'.
The comfort zone	Without much effort we could improve things a bit.
The smart/realistic zone	We could make a significant improvement if we changed things.
The unlikely/visionary zone	In our wildest dreams, we think our students could achieve this.

Types of outcome target

Type	
Elite targets	Target a specific group of students, e.g. raising the proportion of students gaining 5+ A–C grades at GCSE.
Whole group or average targets	Raising attainment across a cohort, e.g. raising the average points score at GCSE.
Reliability targets	Reducing the number of failing students, e.g. reducing the number of students failing to achieve 5 A–C grades.

Principles
- Ensure a balance between process targets and outcome targets.
- Do not set too many outcome targets.

- Set targets in the right 'zone'.
- Make sure that the targets are appropriate to your faculty/subject/year group.
- Make sure that target/action/monitoring process and planning is joined up.
- Use a variety of data and be aware of its limitations.
- Set targets with people, not for people.

Making effective use of data: some case studies

The case studies which follow illustrate how this might work in practice.

CASE STUDY 9.3: HOW A SECONDARY PROGRESS MANAGER USES TRACKING

I use the Key Stage 2 results as the basis to track and set targets for pupils. I have their CATs scores, but find they give me too much data to handle if I want an overview, though our inclusion manager uses them to look at SEN issues and for our Early Intervention Programme. It's also used to identify pupils for the gifted and talented register, and we find it a useful tool when referring to external agencies, as they usually need that sort of data.

Our pupil details are kept on SIMS. Our data manager enters the Year 7 data onto the SIMS for me, and then transfers each pupil's scores electronically onto an individual tracking sheet, so that I can monitor the progress of each pupil. I use this initially to put the new pupils into their forms, so that they are mixed ability. I also draw on information from the feeder schools, so that incompatible children are not put together.

We build up a picture of the progress of the learner on his/her individual tracker. We have an Academic Review day once a term for each student and the subject teachers level their work before each review and use these as the basis for discussions with parents. We also give the pupils an effort score, so we can monitor their attitude and its impact. These levels are entered onto SIMS and transferred electronically to the individual tracker and 'aspirational' targets are set for the core subjects. At KS3 we use SATs levels and at KS4 we use GCSE grades. I can build a year-on-year picture, monitor the individual's progress over the Key Stage, between the Key Stages and the extent to which a pupil meets his/her 'aspirational' targets. It is easy for me to use, and I can see at a glance if things are going according to expectations and it indicates if I should be liaising with parents.

The tracker helps me identify underachievers. The criteria we use are lack of progress or regression. We look at SATs results in English and maths from Year 6 (KS2) and Year 9 (KS3). Students should move two levels, e.g. from Level 3 to Level 5 over the Key Stage   a pupil who hasn't moved up two levels over the Key Stage or who has gone down will go on this list. I have weekly meetings with my SLT line manager about student progress and discuss the pupils identified on the underachieving list with her. The way it works here is that the line manager moves it forward. She will interact with the heads of faculty, who provide subject support and the inclusion manager to organize other intervention strategies, such as mentoring.

I also have access to other software, for example at KS4 I can use the Yellis GCSE projections and I use this when I want more detailed information. I also use SIMS to see how particular ethnic groups are doing or to check the progress of boys or how attendance and punctuality are impacting on progress, though I have to be careful here as we use a swipe system and truanting pupils tend to give the swipe card to a friend, who swipes them in! Luckily we also take hard copy registers daily, so I check SIMS against the class register for the pupil. Similarly, if there is real disparity in a pupil's performance in different subjects I'll talk to the subject teacher to see what factors might be affecting things.

I always use my knowledge of the pupils as well as the data. The data is very useful – targets are much more precise than they used to be and learners know where they stand, but I have learnt to tread carefully because data isn't always accurate and there is always a bigger picture.

Many year leaders feel that they are awash with data and are unclear how to make the best use of it. This case study:

- indicates the range of data available
- illustrates the principles that the year leader applied to enable her to use it effectively
- illustrates how good schools have got at moving a learner forward from his/her own starting point
- illustrates that the data isn't enough on its own – you still need your knowledge of the learner to appreciate the whole picture.

How do you recognize underachievement?

As Case study 9.3 indicates, the main indicators are lack of progress or regression. For example, a group of pupils may come into the school with Level 5s in English and maths. You would expect these pupils to be among your high achievers, but at the end of the Year 7 (or, as a worse case scenario, if you haven't addressed the issue, at the end of Key Stage 3) they are still at Level 5. These students will have underperformed in relation to their grades at the end of Key Stage 2 and the projections which the school will have made for them.

It is your job to unpick the issues affecting their lack of progress and liaise with the relevant coordinators, SLT and parents or carers to put in place strategies which will help these students achieve their potential.

Having access to the data allows you to pick up immediately on any issues that impede learning. It gives you more chance of making a difference if you intervene before the problems become embedded and very difficult to resolve. In Case study 9.3, the year leader had weekly meetings with her line manager which focused on the students identified as not making progress or regressing. In this school, the line manager, a member of the SLT, took the case forward; in many schools the year leader will handle this stage and the SLT will become involved if your approach and strategies don't work.

CASE STUDY 9.4: USING DATA TO GET AN OVERVIEW – AN EXAMPLE FROM A DIFFERENT SECONDARY SCHOOL

We use CMIS to store attendance, contacts, assessments, reports, timetables, free rooms, cover, etc. All the staff has access to this at varying levels. We mostly access this information via an e-portal. This is an intranet page that presents the information in a user-friendly way. So when I log in I am presented with my timetable for the day and associated registers, and any cover is on there with the register. My form register is on there. It also shows me my form events which range from trips to the medical room and merits to behaviour incidents and detentions issued by staff. When I click into a class I am presented with the register which I fill in using the attendance codes. I can click onto each individual student and have immediate access to their contact details, SEN information, at-risk status, form group, all previous assessment data (KS2, KS3, NFER, FFT predictions).

Similarly, I can access students' individual event log, including all their merits, behaviour incidents, exclusions, detentions and medical room trips. Any school reports that are written can be accessed here. This page also gives us information on their attendance and punctuality in pie chart form for quick use, and the student's timetable so you can locate them at any point in the day.

On our front page is the school calendar noting important events, our staff bulletin and a message board for messages that are important to everyone. We are able to add events to each student including behaviour, merits, and detentions. Each incident that is logged requires you to specify when and where the incident occurred and what type of incident it was, how you dealt with it, and whether any follow-up is required. The only downside to this system is that once you hit the enter button you can't go back and edit it later if you have made a mistake. (This could also be seen as a good thing!)

We also use CMIS or e-portal to write our reports, which are then openly available to all staff to read. We can search for students by first or surname and we can also look up a teacher's timetable.

This case study indicates how on a daily basis the relevant staff access information stored on SIMS or CMIS and a year or Key Stage manager is able to get a comprehensive overview of how a pupil is performing.

CASE STUDY 9.5: USING CATS DATA

We consider it very important to start to support our pupils as soon as they arrive in the school. They sit the CATs shortly after they arrive. We analyse the Year 7 pupils' CATs together with their Key Stage 2 results and organize appropriate interventions. Our reading support scheme based on teaching reading through phonics is one such strategy, because a few children arrive unable to read and a significant proportion are well below the reading levels expected for their age. Obviously the main focus is on improving the pupils' functional skills to enable those who are below the expected levels to catch up, but the analysis is also the basis of creating our gifted and talented register.

I liaise with subject leaders to ensure appropriate setting in subjects, SEN support and differentiated SOWs work within each subject area. Progress is then monitored and reviewed by the subject teacher and

I check this half-termly. We make adjustments to settings if there has been progress.

This information is also used as a basis for target setting and mentoring. Targets are recorded in pupils' planners, which are signed by parents to show that they have seen the targets. They are also monitored regularly and adjusted to enable personalized learning at a realistic rate for the learner.

References and web links

DfE guidance materials for using management information systems can be found at: www.standards.dcsf.gov.uk/nationalstrategies (search using the reference number 00756–2008PDF-EN-02). The material provides support on:

- Improving assessment practice
- Using MIS to share information
- Analysing trends over time and summary data for individuals groups and cohorts
- Using core tracking processes
- Predicting likely outcomes and generating targets.

Some useful publications can also be downloaded from this website in pdf format.
MIS commercial providers include:

- Conduct software: www.schoolbehaviour.co.uk
- EduTrack: www.edutrack.co.uk
- Granada Learning's School Centre Software: www.schoolcentre.net
- Groupcall: www.groupcall.com
- Serco: www.serco.com
- SIMS: www.capitaes.co.uk/SIMS

Ofsted: www.ofsted.gov.uk

- For inspections and SEF guidance.
- See the publication *Assessment for Learning: The Impact of National Strategy Support* (Ofsted, October 2008; ref: 070244).

RAISEonline: www.raiseonline.org

- RAISEonline provides interactive analysis of school and pupil performance data.
- To access your school's RAISEonline pages you need the school's URN (unique reference number), and your password. Your administrator will have his/her own password. Check the instructions. For the DfE's guidance for accessing and inputting to RAISEonline see *Data Management in RAISEonline* (DCSF, 2008), which can be downloaded in pdf format from the Ofsted website.

Sleuth user guide and practical demonstration: www.schoolsoftwarecompany.com/sleuthtrial.php

SNIP behaviour audit – based on the QCA document *Supporting School Improvement Emotional and Behavioural Development* and uses a 6-point scale. Download from: www.snip-newsletter.co.uk/downloads.php

Truancy Call: www.truancycall.com

CHAPTER 10

Dealing with parents

Creating an effective relationship with parents is one of the most important aspects of your role. As the year leader you certainly see parents more than anyone else in the school. Yours will be the name that the parents know as the key member of staff with responsibility for the education and progress of their child. This means that as a year leader you can affect the interaction between home and school more than any other manager. How you communicate with and handle the school's interactions with the parents of the students in your year group is crucial to your success. There is also a public relations component of your management role and you will need to think about how you should handle it.

The current situation: the findings of research and their impact on your role

Research into levels of parental involvement

Managing the partnership with parents is currently high profile. Surveys into parental involvement in the life of the school and how they support their children at home have provided an evidence base that influences current practice. It is not surprising, in view of the preoccupation with standards, that the research has increasingly focused on the level of parental involvement its impact on pupil achievement. A summary of the main findings of this research will follow.

- Parental involvement in children's education from an early age has a significant effect on educational achievement, and continues to do so into adolescence and adulthood.
- A very high parental interest is associated with better exam results compared to children whose parents show no interest.
- The quality and content of fathers' involvement matter more for children's outcomes than the quantity of time fathers spend with their children.
- Family learning can also provide a range of benefits for parents and children including improvements in reading, writing and numeracy as well as greater parental confidence in helping their child at home.
- The attitudes and aspirations of parents and of children themselves predict later educational achievement. International evidence suggests that parents with high aspirations are also more involved in their children's education.
- The level of involvement has risen since 1970s. Around half of parents surveyed by the DCSF in 2007 said that they felt very involved in their child's school life. Two-thirds of parents said that they would like to get more involved in their child's school life (with work commitments being a commonly cited barrier to greater involvement).
- Levels of parental involvement vary among parents, for example, mothers, parents of young children, Black/Black British parents, parents of children with a statement of special educational needs are all more likely than average to be very involved in their child's education.

For reflection

Think about the findings of recent research and the government's publications on improving the quality of parental involvement in the context of your own school – how might they affect your approach to dealing with parents?

It could be useful to discuss them as a group of pastoral leaders or with your tutors.

The Every Parent Matters initiative

One example of the government's approach is the Every Parent Counts initiative (2007). It aims to encourage parents to become more involved with their child's educational development and schooling. *Every Parent Matters* (DfES, 2007) describes what this might mean in practice:

- Engaging both fathers and mothers
- Enabling parents to access information so that they can exercise effective choice
- Giving parents the means to influence the shape of services so that they meet their family's needs
- Practitioners providing services to the family seeking to work in equal partnership with parents to maximize the benefits to the children of the services received
- Enabling parents to find and draw down additional information and help to deal with specific issues when they need it
- Ensuring opportunities for fathers and mothers to work in partnership with schools, taking account of the constraints on working parents.

A range of free services called Parent Know How is also being developed to give all parents access to expert advice, and to increase the number of parenting experts working locally in children's centres and schools. You can check the progress of this initiative by accessing the DCSF website.

What are the most important management skills you need for this component of your role?

- Interpersonal skills – you will frequently be dealing with anxious or angry parents; you want a positive outcome from the interaction.
- Communications skills – you must provide clear information in a user-friendly way. In both written and oral communication you will need to think not only about the level of difficulty of the language but also the tone that you use.
- Organizational skills – there is a lot of organization involved in managing an event such as a parents' meeting.

This chapter will focus particularly on four areas:

1. Running an event – managing parents' meetings
2. Dealing with angry parents
3. Dealing with difficult parents
4. Involving parents who are hard to reach

1. Running an event: managing parents' meetings

Parents' meetings are one of the main ways in which you communicate with groups of parents. Most parents' meetings are held to enable parents to discuss their children's progress. It should enable teachers and parents to interact and be constructive, as well as open, about the progress or lack of progress that a child is making at school. Factors such as time pressures, limited staff numbers or anxious parents mean that these evenings can sometimes be challenging for all involved, however. To succeed, the event should be a positive experience for the parents. It needs to be well organized so that is flows smoothly and the parents don't have to spend most of a long evening queuing and don't find the messages that the school wishes to communicate incomprehensible. It also needs to address issues or concerns that the parents have about their child's progress or well-being at school.

Types of meeting
Different styles of meeting suit different schools.

Traditional pupil progress parents meeting
This kind of meeting is usually held in the main school hall for a whole year group. Parents queue for five-minute slots with the subject teachers and the tutors.
  Advantages of this system:

- Everyone is in the same place – ease of access.
- More secure – teachers are not isolated.
- Parents can see all the teachers.

Disadvantages of this system

- Long queues for the teachers who are most in demand – this can take a long time and be a frustrating experience.
- Interviews can overrun – parents can miss their turn for one teacher while queuing for another and often they need to split up.

Variations on this approach include:

- An appointment system can cut down the queues.
- Asking parents to prioritize, four or five teachers rather than see all the subject teachers. If pupils are involved in fixing the appointments, make sure that they don't only choose the subjects/ teachers that they like best.
- Putting the subject teachers in their classrooms rather than in the hall, but there can be security issues when the teachers are dispersed throughout the school at night, so it is not used much.
- Pupil progress meetings when students accompany parents. Where there is a high proportion of parents who speak little or no English, schools often ask the students to accompany their parents.
- Divide the event and hold two sessions so that some subjects are

on the first evening and others on the second session. This isn't very popular with parents as they have to attend twice.

The parent/family sees the tutor

A totally different way to run parents' meetings is to hold them during the day and suspend the timetable for the year group. The student often accompanies his/her parents to the session. They are allotted a 15-minute slot with the tutor. This gives a significant patch of time for the family to discuss through issues. This is normally a target setting session and the targets are explained to and agreed with the family.

An example of this approach could be a Year 11 meeting to discuss GCSE/diploma issues and set targets and to talk to the family about sixth form choices and possible careers.

Events for particular year groups

An example of this is a meeting held for Year 7 parents in the second part of the autumn term. The parents see the tutor who will be in the form room, not the hall. They only get a five-minute slot, but this is sufficient to establish face-to-face contact with the tutor and to reassure the parent about how the child is settling into the school. If real issues arise that need more than five minutes, the parent is asked to make an appointment for a longer session with the tutor or year leader at a future date.

Social events

Some schools make their first Year 7 meeting a more social event for parents which is held in the hall with refreshments, e.g. coffee and biscuits, with the tutors present so that the parents can meet them informally.

Because secondary school teachers have fewer opportunities to talk to parents informally than primary schools, often they use social events to build a sense of community and hold one or two events a term to enable them to meet parents in a relatively informal way. Schools will vary whether the focus is a particular year group or focused on the kind of activity offered.

Curriculum related events/information meetings

Here are some examples: Year 9 usually holds an options evening to inform parents of the choices available and what it means for their child; Year 11 holds sixth form choices evenings; taster sessions for more sensitive aspects of the PSHE curriculum are often provided for parents of the relevant year group.

If there are major changes to the curriculum that will involve particular year groups, e.g. the introduction of diplomas or a proposed change to a baccalaureate qualification, a meeting will be held to inform parents. This kind of meeting, however, is likely to be led by the head or a deputy, and the relevant subject leaders may have to address the parents, but you may have to handle the organization.

Who organizes parents meetings?

Traditionally the year head organized the parents meetings and in your school this may still be the case. Now that functions are split in many schools, however, a non-teaching pastoral leader may do this or one of the school's administrative staff may be responsible for organizing events. Even if you don't personally organize the meeting, you do need to oversee the event so that it achieves its objectives.

When should you hold the event?

You may not have the power to make this decision though you might be able to influence it. There is no right answer here as different patterns fit different schools. The DCSF recommends holding parents meetings early in the year so that parents can be made aware of the academic calendar and important events for the year and the school can enlist their help in approaching any problems that pupils may have. Schools often like to hold a parents' evening to follow a few weeks after issuing a report. This gives the parents time to read the report and be able to raise concerns. It isn't possible, however, to do this for every year group. Choice evenings such as option information sessions tend to be held shortly before the choice has to be made. Most schools have a cycle so that the meetings are spread through the year. They tend to review this cycle every few years as things change.

Guidelines for organizing the event

When organizing a parents' evening, ask yourself what you hope to achieve, and work backwards from there. In general terms your objective should be to make it an arena for honest discussion and productive criticism that will help motivate children and positively affect their learning experiences.

Plan well ahead

Keep a file on your computer with all the relevant information so that you can easily access it. If you are organizing a parents' meeting for the first time, start by checking with the office so that you know what is already in place and you can access and customize the standard letters that the school is likely to use to invite the parents to the meetings and know how much time they require to see that things flow smoothly. Effective liaison with the office will impact on how well the event will run.

Start early

You need about four weeks to get the parents' meeting set up. This doesn't mean that you work non-stop for four weeks, but that you must allow sufficient time for each stage and that you can pre-empt or deal with problems as they arise.

If you want to book a speaker, such as the careers officer, you should see that he/she has the school calendar at least a term ahead and that the date is in his/her diary. Confirm their availability when you start to make the arrangements

Check that all the teachers are available

Customize the staff list to make an alphabetical list of the staff needed for the evening and put the list up on the appropriate board in the staff room about a month before the meeting. Allow a week for them to tick that they can come, and then check those who haven't signed up. Find out whether they have not noticed the list or simply not got around to signing it or whether there is a real problem.

If a member of staff isn't going to be able to attend, you should see the head of the subject department to arrange a facility for the parents to see the head of department. The teacher should do this him/herself, but you cannot rely on this happening so you should take the initiative. The teacher concerned must, however, leave comments on the pupils and to have explained them to the HoD, so that he can talk to the parents.

Liaise with caretaker/site manager and check back before the meeting

Being on good terms with the caretakers in the period up to and including the meeting is vital. The caretaker should arrange the room for you including putting out the staff tables, and clearing them away afterwards. Give him/her a copy of the seating plan well in advance and discuss through any potential difficulties. This means that you should be aware of any constraints of access to the required area and whether, for example, the hall is needed for assembly first thing next morning. Check with an experienced year head what the caretaker is normally expected to do, because if you are inexperienced he may try to do less than usual and you could find yourself having to persuade pupils or parents to move desks or chairs at the end of the meeting. This should not be necessary!

Check out the appointments to make sure it works

Teachers of very popular subjects may need to start their interviews earlier than teachers with a small number of appointments. Sometimes a parent has to come in early for work or family reasons – try to accommodate this.

Post the seating/room plan
A copy needs to be clearly displayed in the staff room and copies need to be prominently displayed in the foyer or entrance to the hall, i.e. where parents can easily see it. Failure to do this usually results in chaos as irritated parents can't easily find the teachers they want to see.

Check whether all the parents are coming
In the week of the meeting ask for feedback from the tutors about the response from the parents in each tutor group. Usually this is done on a form list and it shows up immediately which parents haven't responded or can't come. Again this should be kept on your computer and you should be able to check the parents' track record for attending parents meetings.

Contact parents who can't come
When you find that parents whom staff would very much like to see are listed as not attending, check if they have given a good reason for their non-attendance. Some phone calls/emails home at this stage could be useful. This will help your public relations, and indicate to the pupil and his/her parents that you are aware that they are not coming. It gives you an opportunity for a brief word with parents, who may not need to come in at all but who are likely to be pleased to be given the opportunity for a short chat and the reassurance that everything is OK. In some cases you will have to phone the parents to find out whether they actually received the letter of invitation. In a small number of cases you will want to take the initiative in fixing an appointment at another time.

Brief the staff about possible problems
If the school has a regular slot to give information, e.g. a morning briefing session, it is a good idea to book the slot a day or so in advance of the meeting. This is the time to alert the staff about which parents can't come so they don't waste time waiting for someone who has told the school that he/she will not be present, and for you to say what you are doing about contacting parents who should be seen but are not coming. Sometimes you have to warn staff about possible troublemakers. The usual way to do this is to list those who, if they become argumentative, should be immediately sent on to see you or a member of the SLT.

Quite frequently, teachers find parents will approach them at other events for additional information or to raise issues about their child's progress. Brief your team on how to handle these inquiries appropriately.

Be available and be prepared to trouble shoot

On the night do not overload yourself with appointments, especially those which would be better done on another occasion. As a subject teacher you will have a list which you must see, but you are the section manager so try to keep your list short so that you can be available to see parents who encounter unexpected difficulties or to troubleshoot.

Evaluate afterwards

After the meeting it is useful to check, e.g. at another briefing session, how the staff perceived the evening. This will help you pick up on problems which should have come your way, but haven't. It will also clarify whether the organization of the evening was satisfactory. Keep your record of the evening on file on your computer/memory stick, not just as a guide for next time, but because sometimes you have to refer to it.

Follow-up parents who said they would attend but failed to arrive. This usually takes a phone call but if there are issues, you may need to make an appointment for them to come into school to see you and you would need to collect relevant information from the subject teachers. Occasionally if there is a major problem in one subject you may need to free up the teacher for about ten minutes to see the parents.

Get some feedback from parents and take note of what they say.

This feedback will indicate the extent to which the event achieved its objectives. If you do get requests to make changes to how you run the event, you may not have the power to implement the suggestions so liaise with the SLT member with responsibility for pastoral matters. You may want to raise it at a year head meeting before taking it to SLT so that you have group support for a major change.

2. Dealing with angry parents

CASE STUDY 10.1: THE PERFECT PARENT

Sarah is the kind of parent every school would want to have:

She has three children now in the school, one in Year 7, one in Year 9 and one in Year 10. She is extremely supportive of the school. She attends all relevant pupil progress and information evenings, but doesn't pester the school unnecessarily; rather she uses the parents' section of the school website to communicate with the tutor. The teachers like to have her as a parent volunteer on trips involving her children's classes because she does the right things without needing to be told and she interacts well with staff and children.

Sarah is an active member of the PTA; she has served on committee for the last three years and shown herself to be very capable in the role of events organizer. Recently she has been elected to serve as a parent governor and already her sensitive and diplomatic handling of approaches from parents who have issues with the school has helped to resolve some potentially awkward situations.

Unfortunately, not all parents are like Sarah. As the year leader you will probably have to deal with a higher proportion of parents who are difficult to deal with for one reason or another than other sections of the school's staff. Parents usually want the best for their children but they can be difficult to handle because:

- they are overanxious or unrealistic about their children's abilities
- they have a very limited understanding of their children's programme of studies and find it difficult to work with their children at home
- they are in such challenging circumstances themselves that they cannot support their children and their problems make life more difficult for their children
- they are threatened by the school and teachers
- they are 'know-it-alls'; they believe that their own experience of education means that they know better than the teachers and are instinctively critical of what the teachers are doing
- they are 'political' and stir things up.

Some of these parents are very needy and demanding, some are extremely negative, and a few are aggressive.

The parent who storms into school to defend their child against a teacher or other pupils is a perennial problem for pastoral leaders. Case study 10.2 focuses on a situation in which a working mother feels that the school has got things wrong for her son and that he is being victimized.

Normally the school receptionist acts as a block so that the parents can't simply interrupt a lesson or cause a nasty incident on a corridor. Increasingly, members of the reception staff are being given some training to help them in this task, which can be a difficult one, and many of them handle this well, but sometimes, as in this case study, they add to the parent's anger.

CASE STUDY 10.2: PERCEPTIONS

You are told that there was an incident involving Jimmy Granger's mother and the head asks you to follow-up with the parent so that this kind of incident doesn't reoccur. First, however, you check with the receptionist what happened that morning.

This is what the receptionist tells you about the incident with Jimmy Granger's mother:

> I could see her storming into the reception area. Her whole body language was aggressive. She was moving fast and did not stop at the reception desk, but started to go through the doors onto the classroom corridor. This is against school policy. Parents have to sign in at reception and we have to check which member of staff they are seeing. They can't just come storming in on the bounce. So I called across to her. I'd recognized her by then as Jimmy Granger's mother. We'd had trouble with her before, and Jimmy is regularly in trouble, so I wasn't totally surprised that she didn't follow procedures.

> As I called, I came out of the reception office so that I could stop her going into the classroom corridor before I had checked what or who it was that she wanted. I asked her politely if I could help her, and she curtly replied, 'No,' so I asked who she was looking for and she replied loudly, 'Mr Jones. Where is he? I want to see him now! Where will I find him?'

> I checked that I had heard correctly, as you can't just go stomping in to find a teacher, and Mr Jones is the deputy head. 'Yes, that's him,' she yelled back at me. I tried to talk as calmly as possible, and asked her quietly, 'Is he expecting you? Have you got an appointment with him?' 'No!' she shouted. 'I had an awful letter from him this morning about Jimmy, accusing him of causing a lot of trouble, and I want to see him right now.'

> I tried to speak as calmly as possible although her voice was really loud and she was shouting at me. It could be heard right down the corridor and I was really worried. 'Well, he's teaching at the moment so he's not available. You'll need to make an appointment,' I told her. 'No!' she shouted, 'I need to see him now. It can't wait. I told you that already. Are you deaf or just thick? If

you don't tell me where he is, I'll go into every b***** classroom in the school until I find him. I don't care who gets in the way, so don't you try to stop me!'

She was quite irrational and seemed to think that shouting at me would get her what she wanted, but it just made me more determined not to tell her where the deputy was. Luckily at that moment the head, who had heard the noise, came out of his office and the other deputy also appeared on the scene. If they hadn't come, I would have had to get help because she was becoming more out of control by the minute. The head took her away from the public area, calmed her down and dealt with the matter. I saw her leave quite tamely about 20 minutes later.

This is what the parent told you when you got to talk to her later:

The letter arrived just as I was about to go to work. It was really bad. Jimmy has his moments, but this didn't sound right. Why should he be banned from going on the trip? I couldn't believe it was all his fault and I know that his geography teacher picks on him and doesn't like him, so I wanted to get it sorted out right away. So I phoned in to work and said I had to take the morning off. They weren't pleased and I lost money.

When I reached the school, this woman came out of the office and tried to stop me going into the school. She reminded me of the worst teachers I remember from my own school days. Cold, patronizing and nasty, looking down her nose at me – and she wasn't even a teacher, just the person in the office. Her whole tone was patronizing. Who did she think she was talking to me like that as if I were a badly behaved child?

She stood there blocking my way, with her arms folded and a sour look on her face. She was deliberately being as unhelpful as possible and although I kept emphasizing how important it was to get things sorted out now, I felt I'd never get anywhere with her. She was just wasting my time and trying to stop me from seeing Mr Jones.

I felt so angry. I just didn't have that kind of time to spare. I didn't know what to do to get to see Mr Jones and she was just block-ing me. Luckily, at this point the head came out of his office. The first thing he did was to smile at me and put his hand out to greet me as if I was someone who mattered. He reassured me and told me that I could talk to him and that we'd get things sorted out and we did.'

For reflection/discussion
- What differences did you notice in the two accounts?
- What are the lessons of this case study?

Some points to notice
- The receptionist is focused on protecting the staff from an angry parent.
- She is also focused on following correct procedures.
- The receptionist's preconceptions influence her treatment of the parent.
- The receptionist perceived the school as winning – 'I saw her leave quite tamely' – and the issue as having been dealt with by the head, and this pleased her.
- The office often has to deal with the symptoms of a problem, not the underlying issues – this can be frustrating.
- The parent's resentment of the receptionist's tone, attitude, etc.
- The parent's arrival has been sparked off by what she sees as unfair treatment of her son.
- The parent cared about her son sufficiently to take time off work to come into school.
- She expects to have to do battle on behalf of her son.
- She doesn't claim he is always well behaved.
- The parent doesn't know what to do when the receptionist blocks her, and resorts to shouting.
- The parent lacks the interpersonal skills to handle the receptionist. Upset to start with, she gets even more wound up by the receptionist's tone, which she perceives as patronizing.
- Senior management has to take over and calm down the situation.
- The year leader gets asked to do the follow-up.

Complaints from parents arise when
- they feel that the school has got things wrong
- their child is not succeeding for some reason
- a teacher is victimizing/picking on their child
- a combination of these features is in play.

Sometimes the complaint will be about how you handled things and you will need to review your own approach. More often it will involve at least one other teacher and you will have to handle the situation extremely sensitively. In Case study 10. 2, the mother clearly believed the school had got things wrong and that her child had been victimized. Frequently the complaint goes straight to the head teacher and is handed on for your comments on the situation or for you to deal with before the reply, which you may have to draft for the head, goes out under the head teacher's name. In Case study 10.2, the head has dealt with the short term problem. He calmed the parent down and resolved the issue of whether Jimmy would go on the trip. The year leader is left to try to improve the family's relationship with the school.

This year leader's comment summarizes her approach to dealing with angry parents:

> I always try to make the parent feel that I'm listening to them. I let them have their say and try not to interrupt. They perceive interruptions and even questions as contradicting them and as a sign that I don't believe or agree with them. The listening and attentive posture shows that I am taking their concern seriously, and that their view of events matters. Then I make it clear that the case is not prejudged and that we will investigate carefully. This approach normally defuses the situation and I can fix a time for them to meet me later, when they will be less angry and be more able to think clearly, and we can have a proper discussion. It is important for them to understand how decisions about their child are reached and to be involved in those decisions.

Strategies for making the school a more welcoming and less threatening environment for parents such as Mrs Granger can be found later in this chapter.

3. Dealing with difficult parents

Parents who take on the school always present a problem. The most difficult to deal with are the manipulative parents, who present you with an ongoing challenge. Case study 10.3 gives an example of a manipulative parent.

CASE STUDY 10.3: THE MANIPULATIVE PARENT

Maria Haynes was an above average pupil, but not brilliant. She tended to be isolated within her form group, and appeared to have no close friends. Her form tutor was one of my best tutors, so there was good tutor involvement. The tutor knew Maria well and tried to help her, but she found her efforts to involve Maria thwarted by Maria herself. The girl distanced herself from others in the form. Responsible students in the group told the tutor that Maria acted as if she felt she was superior to them and didn't want to mix with them. Some of them felt strongly that she was subversive, quietly setting pupils or staff against each other. The tutor told me that she couldn't prove it, but she believed that these pupils were probably right about Maria.

Maria's mother found all this very difficult to accept and by this time she had also become a parent governor. In this school the year leaders go up with the year group and I found that there was a flare-up at least once a year. It normally involved how information was conveyed to Mrs Haynes or interpreted by Mrs Haynes. I was never clear how much was misinformation by Maria and how much was reinterpretation by Mrs Haynes as they backed each other up; most probably it was a mixture. A lot of it was 'YOU said this . . .'. Invariably she expertly deflected any points we made and turned things so that she could blame the school. She was extremely articulate both orally and on paper and would send lengthy (two sides or more) letters to me as the year head and would copy these or write independently to the deputy or the head.

Almost always, these were actually small issues; for example, on one occasion the tutor mistakenly marked Maria absent, which was a small mistake and one that could easily be put right. Another occasion, which provoked phone calls and letters, was about arrangements that we made for student taster sessions to help them make their option choices. Maria had been slow returning her form and asked for a group which was full. I got it sorted out in the end, but it was unpleasant and unnecessarily time consuming.

What I learnt from dealing with Mrs Haynes and other parents of this kind:

- The need for consistency so that she couldn't play me off against the tutor or the SLT against me.
- The importance of convincing the parents that their child was being treated fairly or had received the same consequence as other children involved.
- I liaised very closely with the SLT so that senior management was aware of each new incident as soon as it arose and that I could discuss how I would handle it.

- The importance of working closely with the tutor, who checked with me before taking action.
- It was vital to document everything and keep copies. I had to record everything, e.g. what instruction I gave the tutor.
- You have to be very careful how you word things orally (I even had to watch my tone) and even more careful on paper. With this kind of parent, you cannot afford hostages to fortune, so anything you needed to communicate has to be very clear so that it is difficult to misinterpret.
- It is important not to let this kind of parent wind you up (see the key steps to managing your anger below). They will try to personalize things when you need to keep to the issue.

EXEMPLAR 10.1: MEETING RECORD

Notes of meeting with parents/guardian

Student . . . . Form . . . .

Parent/Guardian . . . . School Representative

Meeting arranged by: letter, telephone, face to face (delete as appropriate)

Reason for meeting

Summary of meeting

Action by school

Action by student

Action by parent/guardian

Notes taken by:

Date:

Some strategies for dealing with difficult parents

- Remain calm – don't let the parent wind you up.
- Allow the parent to have his/her say. It is important to let the parents tell you their story; only interrupt if something needs clarifying.
- Remember that what they say is their perception and they will see it as the true version.
- Deflect the aggression.
- A smile can sometimes deflect anger and change a parent's mood (see Case study 10.2, where the mother notices and responds to the head's smile).
- Listen attentively – use all the active listening strategies.
- Make your body language positive and unthreatening.
- Be responsive.
- Concentrate on identifying the real issues, not on what words a member of staff, the child or the parent might have said.
- Try the sandwich approach – start with something positive about the child. This will surprise the parent who is expecting negativity and will show that you care about the child. Put the difficult/negative points in the middle of the session. Always end on a positive, so that this is what the parent remembers.
- Using the problem solving model (see Chapter 6) can help you move the focus from personalities to identifying the relevant issues and possible solutions.
- Consult others where necessary.
- Move the situation forward by offering some solutions – it is important for the parent to see that something will be done about the problem.
- Focus on the best outcome for the child.
- Include the parent in working out the solution.
- Offer to monitor the situation if necessary.
- Shake hands at the end – the contact makes a positive impact.

Common problems and issues and how to deal with them

The list below indicates the kind of problems most frequently experienced by year leaders and some guidelines for dealing with them. The examples come from contributions to pastoral leaders seminars. The seminars were held in different cities around Britain but very similar problems and issues were raised.

Communication difficulties

In our school, which is an inner-city school, the biggest problem I encountered by far was the parents' inability to speak English. If a translator was not available, it could be very hard to communicate effectively. Because we have so many languages and translation is expensive, very few letters or documents are translated into the community languages. Often I had to get the child to translate to the parents. This is one of the reasons why we have the students come with their parents to discussions about their progress.

Perceptions that nothing is being done

A particular problem I often faced was when a child had had something stolen and the parent comes in demanding to know what I was doing about it. Of course I try to retrieve the stolen item but success varies. Often it is only lost. Sometimes it's like opening a can of worms and we retrieve more items than had been reported missing, but more often we can't find property that has gone missing, lost or stolen. In these cases my efforts often fail to calm the parent – they wanted me to perform a magic trick and return the stolen item. We can only do our best. I have to spell out to them everything that I have done so that they can see how much effort the school has made.

Differences in culture

At times when a child was in trouble, informing the parents could have upsetting consequences, such as the parents beating the child or threatening to send them back to a particular country. It is partly that the parents don't know how to handle the situation and partly cultural differences. When I first became a year leader it really upset me if a child came back to me and told me, often in tears, what had occurred as a result of my telephone call or meeting. It made me feel very guilty. Nowadays I try to pre-empt this by the way that we deal with the parent to help them appreciate that an angry or violent reaction will make things worse rather than better (see Case study 10.9 on parenting skills sessions).

Conflict between parents

Frequently I find that the parents try to use me as a marriage guidance counsellor or social worker. They book an appointment, but they have not really come to talk about the pupil. They want to talk about their own problems. Sometimes they simply need someone to talk to. It gives me background about issues that could be affecting the child's progress, but I'm not a trained counsellor and I've learnt that I have to keep my focus on the child and his/her progress at school, so I try to refer the parents to organizations that can help them.

Conflicts between two sets of parents

When two sets of parents are in conflict, often they want the school to sort it out. One parent would phone me and ask me to phone the other set of parents to tell them to stop harassing them and vice versa. In these situations I have to make it clear that I cannot be involved, though we monitor how the children of the two families involved in the dispute deal with each other and try to support them. If the children can resolve their differences, it often solves things.

Parents who lie or cover up their child's truancy

You get to know very quickly which parents regularly cover for their children and collude with them. I find that I need clear evidence before I start any interaction, so that it is difficult for them to refute the facts of the situation. I've learnt that you can't always rely on computerized data to be accurate, so I check very carefully that absences have been entered accurately. This way I don't provide these parents with any ammunition and I try not to let them sideline me or deflect me from the real issue.

Managing yourself

Good self-management helps you deal with manipulative parents. When you are dealing with overwrought or difficult parents, they often try to wind you up. You have to manage your anger as they will try every ploy to get you to lose control.

KEY STEPS TO MANAGING YOUR ANGER

Step 1: Recognize it

Learn to identify the signals that you are angry, e.g. by recognizing that your body tenses up, or you are flushing or clenching your fists.

Step 2: Control it

It is not productive to express your anger to another person until you feel in control. If you need time or space to calm down, step away, or, if the situation allows this, ask for an adjournment which will gain you a breathing space, during which you can calm down. Go for a short walk or find a quiet place where you can swear or mutter aloud to get the anger out of your system or simply relax for a few minutes. If this is not possible use breathing exercises to help you regain control.

Step 3: Decide what you want to do with it
Use a feelings commentary to express your anger or frustration. Remember that your anger belongs to you. Avoid saying 'You made me angry'. Just say 'I feel angry about this'. Be honest. Don't downgrade it by saying 'I'm a bit annoyed' when you mean, 'I'm furious about this!'

Step 4: Express it quietly and calmly
Being able to express your anger or feelings quietly and calmly to the other person is a powerful tool. If you allow your tone of voice to betray your feelings, the other person will pick up the anger and respond to it, without taking in why you are angry. To prevent the situation from escalating and becoming personal, you should express what you want to say in a non-threatening matter and a clear voice.

4. Involving parents who are hard to reach
Ways that you can develop the partnership with parents
- Improving communication
- Improving parental input at home
- Using practical solutions to aid participation
- Overcoming perceived barriers at schools
- Improving parental representation.

Making parents welcome
Here are a series of case studies in which year leaders describe how their schools have tried to improve the way in which they communicate with parents. No school will have the time or resources to use all these strategies, but extended schools funding and the increase in the use of support staff, especially of non-teaching pastoral officers, makes it possible to be more flexible and offer a wider range of opportunities than in the past.

CASE STUDY 10.4: ESTABLISHING A WELCOME ROOM

Many parents in our catchment area have had a negative experience of education themselves and feel threatened by the school. This makes them reluctant to come into school, so we used to have a very poor turnout at parents' meetings and other events and the PTA barely exists. We felt that we had to make a positive statement so, about three years ago, we set up a welcome room. It's just a small room in which we meet parents, but we've tried to make it welcoming. It is painted a warm colour and has easy chairs and a coffee table.

Even if the parents turn up without an appointment, we make sure that someone, usually one of the non-teaching staff, comes to meet, welcome and talk to them. We try to involve them in the life of the school in every way possible. Over the three years there has been an effect. On average far more parents turn up to pupil progress evenings and other functions than in the past. As they began to talk to us more confidently, they told us that at the beginning they didn't ask questions because they didn't know whether they should put up their hands when they spoke to a teacher. Now they help us in a lot of different ways and we are really pleased with the way that our relationship with the parents is developing.

CASE STUDY 10.5: DEVELOPING UNDERSTANDING OF LEARNING ACTIVITIES – TWO EXAMPLES

Case study 10.5A

We were very aware that parents are far more involved with primary schools than secondary schools, so we wanted some of the this relationship to continue into Year 7. We felt that if the relationship got off to a good start, it would give us something to build on. Our Year 7 programme has been modified to make it more of a transition year, so we opened one afternoon a week, for the two lessons after lunch, which we timetable as a double period, for parents/guardians and grandparents to drop in and work with their children's group. It is cost effective for us as we don't have to timetable specific family learning courses. We don't get a huge take-up, but some do come; they enjoy it and they tell others. We have found it has a positive effect on the pupils whose parents come as well as developing the parents' understanding of what their child does in class. It also helps them support the children at home better.

Case study 10.5B

We saw that primary SEAL included materials with activities that children could take home, so we tried this with our Year 7 SEAL programme. It is useful because parents can see what we are doing with their children, but it also addresses emotional intelligence skills, which could help our parents support their children better.

CASE STUDY 10.6: REVIEWING COMMUNICATIONS

At the year heads' meeting we decided to review our existing system of communications. Because we now have non-teaching administrative assistants they could administer it for us. We looked at phone calls, informal contacts, reports, letters, one-to-one appointments, parents events, use of pupil planners, postcards, etc. We used a questionnaire to get parents' views, and got enough returns to make us rethink and revise our existing systems.

Two areas attracted a lot of negative comments. Parents' evenings were a clear cause for concern. We used the traditional system. There were complaints about unclear signposting, which made it difficult to locate subject teachers, the time spent queuing, anxieties that they would miss appointments and teachers overrunning. There were also negative comments about phone calls when they were at work. One parent's comment summed things up. She wrote: 'Why can't we use emails or texting to communicate, then I could pick up messages at work?'

We tried to respond to both these issues. For parents' meetings, we introduced clear signposting to show parents where staff were located and an appointments system in which parents selected five members of staff to see. The year leader checks the choices and where necessary makes suggestions to the parents, particularly about areas that are of concern to us but which haven't been requested.

An email facility is now provided in the parents section of our learning platform. Most contacts are now made via email and tend to get prompt responses. Similarly, parents can leave messages for the year leader in the relevant year mail box which is checked daily. We noticed that as a result the volume of contact increased. Feedback has been positive as parents say it feels less formal and they don't feel that they are wasting our time if they email about something minor. It hasn't replaced one-to-one contacts, but it has given us a very useful additional layer of contact.

The questionnaire also made us realize that not all parents failed to attend because of lack of interest. Cost cutting by the local bus company meant that there is no longer a bus running at night through the local estate and this affected a number of parents who were not car owners, so now we send our mini-bus round a couple of times at the beginning and end of the evening and this has helped attendance. Babysitters are another issue and we are currently piloting a child minding service, using sixth formers for parents who have to bring a small child with them.

The guidance below was included in the school's Year 7 induction pack and also put onto the parents' section of the school's learning platform. The majority of children at this school arrived with levels of achievement below national expectations. Versions of the guidance were available in other languages as English was not the other tongue of many of the families.

EXEMPLAR 10.2: GUIDELINES FOR PARENTS TO HELP THEM SUPPORT THEIR CHILDREN

How parents can help their children succeed at school
- Spend time talking to your children so that you have a good relationship with your child and they can talk to you about issues that matter to them.
- Read with children and listen to them reading.
- Check homework if it is set by the school.
- Listen to their times tables, spellings or other learning activities.
- Provide a quite area for the children to study away from the TV.
- Monitor their use of computers and set limits to the time spent on it.
- Take them to the local library.
- Encourage them to read story books as well as information books.
- Encourage them to be involved in music, drama/PE activities at school or in the community. (Tell us if there are any difficulties that prevent their participation and we will try to help you.)
- Do things with the children in the holidays.
- Encourage the children with speaking, reading and writing in their mother tongue and helping them to value their own culture and background.
- Be a good role model for them – children copy parents habits and mannerisms.
- Come to parents' evenings and other events that the school holds, such as Parent's Association meetings, information meetings for parents and social

events to help you meet other parents. (Tell us if there are any difficulties that prevent your participation and we will try to help you.)

- Ask the right questions when you talk the to your children's teachers – ask about their strengths as well as what they need to do to improve.
- Find out more about what your children are learning in school, e.g. history or science and take them to museums to find out more.
- Contact us – make an appointment to see the year head or the head teacher if you have concerns about behaviour/progress/bullying, etc. Come sooner rather than later as this could stop a problem from escalating.
- Offer help to the school as a volunteer to accompany trips or hear children read, etc. This will also help you to know more about your children's education.
- Take a more active role by becoming a member of the parent/teachers' association, a governor or a parent-helper in school.

CASE STUDY 10.7: USING THE WEBSITE

Our school is in a very deprived area; some 80 per cent of our children are in the lowest 20 per cent for social and economic deprivation, and 50 per cent are on free school meals. Turn out at parents' evenings is reasonable in the circumstances, but as with many schools, too many of the parents you most want to see don't attend.

We checked for internet access and found a high level – around three-quarters – of the pupils could access the internet at home, so we decided to use our learning platform to reinforce contact with parents.

We give each set of parents a unique password, so that they can browse their own child's timetable, day-to-day attendance, unauthorized absences, conduct log, homework diary and current achievement. They can key into estimated grades for Key Stage 3 and how near the child is to achieving the grades and each new target as it is set by the teachers. The data has been simplified a bit for the parents so that they can understand it.

When we introduced the scheme, we ran sessions for parents to explain the process and show them how to use it. To track their child's progress, they needed to be able to use the school's database. We varied the time of the sessions to make it possible for parents to attend and publicized this through the website, the newsletter and letters home. There was a lot of interest and turnout for these sessions was good, and they now play an important part in our relationship with parents. We monitor use and it is high. Feedback has been consistently positive. Features that parents tell us they particularly like include:

- It is accessible 24/7 so working parents can access it when they are free.
- They can find out about the child's progress without having to come into school.
- The information is current – they don't have to wait for a report.
- It is clearer and more factual than reports, which they found bland.
- Children can't hide things from their parents.
- It makes discussion between parents and children easier because parents talk to their children about what they have noticed on the learning platform.
- Children mention things for the parent to look at on the website, especially if it is good.

We like the fact that it helps some of the harder-to-reach parents develop their understanding of their child's programme of studies and be more in touch with their progress or lack of progress. It should no longer be possible for parents to ask us 'Why didn't you tell us sooner?'

There is an email facility for them to make contact with pupil support staff and this is checked daily. We find it is more difficult for parents to argue with data and this has helped us to guide selection of suitable courses. Attendance at our termly target setting reviews, which parents and pupils attend together with the child's personal tutor, has improved since introducing the e-portal. When new features appear, we offer updating training sessions and an introduction to using the e-portal sessions is a feature of our Year 7 parents' programme.

The e-portal hasn't totally replaced other forms of contact, particularly as a quarter of our pupils don't have internet access. We use hard copy homework diaries/planners as the main vehicle of communication for families who are without computers at home and make sure that they receive printed versions of all communications.

CASE STUDY 10.8: IMPROVING ONE-TO-ONE CONTACTS

We are a school with specialist technology status serving an area with a low level of professional parents. We became concerned when the PTA folded for lack of support as this put the onus on parents to contact us and of course just the parents who most needed to do so didn't, and these are the parents most likely not to turn up for parents' meetings.

At a year leaders' meeting chaired by the deputy in charge of the Every Child Matters agenda, we discussed how to improve our communications with parents. One point raised was that many of our parents found it hard to talk to teachers. They lacked confidence and were nervous or tense even though a significant proportion had attended the school themselves. We began to realize that in many cases their own experience of school had not been particularly positive, and as parents they were most likely to see a teacher if their child had misbehaved or was underachieving, which would lead to yet another negative interaction with the school.

It was suggested that perhaps the method of contact should be changed. We now have a non-teacher pastoral officer, Ruth, who handles the attendance issues by phoning home. She has been doing this since the start of the academic year. For us it was very useful because issues could be picked up quickly by someone who had time to keep phoning until contact was made and to do the follow-up calls needed to keep the parents involved in the process.

Feedback from Ruth indicated that she felt her own confidence and communications skills had grown over this period. The scope of the project expanded. For example, we also began to use her to phone parents before parents' evenings if they were hadn't made any appointments; this proved a useful innovation because it contributed to the improved attendance and parents who couldn't come raised and discussed concerns with Ruth and we could pick up on these. At a recent parents' meeting, several parents commented favourably on this innovation. One comment was that talking to Ruth, who was always a friendly voice, had made them more willing to communicate with the school when issues arose.

This made us think about the importance of having friendly unthreatening initial contact for parents, and it was suggested that Ruth would also handle the one-to-one contacts, particularly for parents of pupils who were causing us most concern. Hopefully this would be a less threatening experience than seeing one of us or the deputy head, and a non-teacher, who was also one of our parents, would be able to relate to them better. We agreed to run a pilot for half a term and if it worked well we would expand the team of pastoral officers to create a home–school support team.

At the end of the pilot, we took feedback both from Ruth and from a sample of the parents. Ruth told us that it had been a learning experience for her. She had learnt to look at the parents' body language for signs of tension, especially eye contact and crossed arms. She said that she now realized that if their shoulders dropped they had begun to relax and real dialogue could begin.

Ruth said she had learnt:

- not to talk too much – at first she was too set on the school's agenda
- that you have to listen to them before they will listen to you
- to make her own body language more welcoming, particularly not to fold her arms and to use open gestures ('I hadn't realized that touching my own face gives the message that I am not really listening')
- to copy parents' body language, e.g. the way they were sitting
- to lead them in a non-threatening way ('Tell me about it from your point of view', 'Are there some current issues that could explain why Steven's work is slipping?')
- to use unthreatening questions (such as 'How motivated is Steven on a scale of 1–10?' – this kind of approach makes them think and you can build on the answer. If the parent says 4 out of 10, you can discuss how to get it to 5 or 6)
- that she was using coaching-style techniques to make parents focus on the cause of a problem.

Parents said that:

- their experience improved as Ruth became more confident; at first she was more nervous than she appeared on the phone
- they felt they knew her already from the phone conversations, so they could talk to her
- it was the first time they had really got a chance to say what they felt
- that Ruth really listened to them

- they feel more comfortable about coming into school and that it will be a more positive experience than in the past
- there had been some real progress in helping their children.

The success of the pilot led us to decide to build up a small core of pastorals officers, who would handle first-level contacts with parents.

CASE STUDY 10.9: PARENTING SKILLS SESSIONS

We had major concerns about how the parents of some of our most vulnerable pupils handled the issues facing their children and wanted to find a way that would support them so that they supported their children more effectively. We heard that some schools were providing parenting skills sessions for groups of parents, so we checked the internet and contacted a few of them to see how they organized their schemes and how effective they had been.

The scheme we devised was led by the deputy with responsibility for ECM but mainly run by our non-teaching family support staff. We deliberately kept it small, starting with a group of six Year 9 pupils who were causing us a lot of concern, including one school-refuser. We made the initial contact through phone calls which explained to the families what the scheme was trying to do and to invite them to join. We explain that it is confidential – no one else will know unless they decide to tell people. We phone about a dozen to get six, because not all those who agree actually turn up, but we deliberately keep the numbers low.

There are six weekly sessions, which the pupils attend with their parents. They focus on setting pupil targets which are achievable, such as doing more of their homework and helping the parents improve how they handle interacting with the child over achieving the targets. It basically helps them with their own emotional intelligence, for example to be more patient and less negative with their child. It seems to have an impact; parents have told us that they find it easier to be understanding of the child's situation and to talk issues through with their child. Far more mothers come than fathers but this also represents the level of one-parent families that we have.

Towards the end of the session, the pupils go back to class and the family support officer has coffee with the parents and talks to them about issues that arise and how they feel things are going. The parents like this part of the morning because they can talk to staff in an informal way. The pupils are also positive and many of them have told us that they are pleased that their parent made the time to come into school to help them. Some of the mothers have said that their sons encourage them to attend and don't let them miss any sessions. One mother commented that 'It's almost the reverse of my making sure my son attends school'. This made us realize that having parents involved can have a real impact on the child's motivation.

Involving fathers

Research shows that where fathers have early involvement in a child's life there is a positive relationship to later educational achievement; there is an association with good parent–child relationship in adolescence; and even that children in separated families are more protected from mental health problems. This research indicates that fathers' involvement has increased since the 1970s, particularly with children under the age of 5; there is, however, great variation in the levels of involvement, so that even though levels have increased on average, a substantial proportion of fathers recorded no daily direct interaction time with their children.

It has also shown that there are significant barriers to overcome in improving fathers' involvement in the educational process.

Barriers to fathers' involvement can include:

- Services/schools that are insensitive to fathers' needs and that do not adequately connect with the context of fathers' lives or motivations.
- An overtly female focus and culture among staff, and a lack of confidence to explain and promote the importance of engaging with fathers.
- The underestimation of the significance of a father's involvement if he is not visible to the school or not living with the child.

In practice fathers help less with homework than mothers and tend to be involved in more practical activities such as building and repairing, ICT and maths, and physical play. Schools have built on this preference in the way they work with fathers to encourage them to support their children through participating in school based activities with their children.

CASE STUDY 10.10: DADS AGAINST DRUGS (DAD) – RAISING AWARENESS THROUGH FOOTBALL

We became involved in the DAD programme. It was developed as one approach in response to a local need for good quality education about drugs for children. The programme uses football to develop effective drug awareness campaigns for fathers and their children.

On the understanding that children will only listen to their fathers if they knew what they were talking about, a football team was set up and used as a forum for educating fathers about drugs. This enabled fathers to pass on this information to their children. It is small scale but very useful. An example is John, whose son Sean is in my year group and has some special needs. Usually only Sean's mother came to any meetings or events, so we specifically invited John to a session with Sean's personal tutor.

During the session Sean's tutor mentioned the scheme to John and flagged up that details were available on the school's website. We struck lucky, and John, who disliked the fact that when he came into school he would be told about Sean's problems, got interested and is now a member of the DAD football team. The school promotes DAD because as well as conveying the anti-drugs message, it involves fathers engaging in a team activity with their sons and encourages them to be positive role models. John has told the school that he enjoys being part of the team and that Sean thinks the scheme is really cool. Sean has said that what he likes is that his father makes the time to come into school for the games.

CASE STUDY 10.11: FAMILY LEARNING ACTIVITIES

We now have a parent link outreach worker with a specific link to engage fathers, so we have an ongoing dialogue. We have been working to find out what would encourage them to come into school and we try to build on the fathers' interests to get them involved. Our extended schools funding enabled us to set up some extra-curricular family learning opportunities which attract fathers, for example we have introduced a go-carting club with some real opportunities for mechanical engineering and through the music department we are developing a band in which fathers and children are involved.

Home–school contracts

Some schools still use these but they appear to be far less popular than in the past. Feedback from year leaders is that it can take a lot of work to get the contract set up and the family to sign up, but without real commitment the contract is not worth the paper it is written on and that if the commitment is there you don't need a written contract.

Improving parents' representation

PTAs, governors and parent councils

Government policy is to develop ways that parents can express their views and extend parental representation and although you may not have to lead these initiatives you should be aware of them.

PTAs are the conventional mechanism through which parents become involved in the school's activities. They do sterling work in supporting the school, holding social and fundraising events and events and meetings which focus on particular aspects of the curriculum to help parents to understand their child's programme of studies. They tend to attract their highest membership in the more affluent/middle class areas. Schools in challenging circumstances can find difficulty in keeping their PTA going and it could be worth seeking funding and support from the NCPTA. The NCPTA is a registered charity which promotes partnerships between home and school.

Joining the PTA and becoming a committee member can lead on to becoming a parent governor. Currently about 30 per cent of governors are parents, but they are often not representative of the majority of parents; they are usually the more successful and articulate parents. Some parents come forward because of issues about their own child's progress which can make it difficult for them to be objective.

For these reasons the government is developing other ways to improve parental representation. Parent councils are one example. Only Trust schools have to have a parent council, but the government is encouraging the growth of parent councils because they consider them to be more inclusive than membership of the governing body, and they can create an effective mechanism for consulting parents and getting their views known to the school.

Parents' charters

Some schools make their commitment to parents explicit through a parents' charter. You may feel that it reiterates much of what you say to parents anyway, but sometimes it is important to spell things out. Here is a sample charter:

EXEMPLAR 10.3: A PARENTS' CHARTER

The College makes the following commitments to you as parents

- To ensure a close, three-way relationship between the College, the student and parents in order to help your son/daughter achieve their full potential
- To involve you in matters concerning progress and discipline, even if your son/daughter reaches the age of 18 during their time at College
- To notify you of the results of parents' surveys
- To give you the opportunity to consult with teaching staff about your son/daughter's academic progress and personal and social development
- To ensure you receive regular reports about your son/daughter's academic progress
- To notify you, when appropriate, regarding your son/daughter's attendance
- To consult with you if your son/daughter wishes to change course and seek your agreement where this is the case
- To keep you informed of important dates and events in the life of the College
- To give you information regarding the performance of the College
- To ask you to complete surveys/questionnaires seeking your views on our performance.

To help us, we ask you to

- encourage your son/daughter to meet our expectations of them
- inform us if you become concerned about any aspect of your son/daughter's progress
- notify us about absence, in accordance with our guidelines
- not take your son/daughter on holiday during term time
- respond promptly to College communications
- attend parents' evenings, including regular consultation evenings for parents/carers/guardians with College teachers and tutors plus meetings about higher education, further training and careers.

How to make your views known

- Parents' survey: Every year we undertake a sample survey of parents to find out your views about the College. We will report back to you through the College's regular newsletter and tell you about any changes we are making in response to your feedback.
- Compliments, suggestions and general queries: Contact/write to the Principal.
- Misunderstandings and criticisms: Contact the Tutor, Student Services Manager or Assistant Principal (Student Services).
- Formal complaints: It is College policy to encourage students, parents, employers and members of the community to resolve issues and disagreements informally, wherever possible. In the rare event that a matter cannot be dealt with in an informal way, the College Complaints Policy and Procedure will be put into operation. In these cases, please write formally to the Principal.

References and web links

Web links

DfE: http://parentknow-how.dcsf.gov.uk/default.asp?link=

- Use the DfE website to check the progress of Parent Know How, a range of free services being developed to give all parents access to expert advice and increase the number of parenting experts working locally in children's centres and schools.
- The DfE's Standards Site provides case studies focused on the strategies used by schools to improve parental involvement at www.standards.dcsf.gov.uk/parentalinvolvement/pics
- It also has a range of downloadable publications on parents' evenings, meetings with teachers, school reports, children's homework and other topics in Arabic, Bengali, Chinese, Greek, Gujarati, Hindi, Punjabi, Somali, Turkish, Urdu and Vietnamese. If you have a high proportion of pupils whose parents speak only one language or languages other than English, or who struggle with English to the point that letters and other correspondence from school are ineffective, it could be worth downloading these leaflets.

Directgov: www.direct.gov.uk

- Directgov is the government's portal for information for parents on their children's education, rights and safety, as well as advice on a range of issues including health in pregnancy, adoption procedures and childcare. It is also a useful website for you to use to check latest developments in government thinking about parents and how they might impact on your role.

Education World: www.educationworld.com

- A US website with some useful ideas.

EPPa: www.southgatepublishers.co.uk/eppaindex.html

- EPPa is Effective Partnerships with Parents. You can download free an 8 page pdf leaflet. There is also a toolkit of resources available to purchase. www.southgatepublishers.co.uk/eppaindex.html

GovernorNet: www.governornet.co.uk
- Guidance on parent councils, including a resource pack, is being developed on this website.

The National Confederation of Parent Teacher Associations (NCPTA): www.ncpta.org.uk
- The NCPTA represents more than 6 million parents and teachers through over 12,500 individual PTAs in England, Wales and Northern Ireland. It aims to provide effective partnerships between parents and teachers and to develop learning opportunities both in and out of school.

Scottish resources that are useful both sides of the border, include:
Parentzone Scotland. www.ltscotland.org.uk/parentzone
- This website provides materials to help parents support their children's learning.

TeacherNet: www.teachernet.gov.uk
- TeacherNet is the best site for latest developments as it puts summaries giving a clear overview of new developments. Use the publications section for links to DfE publications and to download relevant publications such as updates to the *Children's Plan; Every Parent Matters*, etc. which could affect your responsibilities in respect of parents.
- Normally these publications have an overview or conclusions which summarize the main points for you. For example, *Safer Schools* is a DfE leaflet which is downloadable from the TeacherNet website. It has advice about undertaking risk assessment, a useful form for recording incidents, and model letters banning or re-admitting parents to the premises. www.teachernet.gov.uk/_doc/1607/safe_school_leaflet.pdf
- TeacherNet will also give you links to other sites such as DirectGov or the Standards Site and has case studies which show you what other schools have done. Be sure to always check old case studies.

Teachers TV: www.teachers.tv
- Teachers TV has some useful programmes on improving communications with parents. Check the menu as new programmes are regularly added to the list.

Union websites can also provide useful resources, for example ATL provides advice on building relationships with parents and dealing with problem parents:
    www.atl.org.uk/help-and-advice/school-and-college/parents.asp

Books

Bender, Y. (2005), *The Tactful Teacher: Effective Communication with Parents, Colleagues, and Administrators*, Vermont, Nomad Press.

Whalley, M. and the Pen Green Centre Team (2007, 2nd edn), *Involving Parents in their Children's Learning*, London, Paul Chapman Educational Publishing.

Glossary

AfL	Assessment for Learning
APP	Assessing Pupil Progress
BACP	British Association for Counselling and Psychology
BeCo	behaviour coordinator
BESD	behavioural, emotional and social difficulty
BESTs	behaviour and education support teams
CAMHS	Child and Adolescent Mental Health Services
CATs	Cognitive Ability Tests – Year 7 tests
CFT	common transfer file – for pupils transferring schools
Child	all pupils under the age of 18
CPD	continuous professional development
DAD	Dads Against Drugs programme
DfE	Department for Education formerly DCSF: Department for Children, Schools and Families (previously Department for Education and Skills (DfES)
EBD	(pupil with) emotional and behavioural difficulties

ECM	Every Child Matters
EIA (2006)	Education and Inspections Act 2006
EWO	education welfare officer (truancy officer)
FFT	Fisher Family Trust – comparative pupil data
HoD	head of department, subject leader
ICT	information and communication technology
IEP	individual education plan
INSET	in-service education and training
LA	Local Authority (formerly LEA – Local Education Authority)
LDSS	Learning Development and Support Services
LftM	Leading from the Middle development programme (run by NCSL)
LSCB	Local Safeguarding Children Board
MAs	management allowances; replaced by TLRs
MBF	Mentoring and Befriending Foundation
NASUWT	National Association of Schoolmasters Union of Women Teachers
NCPTA	National Confederation of Parent Teacher Associations
NCSL	National College of School Leadership (now National College for Leadership of Schools and Children's Services)
NFER	National Federation for Educational Research
NPM Programme	National Peer Mentoring Programme
NPSLBA	National Programme for Specialist Leaders of Behaviour and Attendance
NQT	newly qualified teacher (Scotland: probationer)
PCSCO	police community support officer
Performance management	annual appraisal or professional review system
PMHW	primary mental health worker
PSA	pastoral support assistant
PSHE	personal, social and health education (also PSE – no health element)

PSP	Pastoral Support Programme
PTAs	parent teacher associations
QCA	Qualifications and Curriculum Agency
QCDA	Qualification and Curriculum Development Agency
QTS	qualified teacher status
RAISEonline	interactive analysis of school and pupil performance data
RJ	restorative justice: an approach to dealing with conflict or bullying
SAT	Standard Attainment Test
SEAL	social and emotional aspects of learning
SEF	School self-evaluation form – lead document informing planning and inspection process
SEN	special educational needs
SENCO	Special Educational Needs Coordinator
SHS	School-Home Support
SIMS/SERCO	ICT software programs widely used in schools
SIP	School improvement plan
SLT/SMT	senior leadership team; senior management team – usually comprises the head, deputies and assistant heads
SMART targets are	Specific, Measurable, Achievable, Resourced and Time related
SSP	Safer School Partnerships – partnership with police
TAs	teaching assistants; HLTA is the highest level of TA
TDA	Teacher Development Agency – deals with teacher qualifications and has a CPD database
TLRs	teaching and learning responsibilities – replaced management allowances
Yellis	GCSE grade projections
YH/YL	head of year/year leader
YJB	Youth Justice Board
Pastoral leader titles include	Year Leader; Year Head; Year Manager; Head of House; Director/Manager/Leader/

Head of Achievement, Progress or Learning;
Behaviour Officer/Manager; Behaviour
and Welfare Manager; Key Stage/Phase
Managers

Index

Printed in Great Britain
by Amazon

78115503R00174